Your Clients *for*

The Definitive Guide to Becoming a Successful Financial Life Planner

Mitch Anthony

With Contributions by
Barry LaValley and Carol Anderson

Editorial Director: Donald Hull
Senior Project Editor: Trey Thoelcke
Interior Design: Lucy Jenkins
Cover Design: Design Solutions
Typesetting: the dotted i

Library of Congress Cataloging-in-Publication Data

Anthony, Mitch.
    Your clients for life : the definitive guide to becoming a successful financial life planner / Mitch Anthony, Barry LaValley, Carol Anderson
       p.   cm.
    Includes index.
    ISBN 0-7931-4954-1 (6x9 hdbk)
    1. Financial planners.   2. Investment advisors.   I. LaValley, Barry.
II. Anderson, Carol.   III. Title.
HG179.5 .A58 2002
332.024—dc21

                               2001007550

DEDICATION

To my wife, Debbie,
and my children, Nate, Nic, Sophia, and Alec,
who are constant and joyous reminders
of what this life is really about.

ALSO BY MITCH ANTHONY:

StorySelling for Financial Advisors

The Financial Professional's Guide to Persuading One or 1,000

The New Retirementality

Contents

PART THREE
THE ADVISOR AS EDUCATOR

Acknowledgments

In writing the acknowledgments for a book such as this, I feel like a bird that has built its nest from the strings and strands, and twigs and twine it has found. I fear omitting the acknowledgement of even one person without whose ideas this nascent concept may have not held together. I will do my best to remember where each piece of the nest came from.

Special thanks must start with Barry LaValley and Carol Anderson, who both bring a rare passion and commitment to the idea of marrying life planning and financial advice. Their wholesale contributions to this book form the cornerstones for transporting life planning from a theory to a practical and viable business model.

Many fecund minds have been harvested in the development of this book. Chief among them is Ross Levin, who is a pioneer and a testament to the fact that this idea works for both client *and* advisor. I have liberally quoted Marc Freedman for his inspiring philosophies about what the second half of life could and should be. Oswald Guiness, Richard Lieber, and Ravi Zacharias are just a few of the great thinkers of this age who have challenged me to search, think about, and locate purpose and meaning on every page.

As always, I am indebted to the vision, skill, and faith of the people at Dearborn Trade Publishing. Special thanks to Don Hull for understanding and believing in the idea and for his help in navigating through the process. Thanks also to Cindy Zigmund, Sandy Thomas,

Robin Bermel, Trey Thoelcke, Lucy Jenkins, Courtney Goethals, and Jack Kiburz, whose contributions make this work readable, available, and attractive.

Last of all—as in dessert—thanks to my wife, Debbie, for the many skills she applies to this process. I wish my work were as good as she tries to make me believe it is.

My prayer is that this collection of strands, twigs, and twine can serve as a nest for a new way of doing business and helping people.

Chapter *1*

Financial Life Planning: Merging Money and Life

In May 1953, two men became the first to climb to the top of Mt. Everest: Edmund Hillary, a New Zealand beekeeper, and his guide from Nepal, Tenzing Norgay. On the way down, Hillary slipped and began to fall to a certain death, if it had not been for the quick-thinking Tenzing. He quickly slammed his ice pick into the ice wall creating a temporary brace for the rope—just long enough for Hillary to re-establish his hold. Upon reaching the bottom, they were surrounded by international press. When they heard the amazing rescue by Tenzing, they were quick to call him a hero. Being somewhat of a modest man, Tenzing's only response was, "Mountain climbers always help each other. After all, we are tied together."

Every man and woman has chosen the "Everest" he or she wants to climb in life. Many who have tried climbing without a guide have discovered how treacherous the journey can be. Because of the import of the journey, today's clients have become more discriminating about the skill level of the guide they choose to use. The definition of a good guide is changing. Advisors will want to pay close attention to this redefining of roles, as the fate of the climbing client and the financial guide truly are tied together.

In an article titled "A Look at the Financial Services Revolution," Lewis J. Walker, CFP, declared the trend that will govern our future is the fundamental shift from product to process. But what does that *really* mean? Walker further explained that the future of financial advice will be framed in a "holistic process aimed at the completion of life goals." Similarly, Tracy Herman, a reporter for *Registered Representative,* describes the role of a contemporary financial advisor as a "life planning concierge with a wealth of resources."

Having noted growing interest among advisors in a more personal and holistic focus, the National Endowment for Financial Education (NEFE) invited several "pioneers" to meet and explore the concept of life planning. The group gathered in November 2000 and discussed their individual perspectives on the topic. One participant shared his opinion that the life planning movement comes down to one key question for clients, "Is life just about putting the numbers together, or is there more?" Another participant stated, "I take the approach of first helping clients think about their lives and how they want them to evolve based on their values and goals. Then we assign a financial cost to their needs and wants." And yet another participant explained, "Many of my clients have their retirement and future financial security in place. For them it's like 'enough is enough.' It's what they're seeking for everything else about their lives—values, satisfaction, a legacy—that they're looking to me for help with." (William L. Anthes, Ph.D., and Shelley A. Lee, "Experts Examine Emerging Concept of Life Planning." *Journal of Financial Planning,* June 2001.)

For many advisors skilled in the craft of investing and managing assets, the idea of entering into a dialogue as abstract as life planning sounds daunting and murky. They are intrigued with the concept, recognize the potential, but are confused as to how they can integrate and implement the approach into their own practices.

ONE OPTION

According to James Green, editor of *Investment Advisor* magazine, "Many planners these days are considering becoming life coaches to better serve their clients' total needs." And he is correct. For example, in an interview published on the *Journal of Financial Planning* Web site, Kathleen Cotton, CFP, stated: "We are in the perfect position to add coaching to our services to add another dimension of services for clients. Who else, besides perhaps a therapist, talks to our clients about their fondest wishes and helps them get them? While we have the opportunity to do that, it does require a completely new skill set."

However, in surveying the landscape of financial professionals, planners wishing to become trained life coaches are in the minority. It is a commendable idea for those who wish to pursue this specialized training, but by and large, the majority of advisors have not the time or interest for this course of study. Other planners have partnered with individuals who are trained in life coaching and refer specific clients to these individuals before formulating a financial plan. This approach is equally commendable and works for those who can identify and associate with a coaching professional who is on par with the advisor's competence and professionalism.

THE ALTERNATIVE: THE FINANCIAL LIFE PLANNING MODEL

What we are offering both in this book and in the training we provide is a more practical approach to this revolutionary trend within the financial advice industry. Although a majority of advisors understand the need to take a more holistic approach with their clients, most are not comfortable in exploring and advising in nonfiscal matters. They are concerned that they will be called upon to be all things to all clients and to step outside their areas of expertise. However, in the financial life planning approach, the advisor conversationally explores life issues as they relate to money (most life issues have a fiscal tether), and facilitates dialogue in such a way as to communicate her interest in the client as a whole person. We believe this can be accomplished without taking the advisor too far out into the psychological tide.

Financial life planning is not about having all the answers, it is primarily about asking the right questions (the right questions will be explored in Chapter 5). Financial life planning is simply a matter of broadening the conversation from asset management to money as it relates to each aspect of a client's life.

In this light, financial life planning is *not*

- playing psychiatrist, marriage therapist, or career counselor;
- counseling people in nonfinancial matters;
- advising people on what to do with their lives; or
- giving advice outside your areas of expertise.

Financial life planning *is* about

- exploring what money represents to your clients;
- defining both the tangibles and intangibles that clients expect their assets to provide them;

- anticipating life events and transitions, and making financial preparations for those transitions;
- assisting clients in the process of establishing financial goals that facilitate their life goals;
- initiating discussions on the nonfinancial aspects of retirement preparation and retirement living; and
- developing a network of professionals to whom you can confidently refer your clients.

The following eight tenets constitute the basic assumptions that undergird the philosophy of financial life planning as we see it.

1. *Life is about change.* The purpose of financial life planning is to facilitate successful transitions.
2. *Each person's life is a continuum of unique experiences.* Life experience greatly influences how an individual perceives and responds to change. Financial life planning recognizes that skills, values, attitudes, resources, and relationships that are developed and honed during one stage of life all contribute to meeting the challenges and recognizing the opportunities of the next stage of life.
3. *Each person's life course is unique.* In the past, most transitions have been age-graded and have occurred during predictable times in the life span. However, because of increasing longevity, new perspectives on aging, high incidence of divorce and remarriage, delayed child bearing, multiple career changes, and emphasis on lifelong learning and returning to school for retraining or fulfillment, transitions are less frequently age-graded and predictable. Financial life planning recognizes that a majority of individuals are following an unconventional life course either by chance or by choice.
4. *An adult's orientation to learning is life-centered.* The key to developing a relationship with your clients is to connect with their lives. To engage adults in understanding a product, service, or process, they *must* see the relevancy or direct application to their own lives. Call it the WIIFM factor—everyone wants to know "What's in it for me?" A financial life planner gives financial advice that is life-centered and customized to the tangible and intangible aspects of the individual.
5. *Adults have a strong need to be self-directing.* Most individuals want to feel in control of their lives. Financial life planners will seek

to empower their clients to make wise financial decisions and to develop a sense of mastery in this area of life.

6. *Adults desire balance and meaning in their lives.* Financial life planners help their clients clarify goals in all areas of life and design a financial strategy to support those goals.

7. *Each person's internal compass (values and priorities) guides big and little life decisions.* When a course of action is in conflict with one's internal compass (values and priorities), a sense of inner conflict exists. Life satisfaction results when a course of action is in harmony with one's inner compass. Financial life planners will help clients identify their values and priorities in all areas of life, and then guide them in making financial decisions that are in sync with those values and priorities.

8. *A successful financial life planning practice is built on asking the right questions.* Good communication is more about listening than it is about talking. The goal of financial life planners is to really get to know their clients in order to tailor their advice to each individual's circumstances, goals, and values. To this end, financial life planners will continually seek to perfect their inquiry skills.

LIFE AT THE CENTER

The financial life planning approach is client-centered. For the financial life planner, the life of the client must be the axis around which financial discussions revolve. Although most individuals understand that money is not the end all, they do perceive money as a means to building the life they want—and avoiding a life they will regret. They quickly connect with the individual who possesses the skill to connect their money to their lives. Intuitively, your clients will see the wisdom in developing a plan to use their money to make a life rather than using their lives to make money. Most individuals are quite receptive to the professional who possesses the skill to draw out their vision for their lives and help facilitate the materialization of that vision. Your client's money has powerful meaning to them as individuals. Their money promises the fulfillment of their sense of purpose. That money was obtained with a defined set of values and has within it the seeds of a legacy they intend to leave. To make the life connection, the advisor needs to draw out the intended purpose of the money, the values that created the assets, and the legacy the client intends to leave.

No professional is better positioned for this revolutionary trend of life planning than the financial advisor. Participating in this conversation does not change the traditional role of the advisor, it simply shifts the context for the discussion into the arena where the client is most invested—his own life.

THREE KEY ROLES

We have queried many clients on the role that they desire from their advisor or potential advisor. Not surprisingly, we didn't hear anyone saying, "I need someone to buy financial products for me." Clients are looking for a broader role from the advisor than simply performing transaction-oriented tasks. After putting the question, "What role would you like your advisor to play for you?" to scores of clients, we came away with three roles in which we recommend advisors sharpen their skills.

In the financial life planning model, we feel the advisor plays three essential roles: partner, guide, and educator.

Partner

When commenting on the advisor's role, clients often say things like, "I want them to understand me, my journey, and my dreams. I'm not just Joe Generic, a client with assets. Don't treat me that way." There is an intuitive and tacit expectation undergirding the new partnership that says, "If you don't connect with who I am and where I've been, you really aren't concerned about helping me. You're in it to help yourself." In order to form a satisfying partnership with your clients, you have to really get to know them. We will give clear instructions on how to develop your biographical and inquiry skills in Chapter 5.

Partners share equal status in a relationship. As a partner you will walk alongside your clients as they pursue their life goals, and help them realize their objectives. To earn the status of partner, you will need to "invest" in your relationship by really getting to know your clients as individuals. In this role, you will strengthen your inquiry skills in order to effectively explore the life issues and transitions that are pertinent to each client. As a partner, you will communicate to your clients your ability and willingness to stand by them through the financial implications of all the ups and downs of life. A partner is like a copilot who shares the life journey of the client.

Guide

As a guide, you'll use your financial expertise and in-depth knowledge of your client to develop an individualized financial life plan. This plan will base financial goals on the unique circumstances, values, and priorities of each client. As a guide, you will also advise your clients about viable options and motivate them to make decisions and take action. A guide is similar to a mentor—one who serves as a role model and trusted counselor.

Regardless of age, most adults realize that they lack the discipline needed to stay on track and would welcome guidance from someone they knew had their best interests in mind. Call it a personal CFO or a quarterback, the role that people are longing for the advisor to play is one that leads, affirms, holds accountable, and motivates. They want to win the game called life. Part Two of this book, "The Advisor as Guide," will provide you with the tools to effectively guide your clients.

Educator

Today's clients, by and large, do not want to be left in the dark. They are wary of advisors who can't or won't explain financial concepts or products. In addition, they are annoyed by the use of financial industry lingo. Clients want their own financial tutor who talks in plain English. By grasping the concepts set forth by the advisor, clients feel a sense of growth and self-mastery. We often hear comments like, "I want to know what's going on," "I don't want to be left in the dark," "I'm not stupid, but please try to explain things in terms I can understand," or "It's my money. I think I should know what's going on with it." Be proactive by equipping your clients with the tools to make knowledgeable and wise financial decisions. They will then view you as someone who has spurred their growth. Part Three of this book, "The Advisor as Educator," will provide you with the tools to tutor your clients in money matters.

As a financial life planner, the roles of partner, guide, and educator offer the value-added propositions that today's clients need and want. Also consider that quite often a volatile market brings un-resolved issues and unrealized expectations to a head. Advisors who connect with their clients as partner, guide, and educator will have much less trouble retaining clients when the financial markets sour. In fact, if advisors have coached them properly, these clients will be anxious to take advantage of such markets.

As a financial life planner, success hinges on moving beyond transaction thinking to transition thinking. This involves looking for effective ways to help each client make the connection between their financial life and their goals and priorities in all other areas of life. The purpose of this book is to provide a framework in strengthening client relationships via your roles as partner, guide, and educator.

Moving from Transaction to Transition

Is there a yellow brick road where a true win-win situation exists for both advisor and client? Is there such a place where both advisor and client are rewarded intrinsically and materially throughout the process? Can there be a place where neither buyer's regret nor seller's regret has an opportunity to spawn? We believe that finding the place where the dreams and hopes of clients merge fluidly with those of the advisor is only possible when a philosophical shift takes place in the mind of the advisor from transaction-mindedness to transition-mindedness. We believe this shift takes place when the advisor focuses on

- what is happening in the life of the client;
- what could happen in the life of the client; and
- what the client wishes would happen.

We aren't naïve enough to suggest that advisors shouldn't worry about making a living. We recognize that the financial services business has been very kind to those who consistently generate transactions. Today's financial advisors are paid in a number of different ways for the services they offer. The most common form of compensation is the commission that advisors receive when they facilitate a transaction for their clients. It is estimated that over 75 percent of the compensation paid to advisors comes via this route. The inherent struggle with this system is that it focuses much of the discussion between advisor and client on the ultimate goal for the advisor. As one advisor put it, "We can talk all we want about goals and dreams and retirement with our clients, but ultimately, that conversation has to lead to a transaction where I can be paid for the time spent."

While advisors understand the distance that often exists between product and advice, today's commission structures still bundle the two and clients have difficulty determining the cost of each. To effectively meet the needs and expectations of tomorrow's client, you will have to force yourself to think first about connecting with the life needs of the client (transitions), and second think about how you will be compensated (transaction). We believe that if the conversation is handled properly, there will be a very short path from each life transition to financial transaction. The intuitive radar of today's client is alerted to this ordering of thought. How your thoughts are ordered will ultimately be revealed in your manner of conversation.

GETTING PAID FOR WHAT YOU REALLY DO

Financial planning starts where life planning leaves off. You don't start with the financial plan and then work the life plan into it. You start with a life plan and then build a financial plan to accommodate or accelerate that life plan. This changes the description of the business financial advisors are really in and it also affects what advisors will be compensated for in the mind of the client. Compensation, as the client sees it, can no longer be tied strictly to transactions, because the client clearly receives more value from the discussion than from the facilitation of a trade. Because the client no longer needs that advisor to simply facilitate a transaction, the service that *will* be paid for (either through commissions or fees) will be relevant and customized advice that helps the client negotiate key life transitions.

OPENING THE DIALOGUE

How do advisors make the fundamental and philosophical shift with their clients from a transaction-oriented style to a transition-oriented approach? A veteran advisor told us it starts with the very first positioning statement you make with the client. His first words to a client are these: "Money is a means, not an end. More important than building a pile of money is building a plan for that money. That plan will be as unique as you are. That's the reason I'm going to ask a lot of questions about your life, your dreams, and your plans as well as about your money." This is an effective positioning statement for the advisor who wishes to practice financial life planning as well as an segue into the questions that you will need to ask.

The issues that people deal with on a daily basis aren't whether the markets are up, down, or sideways, or whether they own the right mutual funds. People are more concerned about their children, their grandchildren, their health, their careers, and perhaps pending mid-life crises. In *Selling with Integrity,* author Sharon Drew Morgan calls this the "problem space" inside our heads. This problem space includes those nagging concerns that lurk in the shadows of our minds—issues we need to deal with, but those we do not particularly want to deal with. Equally as important as the problem space is the "dream space" in our heads. This dream space contains the abstract ideas of what we could and should be in our lives as well as the thoughts and visions of what we could do and who we could be if we could sit down with a map and figure out the route from here to there. These concerns can keep us up at night, cause indigestion, or stir every potential moment of tranquility; yet, most of us are not likely to confront the issues until we are led by another to do so. This is where a financial life planner comes in.

Your clients are trying to run their lives, not their money. The two are inextricably bound in their minds—one affecting the other. No matter how much money each of your clients has, chances are that during the course of a day they will think more about where their life is and where they want to be than they ever will about where their money is. For the client, this money is only a means to an end. Are you, the advisor, cognitive of what that end is for each client? Such awareness is the beginning of transition-mindedness.

HELPING YOUR CLIENTS THROUGH THE TRANSITIONS OF THEIR LIVES

Where can the advisor provide the most value for the client? While the answer to this question will be as varied as the number of clients you have, typically you can provide the most value by helping clients through a change that they might be going through, anticipate going through, or want to go through. Advisors will need to hone their skills in helping clients anticipate or deal with changes in their lives.

LOOKING FOR CHANGES

A life change event is a very personal transition and there is usually a financial element associated with it. This gives the advisor the opportunity to provide relevant information on matters that are personal to the client at a time when the client really needs the advice.

If you are aware of the basic changes that your clients go through and you have raised your antennae to the predictable changes, you can increase the value of your relationship with the client by "being there" as a partner, guide, and educator as they navigate through these changes. One of the biggest reasons advisors need to keep in touch with their clients is to stay top-of-mind by having their antennae attuned to each client's problem space. The reason that you want to be in that position is that your clients really need your services on their schedule—not on yours.

When something occurs in their lives that they didn't expect, they are going to want all of the advice that they can access. For those advisors who believe that they only need to update their information on clients once or twice a year, where will their clients turn when something unforeseen happens in the interim? This doesn't mean that you have to be on the phone every month like an ambulance chaser looking for accidents, but you should have a regular communication schedule that will keep you in touch with your client's mind and life agenda as much as possible.

YOUR ROLE IN MANAGING YOUR CLIENT'S UNEXPECTED LIFE TRANSITIONS

Most professional financial advisors are strong when it comes to discussing the financial consequences of an unexpected life change. For many that have experienced bereavement, the first call outside of family and friends is normally to an insurance professional that can provide comfort and reassurance in a difficult time. Advisors have been called upon to deal with divorce, financial windfalls, and financial catastrophes.

The advisor's foray into transition management in these circumstances tends to be reactionary. You are asked by your client to do something because a life change has required a financial transaction of some sort. There often isn't a lot of counseling involved because the time for your advice came during the planning that the client made sometime earlier. This is particularly true if your relationship with the client has only been based on financial products or you have limited your role to simply managing money.

THERE ARE SOME LIFE CHANGES YOU CAN ANTICIPATE

Think about how your own life has evolved to this point. What transitions have you gone through? What transitions do you expect to experience in the next ten years? The next 20 years? As you sit across the table from your clients, what changes do you think that they might be contemplating?

Transition from one life stage to another can be a very emotional passage. When we move from one phase of our life to another, we experience movement and change. Our ability to leave our past stage behind and embrace our new stage is often a function of acceptance, rationalization, planning, and goal setting. Financial life planning is, in part, the process of anticipating and understanding the normal transitions that we are likely to experience and creating a fulfilling vision of the new life phase. We can help paint a picture both by our inquiry and financial advice that connects directly to the transition issue.

As we approach the discussion of predictable life changes, it is important to remind our readers of the anachronistic nature of many life changes these days. People are going through predictable life changes at unpredictable times. There are 75-year-olds getting married and entering into prenuptial agreements. There are 65-year-olds going back to school, taking adventure trips, and acting like they are in their 20s again. There are 70-year-olds caring for 90-year-old parents (Carol knows of one 60-year-old caring for her 108-year-old grandmother who shows no signs of diminishing). There are people entering third marriages who want to adjust their estates accordingly. There are 30-year-olds moving back in with their parents.

Even predictable life transitions have become unpredictable as far as anticipating when a client will pass through them. For this reason, it is important to focus on the individuality of each client. This is the major flaw and oversight of most generational approaches that hold to the view that certain issues pertain only to certain age groups. While certain issues may be front and center for most individuals in a particular age group, it is risky to assume the same for all members of that group.

THE FINANCIAL IMPACT OF LIFE CHANGES

There are financial implications that accompany most of our predictable life changes. The opportunity for you the financial advisor to
reposition yourself as a financial life planner comes in making your
clients aware of the specific financial implications of every potential
life transition relative to their lives. This allows you to open up the discussion on life transitions and financial life planning. After all, as a
financial planner, it is your job to acquaint your clients with the potential fiscal problems that life changes create. Approaching each
life transition as a financial issue gives you the right to carry the discussion further and puts you in a position to provide your clients with
some important nonfinancial information that they may find valuable.

Figure 2.1 lists some life transitions and their most obvious financial implications.

FIGURE 2.1   Life Transitions and Their Financial Implications

Life Transition	Financial Implications	Your Opportunities
Moving into adolescence	• Learning about money	• Kids money camps • Education savings plan • In-trust accounts for children/grandchildren
Moving away from home	• Insurance • Savings accounts • Credit cards • Financial education	• First insurance policy • First investment account • Seminars for young adults • Comfort for parents and grandparents by working with children
Getting married	• Joint financial responsibilities • New home and mortgage • New job and pension program • Credit	• Increased insurance • Long-term investment accounts • Savings programs • Budgeting help • Financial education • Life planning information

FIGURE 2.1 Continued

Life Transition	Financial Implications	Your Opportunities
Having children	• Insurance • Saving for education • Loss of income • Increased expenses • Loss of freedom • Credit	• Increased insurance • Education savings plans • Budgeting help • Financial education • Life planning information
Midlife	• Income levels • Income insecurity • Debt levels • Net worth statement • Ongoing savings and investment • Additional capital purchases • Home upgrades • Aging parents • Financial needs of children • Taxes	• Retirement savings • Career transition • Financial education • Life planning information • Income replacement insurance • Critical care information for seniors • Education information • Tax planning strategies and information • Parental pensions
Empty nesters	• Change in residence • Increased disposable income • Increased opportunities for leisure • Refocus on retirement	• Lifestyle planning • Education programs for young people (children and grandchildren) • Retirement savings information and planning • Financial planning
Preretirement	• New vocation or avocation options • More realistic picture of retirement • Concern about retirement savings levels	• Lifestyle planning • Career transition • Self-employment opportunities • Retirement readiness modeling

(continued)

FIGURE 2.1   Continued

Life Transition	Financial Implications	Your Opportunities
Preretirement (continued)	• Retirement readiness thoughts • Concern about mortality	• Income replacement strategies • Pension plan education
Retirement	• Fulfilling activities • Financial freedom • Income concerns due to markets • Critical care worries • Retirement income	• Critical care insurance • Retirement income strategies and options • Lifestyle planning • Provide investment comfort

HELPING YOUR CLIENT THROUGH THE UNEXPECTED

Figure 2.2 details some of the most common unexpected life transitions that your clients will encounter, the role that you might

FIGURE 2.2   Unexpected Life Transitions and Their Financial Implications

Life Transition Event	Financial Implications	Your Opportunities
Death of a spouse	• Wills, probate, etc. • Insurance policies • Employment-related issues • Inheritance • Burial and final expenses • Financial planning for remaining spouse • Disposal of assets • Loss of income • Change in financial situation	• Approach with empathy as well as advice • Address their fears openly • Take on some tasks that will give your client time to grieve • Provide information and assistance on unfamiliar areas that they need to deal with • Perform same roles with extended family if needed

FIGURE 2.2   Continued

Life Transition Event	Financial Implications	Your Opportunities
Critical illness	• Income replacement • Insurance issues • Asset management • Health care costs • Change in work situation	• Address issues openly (if client asks) • Provide assistance and comfort for family • Take away financial management concerns • Be sensitive to need for lifestyle money in terminal illness situation
Divorce	• Inventory of assets • Disposal of assets • Managing settlements • Day-to-day financial management concerns • Tax implications • Income changes	• Be a partner as well as an advisor • Provide unemotional, rational advice • Recognize and provide information on lifestyle adjustments
Job transfer	• Income changes • Moving expenses • Standard of living changes • Insurance changes	• Reaffirm portability of your relationship and plan • Provide information on new locale
Job promotion	• Income changes • Managing new assets • Reworking financial plan • Insurance changes • Tax planning	• Consider that there may be some uncertainty or insecurity • Address changes in lifestyle and increase in stress level
Job loss	• Income needs • Managing settlement • Tax implications • Inventory of assets • Disposal of assets	• Understand emotional trauma • Help with career transition issues • Provide comfort for family • Provide optimism • Reaffirm partnership

(continued)

FIGURE 2.2   Continued

Life Transition Event	Financial Implications	Your Opportunities
Inheritance	• Financial planning education • Asset management • Asset disposal • Income changes • Lifestyle changes • Tax implications	• Understand the emotional attachments that may come with the money • Provide rational advice or be the voice of reason • Provide information on opportunities • Help other family members deal with new situation
Financial windfall	• Tax implications • Asset management • Spending changes • Income changes • Changes in employment situation • Lifestyle changes	• Understand the emotional side of the windfall • Be the voice of reason and caution • Provide counsel for other family members • Take a financial education approach • Refer to other professionals if necessary • Provide life planning information • Provide information on opportunities

take in helping them through each change, and the opportunities to give them the peace of mind that comes from knowing that the financial implications have been addressed.

HOPEFUL TRANSITIONS

Carol tells the story of a conversation she had with a builder working on her deck who began to inquire about her plans for the property in her backyard. Carol responded that she really wanted to do something nice but was having a hard time deciding exactly what direction to take; consequently, she had done nothing. The builder began asking more specific questions about the designs floating around in her head and began sketching Carol's ideas as she spoke them out. After seeing the sketches, Carol inquired about what it would cost to bring this picture to life and found that it was something she could afford to do right away.

In many ways, the conversation Carol's builder had with her is the conversation financial life planners need to have with their clients. People have dreams, visions, and ideas of redesigning their lives in some way. These ideas are often wistful and nebulous until the individual has a conversation with someone who knows how to sketch out both the image of what the change might look like and plan out the steps to completion and associated costs. This story is an illustration of the right brain function of drawing out the dream and creating a realistic image that needs to precede the left brain function of planning the steps and calculating the costs. Carol was not ready to take action until she had a picture of what she was working toward.

For many clients, very small adjustments can provide tremendous payoffs in their life satisfaction. In the conversation on life transitions, it is not enough to discuss only the predictable and expected, we need to move to the realm of personal imagination and inquire about dreams yet unborn. Many of your clients harbor ideas locked away in a secret place and these ideas are rarely brought out for public display. These dreams may include:

- Pursuing fascinating hobbies
- Embarking on personal growth tracks
- Experimenting with ideas and inventions
- Experimenting with careers
- Building meaningful relationships before it's too late
- Playing a significant role in chosen lives and causes
- Giving oneself the opportunity to fly solo, even if the attempt fails
- Challenging one's abilities on a new playing field

In most cases, these embryonic wishes will die unborn if not explored with someone who can help articulate what we want and assist in mapping the path to completion. We believe a financial life planner can be the facilitator of this process. A financial life planner can ask the questions, draw the sketch, and construct the plan. The entire process can start by simply asking a client to think about the reoccurring ideas the individual has thought about pursuing.

In Chapter 6, we introduce the tools and process for embarking on a life transitions dialogue. The Life Transitions Survey and accompanying worksheets cover over 60 life transitions related to working life, family life, life balance, financial life, and legacy. These tools cover the predictable, the unpredictable, and the "wished for" transitions. You will find these tools helpful for launching and maintaining a life-focused dialogue that continually points to the need for financial preparedness.

"IT'S ABOUT THE CLIENT!"

Nancy Shewfeldt, an investment advisor, changed her approach to business about five years ago. "We began to take seriously our mission statement that said, 'It's about the client.' We want our clients to know that there is a difference between what we do and what they can get down the street." In fact, Nancy's mission statement is even written from the standpoint of the client:

> Commitment is taking the time to ask *my* opinion, and answer *my* questions. Commitment is helping me through all states in *my* life and knowing that *my* life changes are as important as the changes in the stock market.

Nancy sees her role as a support resource when her clients undergo changes in their lives. "We get to know our clients pretty well," she says. "We can't be counselors in the truest sense of the word, but we can show support and provide wisdom in some areas that clients may not have expected."

You can keep their financial houses in order as they experience these various life transitions. Transition-mindedness is the attitude that will help advisors achieve the fluid amalgam between their services and the needs of their clients. When our arrows are pointed at transactions, the experience can be hit or miss for the client, but the arrow pointed at the life of the client will be a bull's-eye every time.

Chapter *3*

Necessary Skills
for the New Partnership

I cannot stress the importance of communication enough.
The number one reason an investor will leave a broker is that
the client's expectations were not met and/or communicated
clearly.

—*Louis Harvey, president, Dalbar and Associates*

Purdue University researchers Tim Christianson and Sharon De-
Vaney conducted a study to examine the interpersonal relationships
that develop between financial advisors and clients. In particular,
they wanted to identify factors that facilitate a client's feelings of loyalty. Of all the factors examined in their study, communication, by
far, had the strongest influence on an advisor's ability to win a client's
trust and commitment.

Of course, good communication alone will not guarantee relationship success, but a lack of communication will guarantee relationship failure. On the other hand, simply telling today's advisors that
they need to communicate more is tantamount to telling a courier to
deliver a package without explaining the route to the intended destination. In this chapter, we will describe the route your communi-
cations should take so you can arrive at the intended destination with
your clients. One advisor gave a wise and succinct description of this
route. "With every client I start my conversation with the heart, move

to the head, and end back at the heart." That description is the ideal road map for communicating with today's client.

What this advisor meant by starting with the heart, was that he made his first connection on the basis of why his clients were seeking financial advice—not in fiscal terms but in philosophical terms. Why did they want their money to grow? What would it bring to their lives? The move to the head was a matter of setting out an investment strategy, selecting investment vehicles that the clients would be comfortable with, and extrapolating how much and how long it would take. He ended communication with the heart by finishing on a chord of hope. There was now a finely defined finish line that they were moving toward that was aligned with each client's unique circumstances and personal values. The clients could feel hopeful that they were moving toward that goal and had taken a step toward self-mastery and life quality.

In my book with Scott West, *StorySelling for Financial Advisors,* we raised the issue of how little the information our industry attempts to communicate actually connects with our clients. What we found was that most advisors, because of the nature and form of the information they were communicating (numbers, charts, rankings, and facts), were making at best a "half-brain" connection. What this means is that these numbers and facts were penetrating the left side of the client's brain that plans, organizes, counts, and controls. What we found to be missing in the advisor-client communication process were the types of communication that connect with the right side of the client's brain such as stories, illustrations, and analogies. The right side of the brain is responsible for sensing, risking, feeling, and "seeing" what it is the advisor is trying to communicate.

What is relevant from that book to this discussion is that if the advisor's primary purpose in communicating with clients is to build trust, then we must start aiming our communication arrows toward the bull's-eye in the right side of the brain where trust is established. No one will argue with the idea that trust is an intuitive function that is established on the feeling or gut level. This is precisely how the right side of the brain operates—at the intuitive level.

SENDING THE RIGHT SIGNALS

It has been observed that the vast majority of people tends to become more conservative as they age. Those pot-smoking youngsters shouting liberal slogans from the psychedelic van in the late '60s tended to tone down their message and appearance once they had children and faced the prospect of working four to five months a year just to pay their tax bill. Do we move to the right as we age? We don't know the answer to that question in a political context, but brain science and gerontological studies indicate that people do move toward more right brain dominance as they age. Your 65-year-old client is much more right brain oriented than your 40-year-old client, for example. But what does that mean to you in practical terms, and how does this affect the role you play with your clients?

As people mature their thought processes change. They no longer make decisions solely on the basis of new information, but on the basis of a lifetime of stored memories and experiences. By drawing from these past experiences and the lessons they have learned about people and processes, the mature individual's thinking has shifted to a right-brained intuitive process. This means they are much more subjective in their decision making. They are no longer so interested in number crunching and analysis. Another factor influencing this shift is the fact that short-term memory function diminishes as we age. Consequently, we are not quite as comfortable wrestling with numbers and facts at 65 as we were at 45. As people mature they learn to follow their instincts, and their lifetime of experiences becomes their best indicator for making decisions. We mention this maturation process and how we must change to relate to it because recent census studies show the average median age in our society is rising. In fact, it is now at an all-time high and growing older. This means that your book of business is also getting older and you will need to develop the necessary skills for staying connected to the shift in mind-set.

It is not just the mature client that requires a balance of right brain-based communication to balance all the left brain-oriented statistics and facts found in most financial presentations. All age groups need assistance to help them "see" and understand what they are hearing from their advisor.

Figure 3.1 compares the means of communicating to connect with the right side of the brain versus the left side of the brain. A short perusal of this chart leads one to the conclusion that the financial services industry has placed a premium on the skills needed to provide services that appeal to the left side of the client's brain. What worked in the past will not work in the future for two reasons. First, the average client age is rising; and second, today's clients, regardless of age, are looking for a value-added proposition from their advisor.

FIGURE 3.1   Left Brain versus Right Brain

Relating to your client's left brain	Relating to your client's right brain
Planning	Teaching
Organizing	Communicating
Managing	Guiding
Detailing	Expressing ideas
Timing	Sensing problems
Implementing	Understanding
Supervising	Supporting
Controlling	Serving
Administering	Trusting intuition
Fixing	Sensing people

The most essential values that today's advisor can add for today's client are the functions indicated on the right side of this chart.

ENLARGING YOUR ROLE

When you look at the words on the left side of the chart you see in an instant how left brain-oriented the financial services professional is trained to be. Although planning, managing, detailing, timing, implementing, supervising, controlling, and administering are all necessary skills, the entrée to be able to display these competencies lies in the advisor's ability to demonstrate the functions on the right brain side of the chart. While the majority of advisors seem to excel at the former, many advisors struggle with the latter. Can you demonstrate your ability to manage a client's investment scenario without first being able to sense where the problems are? Will you gain and retain access to a client's assets without first forging an intuitive connection with that client? It is one thing to plan and implement a specific plan; it is entirely another matter to teach and counsel the client on how that plan will work. As many advisors have found, the degree to which a client complies with a plan can often hinge on how well the advisor has taught, coached, and communicated with the client. The fact that an advisor draws a beautiful road map is no guarantee that the client will follow it.

BASIS FOR THE NEW PARTNERSHIP

Planning, managing, detailing, timing, implementing, supervising, and administering are needed to get the job done but they are not necessarily the skills that will get you the job in the first place. There seems to be a widening gap in our society between what an advisor does and what a client wants. By asking an advisor to play partner, coach, and educator, as well as tactician and strategist, today's client is placing many advisors in an uncomfortable position. Many of these advisors wish that the client-advisor dynamic could go back to the basics—strategy forming and number crunching. But circumstances will not revert; instead they will intensify at a fast-forward pace.

A full-service or holistic approach to client services is rapidly becoming the strategy of choice for many financial planners. In the last decade the concept of client service has undergone profound, client-driven changes. Twenty years ago, clients were satisfied if quality work was done on a timely basis, and if the quarterly reports came in at the expected intervals. Today, clients are demanding more.

—Helene Stein and Marcia Brier, Financial Planning – Interactive
<www.financial-planning.com>

Today's client is looking for an advisor with interpersonal skills as well as market insight and strategic intellect. You could say that the new partnership is based on the advisor possessing equal parts emotional intelligence (EQ) and intellect (IQ)—a merging of insight and information. Today's client is placing an exacting premium on the advisor's ability to relate on a very human level.

How do you differentiate between EQ and IQ? That may be best answered by asking the question, *Have you ever known someone who was incredibly smart but really stupid at the same time?* Chances are that you have. When you bring those individuals to mind, what specific behaviors caused you to think of them in this way? Are they rude, impatient, insensitive, or self-sabotaging? Generally, when we ask this question of our audiences they characterize this sort of person as lacking common sense or people skills.

It should interest advisors to know that when we ask clients what they are seeking in an advisor, much of what they say falls directly into the emotional intelligence arena. They desire good communication and social skills, intuition and empathy, sufficient patience for teaching and coaching, and genuine concern and support. All these skill sets can be viewed as emotional competencies because it takes an emotional investment on the part of the advisor to succeed with a client. Teaching, coaching, communicating, and demonstrating concern are expressions of this skill set. You might say that today's client is tacitly saying, "I'll invest more assets with you when you demonstrate that you're willing to invest more energy and concern with me." Another quote by Stein and Brier is appropriate here: "Client loyalty is based on more than quality number crunching. When a client receives an excellent product and feels cared about, he will remain loyal to you and your firm, and it is likely the next generation will as well."

HOW HIGH IS YOUR EQ?

Daniel Goleman's breakthrough book, *Emotional Intelligence,* documented the fact that the basic assumptions about what makes a person successful are changing. It was once believed that a high IQ was the most important precursor to career success. However, recent studies seem to contradict this assumption. Studies indicate that a high IQ is somewhere between a 5 and 20 percent indicator of success, and that a high EQ is an 80 percent or more indicator of success. These conclusions caused quite a stir in the academic community in the mid-1990s when they were published because many in that community held fast to the idea that IQ was the most reliable success indicator. Many were troubled to think that a "soft" indicator such as emotional competence could replace a statistical indicator such as having an IQ of 124. However, when we stop and analyze IQ for what it is, we realize that it basically measures one's mental agility with numbers and language. Emotional intelligence (EQ), on the other hand, measures the following:

- *Awareness.* By this we mean awareness of one's own emotional state and the impact of those emotions on our behavior.
- *Restraint.* This is the ability to restrain negative emotions from affecting our behavior.
- *Resilience.* This is the ability to rebound and grow from failure, disappointments, and injustice.
- *Empathy.* This is the ability to discern others feelings and motives.
- *Social skills.* This is the ability to communicate, resolve conflicts, and relate to and lead others.

What are the practical implications of developing emotional intelligence in the business of advising clients on how to invest wisely? It is easy to draw a correlation between these basic principles of EQ and the conversations that take place daily in the life of the advisor.

- Awareness is necessary so advisors can realize the impact and perceptions of their personality on the psyche of their clients. Are you increasing or diminishing the distance between yourself and your clients? What sort of emotional response do you evoke in your clients?
- Restraint is necessary for keeping the emotional part of the brain from hijacking the rational part of the brain when we are agitated or perplexed with a client's behavior. Are some clients causing you to lose it or to sour your attitude?
- Resilience is necessary so the advisor can fight through career obstacles, negative surroundings, disappointments, and inevitable failures. Are you able to learn and grow from negative experiences?
- Empathy is necessary because it is the emotional radar that helps advisors read their clients' motivations, concerns, and feelings which will ultimately determine their level of satisfaction. Are you able to read between the lines and respond in a manner that assures and calms?
- Social skills are necessary to communicate, resolve differences, relate to a broad variety of personalities, and develop a dynamic of persuasiveness in your own personality. Are you able to lead people in the right direction without pushing?

FROM THE CLIENT'S POINT OF VIEW

While we view all of the above emotional competencies as being critical to an advisor's success, we want to spotlight the competency of empathy here. We do this for the simple reason that if we don't begin to see the world through the eyes of our clients, then they will move to someone else who is willing and able. Empathy is perhaps the most critical cornerstone in the process of building client trust. If we are not connecting with our clients' frustrations and hopes, how will they ever feel comfortable turning over their psychologically laden assets to us? Those assets, in many respects, are representative of who they are, where they've been, and where they hope to go. "Get

a handle on who I am before you try to get a handle on my money"
is the ultimatum playing out in the psyche of today's client.

Empathy helps to forge essential connections on three levels in
the client-advisor relationship. First, clients want the advisor to understand where they have been, where they are, and where they want
to go. They want you to truly understand the people and goals most
important to them and the concerns they have pertaining to these
life priorities. They want an advisor to connect with their mission and
to work with them in the context of that mission. Second, each
client, depending on personality, will want their advisor to play a
slightly different role. Some want a deferential, supportive role, and
others want a more assertive, leadership role. It is up to the advisor
to read between the lines and figure out exactly what role each client
needs the advisor to play. This task requires the competence of empathy. Third, the client wants to connect with an advisor who views
financial products and strategies from the client's own perspective
rather than from the perspective of the firm vending those products.

To illustrate in practical terms the role that empathy plays in
viewing financial products through the client's eyes, we have prepared the charts in Figure 3.2 that illustrate the gulf of perception di-
viding the advisor's and client's views of the same investment issues.
The first chart presents financial planning issues that an advisor will
ultimately address from an advisor's perspective. The second chart
simply restates the financial products and services in terms of the
client's life.

After contrasting these two views of the financial products and
services, we cannot help but notice that the client's view of financial
planning is largely *emotional* in nature. This is one fact of financial
life planning that advisors must fix their sights on and not let out of
their crosshairs. Money arouses emotion. Money is tied to deeply
held hopes and dreams that were obtained with profoundly emotional toil and stress—or perhaps dashed hopes and dreams. Money
can result from unhappy circumstances such as a divorce settlement,
an inheritance that is accompanied with profound guilt or grief, or
an early retirement package that shoved a worker out the door earlier than expected or desired. To form a partnership with our clients,
we need to start seeing their money through the same lens that they
see it. This is empathy. As we set out to perform simple transactions
regarding estate, education, retirement, or taxes, we must bear in
mind that each step has an emotional connection in our clients'
minds. While we may be advising them for purely rational reasons,

FIGURE 3.2 Advisor's View versus Client's View

		Advisor's View		
Tax	**Estate**	**Investment**	**Family**	**Business**
Revenue deferral	Life insurance	Asset management	Education savings	Business investment
Income splitting	Wills	IRAs, 401(k) pension plans,	Savings accounts	Succession planning
Tax sheltering	Trusts	RRSPs	Mortgages	Disability
Tax efficiency	Heirs	Personal investments	Loans	Business insurance
	Planned giving/ charitable remainder	Real estate	Revolving debt	

		Client's View		
IRS / Revenue	**After I am gone**	**Long-term money**	**My family and life**	**My business**
Tax refunds	Protect my loved ones	Protect savings	Assist children	Money to finance dreams
Pay less taxes	Pass on my assets	Look after retirement	Assist parents	Pass on assets
Contributions to 401(k), IRA, 403(b) (U.S.), RRSP (Canada)	Gift loved ones	Give me lifestyle money	Family home	Protect family
	Give to charity	Make big purchases	Lifestyle money	Protect business
	Don't give to IRS	Make my money grow	Desired lifestyle money	

they are motivated to follow through for reasons that are emotional in nature.

When we talk about funding their children's education, they may be thinking about the competing financial needs of aging parents. When we talk about life insurance, our clients may be thinking about individual and specific concerns such as the exceptional long-term needs of a disabled child. We may discourage revolving debt, but our clients may be thinking about what they need in order to make them feel successful. When we talk about retirement savings, our clients may be thinking of starting that business they always dreamed of or of telling their megalomaniacal boss good riddance. Clients have emotional reasons for doing what they do. If emotion isn't involved, there is no personal connection and, therefore, little motivation to follow through. Empathetic advisors study and query their clients until they are fully aware of their clients' motivations.

UTILITY MAN

In the 2000 Major League Baseball season, the Minnesota Twins' Denny Hocking received some notoriety because he played seven different positions in a number of games during the season. His versatility is a rare commodity in a world where even in sport highly specialized performers are the order of the day. Similar versatility in people skills is what we think today's advisor needs to aim for. To be successful in the new partnership, advisors can no longer dictate how they will relate to clients. Advisors need to possess the versatility to play to their clients' needs—whether it be director, facilitator, strategist, or coach. We recently saw a print advertisement for a financial services company that asked:

> "Need a secret weapon?"
> "Who will be your quarterback?"
> "Are you looking for a copilot?"

The advertisement depicts a female professional advisor who is willing to operate as secret weapon, quarterback, or copilot depending on which role is most advantageous to the client. This is the financial services equivalent to the utility man.

This is the diversity clients are looking for in a financial advisor. An advisor who knows how to play the game can help them strategically and guide them throughout the journey.

Chapter 4

Forming the New Partnership: A Business Transition Story

Within the financial services industry, a trend toward a more holistic approach to product and service delivery is rapidly gaining momentum. For those advisors who see the value of this movement, the financial life planning perspective can provide a framework for developing a more client-centered practice. Whether your current compensation structure is commission-based, fee-based, or a combination of both, the underlying principles of financial life planning will bring more value to clients and help your business to grow.

Ross Levin, CFP, transitioned to a more client-centered approach several years ago and is now a well-recognized and often-quoted expert in the field of life planning. Over the years, Ross's firm, Accredited Investors of Minneapolis, has evolved into a high-end, fee-only, life-planning practice.

Accredited Investors currently has around 230 clients who pay $10,000 per year, or a percentage of assets under management equal to or greater than that amount. It is a business that has great appeal to high net worth clients who are interested in a more holistic approach to their money. Accredited Investors has a highly predictable cash flow because it derives no other income aside from fees. It is an up-front proposition regarding costs, and Ross's firm provides whatever level of administration and service the client and advisor deem necessary.

Ross Levin works with three partners, financial planning assistants, and an administrative staff. In the words of Levin, "Delivering comprehensive planning is more expensive than other financial service models, but it is also a much more cohesive relationship with the client." Levin says that his firm does so much for some clients that "leaving would be unthinkable for them." Levin warns that many have tried unsuccessfully to establish this sort of business model, and that those who succeed will do so by virtue of a good mix of competency, sincerity, and a strong relationship with clients.

In this chapter, we will take you through a tour of the following aspects of Ross Levin's practice:

- The dialogue at the initial prospect meeting
- Where clients come from
- The Wealth Management Index™ that the firm implements with each client to keep score of progress

A DIFFERENT SORT OF CONVERSATION

Within the first minute, clients meeting with an Accredited Investors advisor know that this is going to be different than any other conversation they previously have had with a financial services professional. The stage is set with the very first question, and the interview is not complete until the advisor has plumbed the depths of what clients want out of life and what they want from their advisor.

Levin emphasizes the fact that asking the right questions is critical to the process of letting clients know that you are serious about helping them get what they want out of life and in differentiating your services from what is commonly found in financial services. He states that the answer to one question in particular is a sure sign that the individual has moved from a prospect to a client.

Following are the five questions prospects at Accredited Investors are asked and the reasons for asking.

Question 1: Why are you here?

Reason for asking: To ascertain real issues.

Levin states that there are real, visceral reasons—that transcend simply building wealth—which motivate people to approach a financial professional. Wealth is representative of deeper desires, hopes, and dreams for our lives and those close to us. For this part of the interview, Levin uses the *values ladder* approach, advocated by Bill Bacharach is his book *Values Based Selling*. In this model, if a client says she wants more money, the advisor responds by asking *why* she wants more money. If the client responds that she wants more freedom, the advisor responds by asking *why* she values freedom, and so on and so forth, until the advisor has aided the client in distilling her answer to the most basic level. The intent of this question is to move past what clients want financially to why they want it to happen.

Levin talks about how prospects might state that they want more money so that they can have more time with their families. Levin asks prospects to talk about the family members they want to spend more time with. When prospects mention a child, a spouse, or a parent, Levin then asks, "What kind of parent (or spouse, or child) do you want to be?" As you can see, Levin has no qualms about going right for the emotional base that is motivating the individual to seek out financial help. He informs us that prospects enjoy this sort of opportunity to discuss the things that matter most to them.

Question 2: What is going on in your life and how do those events make you feel?

Reason for asking: To discern the client's desired quality of life.

This question aims at uncovering what life events are arousing financial uncertainty. One scenario that illustrates this well is that of divorced women who are facing a great deal of uncertainty in life and with their finances. From their answers, the advisor can develop a financial plan that will work toward their goals, abate their fears, and remove the stress associated with having to orchestrate these affairs on their own.

People will talk about relationship problems, work problems, health problems, extended family problems, and any other issues that are interfering with their quality of life or events they suspect may be upsetting their contentment. It is not the event itself that brings clients to the advisor, but rather the feelings the event has forced to the front of their psyche. Fear, uncertainty, insecurity, or any other haunting emotion can easily rob clients of their life enjoyment until they address the issues necessary for resolution—and many of these issues are fiscal in nature. Levin believes in getting these life events and the related feelings on the table so clients can get a good grasp of their motives for seeking help.

Question 3: What money messages did you get growing up?

Reason for asking: To raise client awareness of the link between early messages and current financial behavior.

"We are creatures of our past," says Levin, "so, this simple question allows people to discuss how their family background shaped their money profile. It's amazing how frequently people will recognize that many of their feelings surrounding money evolved around the dinner table."

Some people have learned to treat money as if there may never be another dollar, while others have learned to act as if they had an orchard of money trees growing in their backyards. Some people have learned that money issues are private and should not be discussed, while others avoid money conversations because they are always filled with stress. Some have learned that to make money you have to take risks, and others have learned to never stray near the slightest risk. There is little doubt that people carry the internal money issues learned at home well into their adult lives. Many people do not fully understand why they think and/or behave the way they do until they reflect on this question.

Question # 4: If you were diagnosed with a terminal illness and you didn't know how long you had to live, what would you want to do with your life?"

Reason for asking: To distill life to its most basic desires and motivations.

This question cuts to the soul of life satisfaction and arouses clients to examine whether or not they are getting their money's worth out of life. If an individual is running down a stressful occupational track, living a chaotic lifestyle, feeling displeased with the direction of his life, or shelving important life goals, this question will bring these emotions to the surface. Ross Levin informs us that this is a pivotal query in the life-planning interview. *"If they answer this question, there is a 99 percent chance that they mentally moved from being a prospect to a client."*

By asking this pointed and searching question, Levin communicates to prospects that he is serious about helping them get their lives on the right track. The fact that these prospects have money (all Accredited Investors must have $1 million in investable assets) by no means ensures that they have their lives and money on the perfect track. Because of their willingness to ask these pointed questions, Levin and associates have been able to guide their clients into meaningful transitions.

One client who had just sold a business expressed a desire to move into the venture capital arena. Ross was able to put him in touch with some board members of nonprofit organizations who were venture capital veterans. Through this nonprofit involvement, Levin's client became well acquainted with these individuals and consequently segued into the venture capital business himself. Another client, quite successful in his field, was both rich and miserable. He voiced a desire to write a novel, and Levin helped him to arrange his financial affairs in a way that would afford him the opportunity. A doctor, whose husband was also a doctor, was feeling like she was missing too much of her young children's early years. With Levin's help, she decided to tack on a few earning years later in life and take advantage of the present to satisfy her need to be with her children.

When advisors ask these types of questions, they can and should expect clients to open up their storehouses of hopes, aspirations, and dreams for their lives. As clients articulate their dreams, the advisor becomes something akin to a personal CFO who manages the financial functions and technicalities that ultimately give life to these dreams.

WHAT DO YOU WANT FROM ME?

At this point in the process, Levin and his associates move from examining the client's life path and heritage of money issues to querying their expectations of and relationship to financial professionals. In the penultimate question, clients get a chance to paint a portrait of the impact they expect from their relationship with Ross— and in the last question, he obtains a biographical sketch of their associations with other professionals.

Question 5: If we were to do a great job for you, what would that look like a year from now?

Reason for asking: To establish client expectations in the advisor-client relationship.

Ross Levin believes that most clients fall into one of four types in their relationship to money. This question can help establish which description fits each client. The types are:

- Relationship clients
- Fear-based clients
- Curious clients
- Greedy clients

Relationship Clients

These individuals want to develop a long-term relationship with someone they can trust. They tend to be easy to talk with and relate to. It is important to spend time listening to these clients. They want to be comfortable. They tend to be very good long-term clients and very nice to work with. They may follow your recommendations, but they want to be involved in the process. After meeting with the relationship client, summarize the business aspects of your meeting in a letter. This is helpful in keeping the business end of the relationship moving forward.

Fear-Based Clients

These are typically financial novices. They may be the recent benefactors of an inheritance or the financially uninvolved spouse in a divorce. They also can be busy professionals who are in control of all areas but money. These clients will be reliant upon you. They will need educating, even if they do not ask for it. Try to work with them, not just for them. You have to help them gain confidence in their ability to manage money.

Curious Clients

These people are typically working with you because they are busy people. They will show a great deal of interest in what you do and sometimes imply that they would like to do what you do when they retire from their current profession. These clients will have done some self-education and have preformed opinions. You must talk with these clients in great detail about their money beliefs that you may feel are false. They will be very good long-term clients if you speak their language and provide support for what you are doing. As these clients get to know you better, they may begin to resemble the relationship type of client. Just don't forget about their need for information and control. After you have made decisions together, continue to support those decisions through articles that you find and third-party endorsements of your ideas.

Greedy Clients

This type of client usually has unclear, constantly changing goals that are measured by short-term performance. They may be charming with a high energy level and a quick mind. They tend to put you on a pedestal at the outset and spend the rest of the relationship trying to knock you off that pedestal. It's all about short-term returns with the greedy client.

Levin says that he tries not to work with these clients as they end up creating trouble for him and his staff by making unreasonable or unappreciated requests. Eventually, this type of client ends up leaving. Levin gives the example of a client who was furious with his firm for not having him fully invested in international funds in a year in which they beat U.S. stocks. He says, "In Roger Gibson's paradigm [from the book *Asset Allocation: Balancing Financial Risk,* Irwin Professional Publishing, 1990], the greedy client would believe in market timing *and* stock selection!"

MANAGING CLIENTS WITH THE WEALTH MANAGEMENT INDEX

One of the first objectives of Accredited Investors is to help the client redefine what it means to manage wealth. We live in a world where many clients' scope of wealth management is narrow and dominated by short-term performance numbers. If you bill yourself as a money manager, you are setting yourself up for failure because you will be compared—and come up short—to some index or another money manager. Levin's group prepares clients for the fact that in a roaring bull market a properly allocated portfolio is destined to trail most of the U.S. indices. A major educational objective is to help clients grasp the fact that an appropriate risk-adjusted plan tied directly to the client's objectives is more meaningful than absolute total return.

This is where the Wealth Management Index comes in. The Wealth Management Index is a tool to quantify clients' annual success toward reaching their stated objectives. This index has five major categories and several subcategories within each major category. In the process of building and maintaining wealth, a weighting is assigned to the five cornerstones of the index as follows.

Wealth Management Index

1. Asset protection (preservation): 25 percent
2. Disability and income protection (protection): 20 percent
3. Debt management (leverage): 10 percent
4. Investment and cash flow planning (accumulation): 25 percent
5. Estate planning (distribution): 20 percent

Levin and his clients set targets for measuring success that are measured against the Wealth Management Index—and not against popular indices. Levin demonstrates to his clients that their success hinges as much on their behavior staying aligned with the plan as it does on Accredited Investors following through with its service and functions.

A client may place more emphasis on one area than the others, but that does not diminish the importance of visiting those other areas. Most of Levin's work with clients will be in the areas where they may feel the greatest deficiency. Each year the client's stated goals are measured against the agreed upon Wealth Management Index. The index—supplanting other popular measures as the standard for success—is the linchpin in the life-planning strategy that Levin uses. Measuring success by factors you cannot control is an exercise in futility that only leads to dissatisfaction on both the client's and advisor's part. There is an inherent disappointment built into measuring success by anything but progress toward a client's personally stated life goals and objectives.

Figure 4.1 details the subcategories and percentage allocations assigned to the five areas measured in the Wealth Management Index. These categories are constantly revisited and progress is measured specifically against them.

Individual Components and Percentage Allocations

The 21 individual components of the Wealth Management Index represent the following percentage of the total scale.

1. Is your asset allocation appropriate? (10%)
2. Were your annual contributions or withdrawals on target? (10%)
3. Are your business interests adequately covered? (8.5%)

**FIGURE 4.1   Subcategories and Percentage Allocations
(within each category)**

1. **Asset Protection (Preservation)**
   34%   Are your business interests adequately covered?
   33%   Do you have an appropriate amount of life insurance consistent with an articulated philosophy around this insurance?
   33%   Have you protected yourself against catastrophic loss due to long-term care, property losses, or liability issues?

2. **Disability and Income Protection (Protection)**
   40%   Do you have too much or too little disability protection given your assets and income? Will it pay you should you be unable to work?
   20%   Did you receive in income from all sources (earnings, gifts, social security, pensions) what you expected to this year?
   20%   Did you spend according to plan?
   20%   Did you use all reasonable means to reduce your taxes?

3. **Debt Management (Leverage)**
   40%   Is your current ratio stronger than 2:1 and is your total debt reasonable as a percentage of your total assets?
   30%   Have you access to as much debt as reasonably possible and at the best available rates?
   20%   Have you managed your debt as expected?
   10%   Is your debt tax-efficient?

4. **Investment Planning (Accumulation)**
   40%   Were your annual contributions or withdrawals on target?
   40%   Is your asset allocation appropriate?
   10%   How did you do against your established rate-of-return target (CPI plus stated percentage)?
    5%   Was the portfolio income tax-efficient?
    5%   Have you set aside enough cash for anticipated purchases in the next three years?

5. **Estate Planning (Distribution)**
   40%   Does your will match your wealth transfer wishes?
   25%   Are your assets titled correctly and are all beneficiary designations appropriate?
   15%   Do you need and have . . .
      • A power of attorney?
      • A health care declaration?
      • A living will?
   15%   Have you established and funded all necessary trusts?
    5%   Have you made your desired gifts for this year?

4. Do you have an appropriate amount of life insurance, consistent with an articulated philosophy around this insurance? (8.25%)
5. Have you protected yourself against catastrophic loss due to long-term care, property losses, or liability issues? (8.25%)
6. Does your will match your wealth transfer wishes? (8%)
7. Do you have too much or too little disability protection given your assets and income? Will it pay you should you be unable to work? (8%)
8. Are your assets titled correctly and are all beneficiary designations appropriate? (5%)
9. Did you receive in income from all sources (earnings, gifts, social security, pension) what you expected to this year? (4%)
10. Did you use all reasonable means to reduce your taxes? (4%)
11. Did you spend according to plan? (4%)
12. Is your current ratio better than 2:1 and is your total debt reasonable as a percentage of your assets? (4%)
13. Have you established and funded all necessary trusts? (3%)
14. Do you need and have a power of attorney, a health care declaration, or a living will? (3%)
15. Have you access to as much debt as reasonably possible and at the best available rates? (3%)
16. How did you do against your established rate-of-return budget (CPI plus stated percentage)? (2.5%)
17. Have you managed your debt as expected? (2%)
18. Have you set aside enough cash for purchases to be made in the next three years? (1.25%)
19. Was the portfolio income tax-efficient? (1.25%)
20. Is your debt tax-efficient? (1%)
21. Have you made your desired gifts for this year? (1%)

Each year clients are scored on a ten-point scale within each category. That point total is then multiplied by the percent within the category to give points toward the index. All of these points are then added up to give the client his or her total Wealth Management Index score. Here is how the point totals are interpreted:

- 100–85   Financial plan should meet your objectives
- 84–65   Financial plan needs to be more focused on your needs
- Under 65 Planning overhaul is necessary

According to Levin, "As you score the Wealth Management Index with the client, you create a whole new set of talking points. Values may be redefined. The reason the client needs to be a part of the scoring process is because it brings the index down to an emotional level—a level that will help the client to see how he or she is vulnerable."

There are many ancillary benefits of revolving your life-planning and wealth-building conversations around this index.

- You have clearly aligned yourself as the client's advocate.
- You have honestly assessed the client's situation and have taken joint responsibility for the effectiveness of the financial plan.
- The client is engaged in the plan with you.
- Interdependence is established that leads to a mutually beneficial long-term relationship.

In his book, *The Wealth Management Index: The Financial Advisor's System for Assessing & Managing Your Client's Plans and Goals,* Ross Levin guides advisors through the intricacies of administering the Wealth Management Index. He illustrates the processes of establishing a work plan and working through each component of the index to provide strategic decisions around each point. Levin's book and system are highly recommended for advisors who desire to move their practice to a life-planning focus and to a more comprehensive financial model.

Levin made this transition after experiencing the market blowup of 1987 and found himself wondering how he could better serve clients and still make a living in the process. His business went through some years of evolution between commissions and fees until he arrived at the current model of a flat yearly fee for each client.

His business has grown organically with no expenditure for advertising and marketing. All of his clients come on a referral basis because they have heard that Levin is a more holistic planner and are interested in a life-planning approach to their money management. His clientele is diverse and includes executives who have been motivated to come for stock-option planning, divorced women and widows, and professional couples.

Levin summarizes the benefit of totally transporting a practice from transaction orientation to life planning in philosophical terms, "I've tried to align my life and practice with the laws of abundance.

What that means to me is that if I bring true value to my clients and I am up-front about what value I can and cannot bring, then abundance will follow."

Some call it the law of sowing and reaping. In this case, planting the seeds of life fulfillment has provided a rich harvest for both clients and advisors.

Chapter 5

Questions about Life

Elissa Buie, CFP and former president of the FPA, specializes in what she calls "spirit of life" financial planning. When asked how she got started along these lines, she gave this answer:

> I had hired a business consultant and he pushed me to evaluate who were my best clients. I realized I had no typical profile: I had clients from all walks of life, income levels, vocations, and avocations. The common thread was that my best clients were the ones I knew the best. So I flipped that around and realized I had to make sure I knew all our clients as best I could. I started taking a life history of all our clients and from that evolved the goal-setting capabilities.

—Journal of Financial Planning, *9/10/01*

Buie's discovery was that comprehending a client's history was critical to knowing the client and to setting appropriate goals. Financial planning can be a brilliant process, but it is only as good as the targets that are set. We won't find the proper targets until we ask the right questions. This chapter is about asking the right questions.

We would like to open this chapter by applying the very craft we recommend for your practice—*asking questions that cut to the core of the issues at hand.*

- How important is asking good questions to your business's success?
- What do the questions you ask your clients say about you?
- Could you be more efficient by using better questions in the discovery process?
- Are you asking your clients the kinds of questions that help build their trust and confidence in you?
- Do your questions help you learn about your clients' life goals and priorities as well as the distribution of their assets? Do you know *who* your clients are as well as *what they have?*
- Do you customize your list of discovery questions for each client?
- Do you continue to ask important questions even after you "land" the client?
- Do you ask questions that give you a clear understanding of your clients' values?
- Do you demonstrate a keen sense of curiosity and interest in your clients' lives or just in their financial situations?

Most of the preceding questions are Socratic in nature and are simply intended for you to *question your questions.* We are of the opinion that nothing communicates who we are to others like the questions we ask. So much is revealed about our nature and character by the manner and intensity of our queries into the lives of others. What we have found is that the majority of people are a shade too self-centered or simply lack the curiosity to make significant and meaningful inquiries into the lives of others.

My favorite example of narcissism is the fellow who said, "Enough of me talking about me, how about you talk about me for awhile." Peruse the conversation patterns with the next ten people you meet and see how true this idea is. It is amazing how you can stand out from the crowd simply by the questions you ask. Think back to the last time you had a conversation with someone who could not learn enough about you. Chances are such conversational events are few and far between—so far, in fact, that you possibly cannot remember such an occurrence. If you have had such a conversation or know a person who converses in this way, you no doubt fondly remember that occurrence and person. In part, this chapter is about helping you become that sort of person in your clients' memory banks. This chapter is about doing a better job of what we are charged with—to help our clients achieve the quality of life they desire. To accomplish this goal, financial life planners will focus on ways to get to know their clients better.

Know thy client is the foundation from which all successful client relationships are built. The sad truth is that many professionals have never developed the skills of inquiry to the degree that they know what really matters to their clients. For a best practices spotlight on the *Journal for Financial Planning* Web site (April 30, 2001), Kathleen Cotton, CFP, was asked, "What do you recommend planners do to improve their services to clients?" She replied: "Focus on the client during the meeting and not on your brilliance. Instead of looking on the meeting to expound and impress, look at their situation and take action for them. Clients want to know they have been heard. Listen to them and then take action."

There are some good models out there for client discovery; however, most of them fall woefully short in the department of framing the life goals, transitions, concerns, and hopes of the client. Most discovery models major in discovering *what* the client has and minor in discovering *who* the client is. How can we find solutions for our clients' lives if we only have a marginal understanding of the aspirations and dramas playing out in their lives? In an article titled "Values-Based Planning: Seeing the Whole Client," Kris Arnzen (*Journal of Financial Planning,* March 1999.) commented that clients will directly and indirectly give you clues about what is most important to them. She continued: "And when you know the who, what, and why about your client, you do them the greatest service by designing plans that help them address those values. Doesn't it make sense that the client would want to act on those ideas faster than they would act to buy a particular mutual fund or life insurance policy? This is because you have been able to frame the plan in terms of their life. They told you what's important and you listened."

The majority of inquiries conducted by most advisors is focused on the size allocation and location of assets and the minority of inquiries is focused on the lives of the clients (the purpose of the process). It should come as no surprise then to learn that many clients are notably underwhelmed by their conversations with this type of advisor. It must also be noted that advisors who fail to ask the proper life questions miss many opportunities for promoting their own products and services. Here is a good example.

An insurance agent sat down with my wife and me and began to tell us that a major motivator for purchasing a life insurance/investment policy should be to provide for our children's college education. We thought it was rather presumptuous of this fellow to tell us what our motivations should be rather than ask us how we felt about funding our children's education. Both my wife and I had worked our way through school with negligible aid from our parents. We had discussed this issue and felt the experience had helped fortify our work ethic and mold our character; and we both had seen too many of our classmates on a free ride from their parents fritter and party away their opportunity to learn. We had decided that our children would (1) earn money toward college; (2) receive matching funds from us based on their earnings; and (3) take out a student loan for the shortfall. Had the insurance broker bothered to ask, we would have explained our philosophy.

He didn't get our business.

The next agent that visited us started by asking the story of our lives. That was the best move he could have made. What he discovered was that my wife had lost her first husband to cancer after six months of marriage when she was just 21 years old. Before he died, he had forgotten to sign a document that would have reassigned the benefits of his life insurance policy from his parents to his wife. For some unimaginable reason, his parents kept the benefit after his death, leaving his widow both bereft and broke.

Consequently, my wife had a morbid fear of another complication in her support should I precede her in death. With the way she felt, no amount of life insurance would suffice.

Because he bothered to ask, that agent got the sale.

—Excerpt from StorySelling *by Scott West & Mitch Anthony*

As the preceding example illustrates, a searching inquiry into the life of the client can open up more opportunities than a product-focused inquiry because the life-focused inquiry exposes both the experiential and emotional footing for the services you will provide. The client does not question the relevance of the service or product you offer when it is directly tied to their life experience or future life path. The first representative in the above story assumed that he understood what the clients wanted and proceeded to forge ahead with a product-focused approach that failed to connect with the clients.

WHY DO YOU ASK?

We would all do well to analyze the questions we are asking our clients and prospective clients to ascertain whether our inquiry process is designed to benefit the client or ourselves. There are four types of questions we can ask clients and each type of question has a unique objective. The four types of questions are:

1. *Data questions.* These are designed to get information (e.g., most questions on a financial questionnaire; the summary of assets and where invested, etc.).
2. *Intuitive questions.* These questions allow you to read between the lines (e.g., "If you were to teach one financial lesson to your children or grandchildren, what would that lesson be?"). These are the questions that help you hear what your client is thinking but not saying.
3. *Socratic questions.* These are designed to stimulate necessary thought (e.g., "If you had the money, what would you do differently?").
4. *Biographical questions.* These are designed to build understanding of the client's life history and to strengthen the relationship between advisor and client (e.g., "Tell me about your life's work" or "Tell me about your father. What kind of work did he do?").

Trust is the irreplaceable cornerstone of a lasting relationship. If we look at trust building as the goal, then all our processes should be contributing toward that goal—most significantly, the discovery process. Clients learn their most valuable information about us through the questions we ask about them.

Many advisors in the financial services industry are data-oriented rather than life-oriented. They are aimed primarily at deciphering their clients' current financial status without sufficiently exploring who their clients are. Kris Arnzen compares the inquiry strategy of many advisors to the *Dragnet* television hero of yesteryear, Sgt. Joe Friday. But she warns against this strategy because life is about much more than "just the facts." "As financial planners, we too risk being taken 'off the air' in the new millennium if we continue to solely concentrate on the technical part of the planning process."

Planning must encompass more than the material assets of the person. Even some of the better models for discovery fall short in this area. Critique the questionnaires you are using—and the questions

---

FIGURE 5.1   Inquiry Query

---

(1) Data—questions that gather information

Grade yourself _____

(2) Intuitive—questions that reveal values, beliefs, personality, and priorities

Grade yourself _____

(3) Socratic—questions that cause the client to think about goals, hopes, and direction of life

Grade yourself _____

(4) Biographical—questions that help you understand the client's history and life path

Grade yourself _____

---

you are asking—in your discovery process against the form in Figure 5.1 and give yourself a grade under each category. How do the questions you ask your clients, either verbally or in written form, measure up? Give yourself a grade for each category.

WHAT INFORMATION DO YOU NEED?

The kind of information that you require to build your framework for financial life planning will be somewhat different than the standard questions that are found on most financial planning data forms. For example, let's take a look at the first three elements of the CFP financial planning process, detailed in Figure 5.2, from a financial life planning perspective.

It is clear that to make a better connection to the life of the client we need a better process of discovering what the client's life and goals are all about. You cannot compartmentalize money into a sep-

---

FIGURE 5.2   The Financial Life Planning Approach

Step	Approach	Information Needed
Step One	Identify the client's personal and financial goals	• Discover the extent that the client has built a life plan for the future. • Clarify the client's short-term and long-term life priorities in all areas of life. • Redefine such vague terms as *retirement* and *financial independence* in terms of client's life plan. • Client must understand core values and needs as a first step in creating goals. • Identify all people who will be affected by the life plan and financial plan.
Step Two	Clarify the client's present financial situation	• Identify gaps between where the client is today and where he or she wants to be in life. • Discuss the client's views and beliefs regarding money. • Ask how the client arrived at his or her present situation.
Step Three	Identify financial problems that create barriers to achieving financial independence	• What are the important life stressors that could affect the financial plan? • What transitions in the client's life might occur soon? • How does the client's view on and habits with money relate to a view on life? Are there conflicts? • Does the client plan on working and earning in the post-retirement years?

---

arate discussion apart from how and where the client attains the money, and how and to whom that money will be distributed. In this arena the advisory industry must take steps in the client's direction.

In financial life planning we offer a unique discovery process that is more client-centric than most approaches used in the past. The chart in Figure 5.3 illustrates the inevitable conflict that results when advisor goals fail to connect with client goals.

In the advisor-centric model, the motivating factors are the advisor's business and production goals. The advisor then looks for human contacts through which those goals can be achieved. With each contact the advisor strives to maximize transactional opportunities with the hope of also benefiting the client's net worth. In the twenty-first century, this approach can and does lead to both buyer's regret and seller's regret. It is unlikely to be effective in attracting and retaining life-long clients, especially during difficult market conditions and market downturns.

In the client-centric model, the advisor simply strives to draw to the surface the issues and concerns that are near and dear to the life of the client, and then provides the necessary financial transactions and services to address those issues and concerns. At the core of this process is the objective of aligning the clients' financial goals with values and priorities in life. Chances are great that the client has not yet fully clarified what these goals are. This is the first place the advisor can help. Next, clients know—and feel uncertainty about—many of the transitions they are currently facing or will be facing in the future. Again, the advisor can help clients focus on these transitions

FIGURE 5.3   Advisor-Centric versus Client-Centric

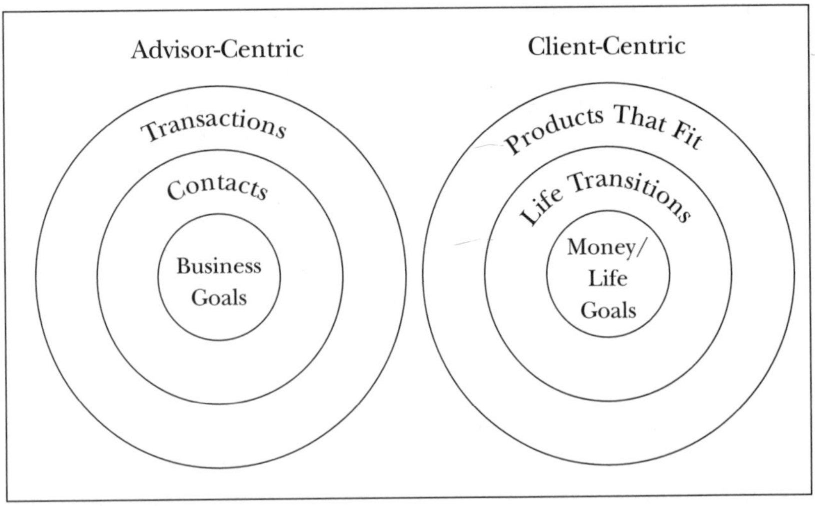

and the financial implications of each. Finally, in the client-centric model, clients want transactions and processes in place that tie directly to the goals and transitions in their lives. Financial transactions and processes must link directly to life goals and transitions or the client will doubt the necessity and validity of the transactions the advisor performs.

PAST, PRESENT, AND FUTURE

Of the four types of questions we can ask—data, intuitive, Socratic, and biographical—the financial services industry has done the best job with data questions. Advisors typically get a snapshot of the financial past and present of their clients and try to build a plan that will help to project the future. If we narrow our discovery process primarily to data gathering, clients may feel that we know their numbers but we don't know *them.*

Figure 5.4 lists questions of the intuitive, Socratic, and biographical variety to help you understand the past, present, and future of your clients. We will not attempt to add any more data questions to your existing process. We have interviewed scores of advisors to find out which questions they have found to be most helpful in gaining a better understanding of their clients' lives in order to build more credible relationships with them. With each category we offer both the questions asked and the reasons behind asking the questions.

FIGURE 5.4   Questions to Help Determine Your Client's Past, Present, and Future

Review Your Client's Past

- *Where are you from?*
  Reasons for asking: Reveals a client's roots and values; creates the possibility of a connection between someone or someplace both the client and advisor know; enlarges understanding of client

- *What have been some of the best financial decisions you have made in the past?*
  Reasons for asking: Reveals financial knowledge, risk tolerance, and experience; may also reveal mistakes and shortcomings

(continued)

FIGURE 5.4   Continued

Review Your Client's Past, continued

- *How did you accumulate what you have today?*
  Reasons for asking: Reveals financial disciplines or lack thereof; indicates need for structured savings program (Did they build their assets through disciplined process or fortuitous circumstance?)

- *What lessons about money did you learn growing up?*
  Reasons for asking: Reveals values regarding money, level of financial instruction, and whether client's relationship to money is conflicting or harmonious

- *Tell me about your life's work.*
  Reasons for asking: Reveals goals, directions, and life course of client; may also reveal work satisfaction and/or entrepreneurial ambitions

- *In the past, have you known anyone who has retired successfully, and what factors contributed to that success?*
  Reason for asking: Reveals client's vision (or lack thereof) for retirement (Do they have a realistic picture of what will keep them content in retirement years?)

Establish Your Client's Present

- *Tell me about your family?*
  Reasons for asking: Reveals the needs of others that will be affected by the financial planning process

- *Who else is affected by the financial decisions you make?*
  Reasons for asking: Reveals family, extended family, and others for whom the client feels a sense of financial responsibility

- *What is the most important thing that your money gives you today?*
  Reasons for asking: Reveals the client's values and priorities; helps to determine what money represents in the life of the client

- *What are some of the factors or circumstances in your life that could affect your financial plan?*
  Reasons for asking: Reveals concerns and fears that may take financial plans hostage; may reveal need for insurance and financial security products

- *What transitions are you and your family presently experiencing?* (See the Life Transitions Survey in Chapter 6.)
  Reason for asking: Reveals present situations that may need to be addressed at financial planning, transactional, or educational level

---

FIGURE 5.4 Continued

Establish Your Clients Present, continued

- *What would you do differently if you "had the money" (if money was not a limiting factor)?*
  Reasons for asking: Reveals contentment with current life/work situation; reveals client's most cherished goals; reveals client's realistic/unrealistic expectations of money

- *Are there any investments that you will not make because they go against your principles?*
  Reason for asking: Reveals the client's level of desire to be socially responsible and conscientiously satisfied with personal investment decisions

- *Who or what are your chief information sources regarding financial decisions?*
  Reasons for asking: Reveals sophistication and level of client's financial education and how current that education is; reveals degree of dependence on other individuals for making financial decisions such as a spouse or parent or another financial professional such as an accountant

Uncover Plan for Your Client's Future

- *How do you plan to change your lifestyle (if at all) when you retire?*
  Reasons for asking: Reveals transitions that will affect client's financial picture; indicates the lifestyle client desires

- *What will you miss most about the job you have today?*
  Reasons for asking: Reveals aspects of the working life that the client may want to contemplate perpetuating in retirement years; opens up discussion on personally defining "retirement" stage of life

- *What are your biggest fears about your retirement?*
  Reasons for asking: Reveals economic, social, and psychological concerns that the client has seen other retirees face; helps client begin the process of designing an individualized retirement plan

- *What are you most looking forward to when you are retired?*
  Reasons for asking: Reveals if the client is running from a problem or moving toward a goal in retirement (the healthiest retirement experiences are those filled with purpose and balance); reveals intangible benefits of retirement that are most meaningful to the client

(continued)

FIGURE 5.4   Continued

Uncover Plan for Your Client's Future, continued

- *What would the ideal week in your retirement life look like? How will you invest your time?* (See section on ideal week in Chapter 13.)

  Reasons for asking: Reveals whether or not client has a balanced and realistic vision of retirement (e.g., Do they only have plans for golf? Is that enough to satisfy?)

  - *What are the top five to ten things you want to do while you still can?*

  Reasons for asking: Reveals shelved dreams, fantasy adventures, and delayed desires that will motivate a client to build a plan and stick to it

  - *What transitions do you anticipate facing in the next five years? What transitions do you want to prepare for that you anticipate experiencing in your retirement years?* (See the Life Transitions Survey in Chapter 6.)

  Reasons for asking: Reveals life transitions that the client anticipates and either desires or fears—or perhaps both; opens the door for discussion regarding financial preparation for each transition

---

FOCUS ON TRANSITIONS

We encourage you to familiarize yourself with the Life Transitions Survey explained in detail in Chapter 6. This survey will open the door to discussions that will help your clients navigate through the financial implications of both predictable and unpredictable transitions of life. This process is a succinct but powerful means to illustrating the financial implications of each transition. Each life event presents an opportunity for you to provide a meaningful service to your client. This process is designed to help your client better understand the inextricable tie between life and finance. Using this tool as a foundation for your discovery process creates a new way to facilitate the advisor-client dialogue. The axis for future conversation is not, "What's going on with the Dow?" but rather, "What's happening in your life these days?" and "How can we help you successfully navigate this transition?"

We believe that the discovery process you use is critical to sending a message to your clients about your interest and intentions in their affairs. This process is the linchpin in attaining and maintain-

FIGURE 5.5   The Trust Cycle

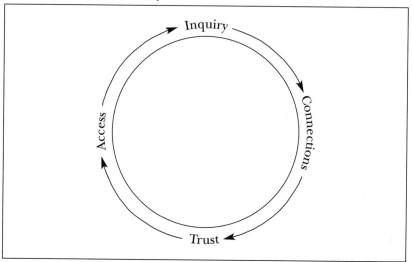

ing trust. Figure 5.5 illustrates the pivotal role that your process of discovery plays in developing a lasting and comprehensive role with your clients in their financial lives. It details how the trust cycle is affected by the questions you ask.

Inquiry

The questions you ask differentiate you from the pack because the questions are life-focused rather than financial-focused. By asking the right questions, you not only lead your clients to a financial product or service but you also create a foundational framework in their minds. You are now *connected* to the life of the client.

Connections

Clients want to work with an advisor who understands their lives and goals. When an advisor makes sufficient inquiry into the lives of his clients, they begin to feel that the groundwork is in place for building trust because the advisor is now connected to their lives and goals—as well as their account balances.

Trust

If an advisor knows little to nothing about what is happening or will be happening in the life of the client, then the trust level of the client is hinged exclusively on the performance of the advisor. In this paradigm, as soon as performance dips, the trust level dips with it. If, however, the trust level is built on knowledge and understanding of the client as well as investment performance, the fluctuation and temperament of trust is changed. If performance is below par, the client may contemplate changing advisors. However, the client is now faced with the prospect of working with someone who does not understand her life as well as her current financial advisor. Trust is at the core of why a client will give *access* to any or all of her assets to an advisor.

Access

If your connection to your clients is based on their lives, then they will expect you to help them navigate through the financial implications of each life transition. Access to their financial resources is the natural outcome of this process. Your access is no longer predicated on getting a better return but rather on answering the financial challenges they face. Access is evidence of trust. An intelligent and comprehensive inquiry process is necessary for initiating this level of trust.

Good questions are the key to a better advisory business. Good questions reveal as much about you as the answers reveal about your client. Think of the people you personally trust the most and reflect on the level of discovery they have done in your life. Chances are they have intimate knowledge of your life because they cared enough to ask the right questions and had the time to listen to your answers. In the psyche of clients, your level of inquiry indicates your level of caring.

Why would any clients want to trust an individual who only inquired about their account balances? Such inquiry is a poor foundation for establishing trust at any level—especially at the level required to maintain long-term relationships and endure turbulent markets. Your future hinges as much on your process of discovery and the care and curiosity that drive that process as it does on your ability to manage and invest the assets entrusted to you. Begin today to increase the depth and breadth of your inquiry process and witness the transformation it can bring to your client relations—and ultimately to your business success.

Using the
Life Transitions Survey

How do we measure the degree of separation between what the vendor vends and what the buyer buys? In the minds of most people, it comes down to motivation: Why is the vendor vending, and why am I, as a consumer, buying? This inexact and nebulous measure of motivation is often the hinge upon which the door of opportunity swings.

Clients come to professionals for practical reasons, emotional reasons, or sometimes both. In matters where clients understand precisely which product they want to fill a specific need, they are likely to take a practical approach and simply compare products and prices. Such pragmatic prospects are likely to be quite sensitive to price point.

On the contrary, those who come to professionals to answer a nagging concern are more sensitive to relational factors than price. More than desiring the lowest price solution, they want to know that the individual they are working with understands their needs and will provide a solution that is sensitive to the subjective as well as objective nature of the problem. They want a solution that will still the stirring emotion. In other words, these clients come to a financial advisor with a perceived problem hoping to connect with the kind of professional who can empathize with their needs and concerns. For these individuals, the specific product solution is a secondary priority.

Because the decision to partner with a financial professional is grounded in emotional concerns, these clients are most likely to partner with the professional who can connect with them at the level of their specific emotional concerns. With this thought in mind, we need to take an honest look at the client profile tools that are currently being used in the industry and ask how well these instruments communicate this ethos of concern for clients. Do they adequately address emotional as well as rational concerns?

We have seen a trend recently on the part of financial services companies to soften the feel of their profiles and financial surveys. An example would be a financial profile used by an insurance firm that uses terminology like "dying too soon" to introduce life insurance products or "financial concern" and "living a long life" to introduce retirement planning. This particular profile displays further emotional awareness by asking clients such questions as how they feel about providing for their children's education, or what they feel a reasonable rate of inflation would be for making financial calculations for the future. This is an enlightened approach in that it does not automatically assume that the provider knows what the client wants, and that the provider does not perform calculations with numbers she assumes the client will agree with. Other companies have made attempts to link financial and emotional issues by using more visceral language.

Another example is a checklist distributed by a mutual fund company that uses language like, "helping yourself," "helping your parents," and "helping your children," and asks questions such as, "What is it that keeps you up at night?" before presenting topics that address a wide variety of life topics. This particular checklist is on the right path because it offers to send clients nonfinancial information on their areas of concern. A common shortfall of other hybrid instruments is that they try to marry emotive language with financial industry jargon that most people outside of the industry don't understand. Consequently, some of these profiles succeed in making clients feel warm and fuzzy, but they still feel completely confused about the course of action to take.

A good example of a financial tool moving in the right direction is Lutheran Brotherhood's *Life Map*™—a financial life planning process that focuses on clients' values, goals, and plans for their life. The *Life Map* process helps clients plan for their lives and legacies and covers all their financial bases in the process. This sort of planning is a relatively easy transition for a company that works in a closed system and markets its services to members of Lutheran congregations.

Our assessment of scores of financial profile instruments is that, by and large, their use of life planning vernacular is token at best.

The intent of these profiles at times appears to be trying to soften the language in order to get the same hard facts; and that is, "How much do you have and where is it?"

ESTABLISHING A NEW CONTEXT

For this reason we are introducing a tool that sends a different sort of message to clients—a message that succors their emotional rumblings and concerns for the future. The Life Transitions Survey is a component of the Financial Life Planning Toolkit distributed by Money Quotient, Inc. The intent of this instrument is to help clients articulate their concerns, fears, and hopes as they relate to all aspects of their lives and to their financial lives. The Life Transitions Survey is intended for use as a conversation starter and as a way to initially identify clients' most pressing financial concerns. In conversations that follow this survey, this instrument can be used as a point of reference for measuring progress in answering these concerns. It is also our intent that the Life Transitions Survey will be used as a means of establishing a financial life planning framework for building your relationship with your clients.

The Life Transitions Survey, shown in Figure 6.1, categorizes common life transitions into four categories.

1. Work transitions
2. Financial transitions
3. Family transitions
4. Legacy transitions

Clients are asked to select the transitions relevant to them and to classify each selected life transition as either current, short-term (one to three years), or long-term (three or more years).

SETUP

Here is an example of dialogue you might use to introduce the Life Transitions Survey to your clients.

Mr. and Mrs. Client, one of the things we try to do is correlate our services to the current and anticipated life experiences of our clients. Our strategy is to discover what changes you are now facing or those you expect to make, and find ways to help you make successful transitions. Please take a couple of minutes to complete this Life Transitions Survey.

FIGURE 6.1   Life Transitions Survey

Work Transitions	Experiencing now	Anticipate short-term (1–3 years)	Anticipate long-term (3+ years)
1. Career change	❏	❏	❏
2. New job	❏	❏	❏
3. Promotion	❏	❏	❏
4. Loss of job	❏	❏	❏
5. Job restructure	❏	❏	❏
6. Education/retraining	❏	❏	❏
7. Sell or close business	❏	❏	❏
8. Transfer family business	❏	❏	❏
9. Gain a business partner	❏	❏	❏
10. Lose a business partner	❏	❏	❏
11. Downshift/simplify work life	❏	❏	❏
12. Sabbatical/leave of absence	❏	❏	❏
13. Start or purchase a business	❏	❏	❏
14. Retire	❏	❏	❏
15. Phase into retirement	❏	❏	❏
16. Other _____	❏	❏	❏

Financial Transitions

1. Purchase a home	❏	❏	❏
2. Sell a home	❏	❏	❏
3. Relocate	❏	❏	❏
4. Purchase a vacation home/ timeshare	❏	❏	❏
5. Re-evaluate investment philosophy	❏	❏	❏
6. Experience investment gain	❏	❏	❏
7. Experience investment loss	❏	❏	❏
8. Debt concerns	❏	❏	❏
9. Consider investment opportunity	❏	❏	❏
10. Receive inheritance or financial windfall	❏	❏	❏
11. Sell assets	❏	❏	❏
12. Other _____	❏	❏	❏

FIGURE 6.1   Continued

Family Transitions	Experiencing now	Anticipate short-term (1–3 years)	Anticipate long-term (3+ years)
1. Change in marital status (marriage)	❑	❑	❑
2. Change in marital status (divorce)	❑	❑	❑
3. Change in marital status (widowhood)	❑	❑	❑
4. Start a family or expect a new baby	❑	❑	❑
5. Hire child care	❑	❑	❑
6. Child moving into adolescence	❑	❑	❑
7. Child experiences/special needs (orthodontics, extra activities, etc.)	❑	❑	❑
8. Child education, pre-college expenses (private school, tutoring)	❑	❑	❑
9. Child going to college	❑	❑	❑
10. Child getting married	❑	❑	❑
11. Empty nest	❑	❑	❑
12. Family special event (trip, Bar Mitzvah, etc)	❑	❑	❑
13. Expecting grandchild(ren)	❑	❑	❑
14. Grandchildren need help (education, etc)	❑	❑	❑
15. Declining health of a parent	❑	❑	❑
16. Concern about health of a spouse or child	❑	❑	❑
17. Family member needs caregiving			
18. Concern about personal health	❑	❑	❑
19. Provide for long-term care of parent, spouse, or self	❑	❑	❑
20. Disability/hospitalization (self or family member)	❑	❑	❑
21. Other _____	❑	❑	❑

(continued)

FIGURE 6.1   Continued

Legacy Transitions	Experiencing now	Anticipate short-term (1–3 years)	Anticipate long-term (3+ years)
1. Increase benevolence planning/charitable giving	❐	❐	❐
2. Give special financial gifts to children (annual gifting, downpayment for home, etc.)	❐	❐	❐
3. Give parental pension (monthly stipend for parent)	❐	❐	❐
4. Develop an estate plan	❐	❐	❐
5. Change estate plan	❐	❐	❐
6. Develop an end of life plan (funeral expenses, living will, etc.)	❐	❐	❐
7. Other _____	❐	❐	❐

© 2001 Money Quotient, Inc.

Each transition for which clients express concern, the advisor can present a set of questions that will enable the clients to clarify the issues and understand the financial implications. This set of questions is presented as a Life Transitions worksheet. For example, if a client indicated that she is facing a possible or imminent job loss, the advisor can personally ask the questions on the worksheet and advise the client on which services could benefit her during this transition, or send the client home with the worksheet and agree to discuss the answers at the next meeting. In this case, the advisor informs the client of the importance of thinking through all the implications of such a transition.

Figure 6.2 is an example of a Life Transitions worksheet you could use if a client was facing a job loss.

There are numerous benefits to broadening the context of your conversations from financial transitions to life transitions. The irony of this change is that the conversations will end up leading to the same sort of transactions and services you have performed in the past, only now the client is emotionally anchored to the transaction. It was the client's life transition that made the financial transaction necessary and sensible. If the financial transaction is made necessary

FIGURE 6.2   Life Transitions Worksheet

Work Transition: Loss of Job

1. Are you contemplating a transition into a new type of career or working arrangement?

2. What are your plans for reemployment?

3. Are you contemplating any lifestyle changes as a result of the job loss?

4. How long can your current savings carry you?

5. Did you or will you receive a settlement or severance package? If so, what are your plans for it?

6. What arrangements are you contemplating for your retirement assets (401(k), IRA, etc.)?

7. Are you contemplating selling assets at this time?

Financial Implications

- Change in income
- Change in standard of living
- Retirement plan adjustments and transfers
- Insurance coverage review
- Transition cash flow plan
- Impact on retirement plan

---

by virtue of the client's life transition, the chances of buyer's regret and seller's regret are largely diminished. With this approach you have

- displayed awareness of the issues that affect your clients' quality of life,
- enlarged their perception of the role you play both in the present and as they face future transitions,
- helped increase your clients' awareness of the financial implications of each transition they face in life,

- broadened your job description from financial advisor to financial life planner, and
- removed some of the obstacles that cause clients to compartmentalize life matters and financial matters.

After working through a Life Transitions worksheet, the client now has a highly relevant context for the many services the financial advisor may choose to introduce. In the example of transitioning through a job loss, the client had both the opportunity to talk through her options and to confront the financial implications and opportunities brought to the fore by the transition. The client now understands that going through this transition cannot be compartmentalized from her financial life. There are financial implications to be dealt with. In the case of transitioning through a job loss, the financial implications include: changes in income, changes in standard of living, retirement plan adjustments, insurance coverage review, cash flow planning through the transition, and the long-term financial impact on retirement plans.

As a financial life planner, you also have the opportunity to make other observations or suggestions that might facilitate a successful life transition. Maybe a job loss is a time to sample a new lifestyle such as "downshifting" in order to experience a better work-life balance. Or maybe this is the time to shift careers. Is there something else the client has really wanted to do? Or if finances permit, you could suggest a sabbatical—a time to rest, refresh, and reflect on the next steps.

This process has now given the client much to think about regarding the impact of life on finances, and vice versa. This contemplation will help the client appreciate the expertise that a competent financial life planner—a partner, guide, and educator—can bring to the table. The client will want to know what he could (and should) do. The client will need to comprehend obstacles and options. Facing financial implications of life transitions alone is a daunting and draining task, and the odds of dealing with each issue appropriately are negligible. The need for professional financial help is obvious.

POSITIONING STATEMENT

My job is kind of like that of a personal CFO. Only in this case, the "corporation" is made up of you and your goals. You are the CEO of your own life. You will be the one to make the important decisions because you and your family members are the ones who have to live with those decisions. My job, as I see it, is to advise you of the financial pitfalls and opportunities at each transition in your life.

The life transition conversation allows the advisor-client relationship to grow in a manner that is advantageous for both parties. It is good for the advisor because it creates a better sense of understanding for what is happening in the life of the client and it creates more cohesiveness in the relationship. The advantages for the clients include a greater understanding of the relationship between their money and their lives, an appreciation of what impact sound financial advice can present, and an opportunity to talk through important life decisions with someone who has observed similar transitions with many other clients.

In short, the Life Transitions Survey is the beginning of new sort of conversation between advisor and client where the client's perspective is broadened and the advisor's role is expanded and more defined. Figures 6.3 through 6.5 are samples of Life Transitions worksheets clients would receive upon indicating the life transitions of loss of a business partner, a new job, and education/retraining.

Using these types of "know thy client" instruments will not change the products or services you offer, but these tools will change the context in which you present those products and services. This approach will work best for those advisors who have a network of professionals who can offer services that fall outside the advisor's personal arena of expertise.

Some life transitions will require insurance solutions. Other transitions will require estate or tax work. These are common referrals for advisors to make. By placing this tool in the discovery phase of your interaction with clients, you begin placing yourself in the role of general contractor as you either perform the service(s) they need or coordinate the appropriate referral.

In this age where transactional brokers and advisors abound, it is of paramount importance to set yourself apart with a process that differentiates you from the transactional crowd. We believe that establishing a fresh context for your relationship with clients is a critical step in that process. This sort of tool can help you do that. Opportunities are the offspring of well-thought-out questions. The Life Transitions Survey is an example of the kind of tool that can help you in that process. This tool and this process are premised on the princi-

FIGURE 6.3   Life Transitions Worksheet

Work Transition: Loss of a business partner

1. How does this transition affect your business goals?

2. How does this transition affect the day-to-day operations of your business?

3. How does this transition affect your outlook?

4. Has this change revealed any vulnerabilities in your business?

5. Will this transition have an impact on your personal financial situation?

6. How will this transition affect your business planning for the future?

7. Have your priorities changed as a result of this transition?

Financial Implications

- Impact on estate plan
- Impact on personal retirement plan
- Disability issues
- Emergency fund planning
- Effect on revenues

ple of asking questions to find out where clients are before telling them what they need to do. In this approach, clients are convinced of their need for your services *before* you ever discuss the service or transaction because the recommendation you make is directly tied to a life event or expected transition.

FIGURE 6.4   Life Transitions Worksheet

Work Transition: New Job

1. Does the new position have a pay increase or decrease?

2. If there is an increase, what plans do you have for the additional money?

3. Are there increased or decreased retirement benefits with the new position?

4. How will the change in benefits affect your retirement plan?

5. Have you made arrangements for transferring your 401(k), IRA?

6. Do you plan on living standard adjustments?

Financial Implications

- Change in income
- Relocation expense
- Managing new assets
- Insurance adjustments
- Retirement plan adjustments and transfers
- Tax planning
- Living standard adjustments
- Cash flow planning

FIGURE 6.5   Life Transitions Worksheet

Work Transition: Education/Retraining

1. What will the education costs be per year? How long will it take?

2. What impact will this have on your current earning power?

3. How will this education impact your future earning power?

4. Are you contemplating lifestyle changes through this period? If yes, what changes?

5. Are you contemplating selling assets during this period?

Financial implications

- Tuition costs payment plan
- Loss of income
- Cash flow planning
- Impact on retirement plan
- Impact on lifestyle

7

The Intuitive Advisor

Great technologies eventually reach a point where they surpass the capacity of humans to manage them. For example, we could build automobiles so that they all had the capability to go over 200 miles an hour, but if we did, our highways would become one large demolition derby. Our information technologies have now reached the point where we are being deluged with more information than our finite brains can successfully manage. While the world of information technology operates according to a law that demands doubling capacity and speed every 18 months, the human species operates according to an opposing law because our capacity for processing information diminishes with the passing of time. Consequently, even though technophiles still laud and extol the virtues of voluminous overload at breakneck speeds, the information age has already reached the point of diminishing returns with its intended audience. Perhaps nowhere is this truth better illustrated than in the financial services realm.

Consider the following facts regarding the growing tension between technological progress and human capacity as it plays out in the financial services arena. The typical *Morningstar* report contains 167 statistics. The average prospectus contains 390 numbers. If you were to type in the keyword *invest* on Yahoo!, you would receive 10,381 responses. Now contrast those figures with statistics from the human front. If you were to read 24 random numbers to a 20-year-old, a 40-year-old, and a 60-year-old, and ask them to recall as many of those numbers as they could, you would see the following results.

- The average 20-year-old would be able to recall 14 of 24.
- The average 40-year-old would recall 11 of 24.
- The average 60-year-old would recall 9 of 24.

There is a simple physiological explanation for this recall problem: short-term memory diminishes as we age. While information technology races in one direction, the human capacity for it withdraws in the opposite direction. You've probably heard statistics regarding the "graying" of America such as the fact that there are now 31 million Americans over the age of 65, and that there will be over 63 million in that age group by 2025. You may have also heard that the average 65-year-old's nest egg is nine times larger than the average 40-year-old's nest egg. However, this issue is more influential than the maturing of the marketplace and the impact of that demographic trend on your business.

The larger issue is that for the past few years we have been told that more information and better information technologies were the keys to building a better business in the information age. That would be all well and good if we were still in the axis of the information age—but we are not. Because of the superfluity of information and the paralyzing effect of receiving excessive and seemingly contradictory input, the consumer has quietly crossed into a period that we would characterize as "the intuitive age."

FROM INFORMATION TO WISDOM

Today's consumer now has access to too much information. Consumers have difficulty making decisions because they are suffering information overload. This forces their analytical abilities to "tilt," and they then defer to the feeling, sensing capacities in their brains and make important decisions at the intuitive level. In short, the proliferation of information and its prodigious pace has created a market for something that supersedes information. That something is called wisdom.

Today's clients are desperate for a conversation with someone who can make sense of everything they are hearing—and that someone better be able to connect with them at the intuitive level. While the rest of the world is racing toward artificial intelligence, tomorrow's advisor should be striving for emotional intelligence. If you were forced to choose between technological or intuitive skill for your future, we would advise you to take the intuitive path. Many dot-com observers seemed genuinely shocked by the fact that every consumer didn't capitalize on a great technology (the Internet) and begin to shift the majority of their consuming online. Those with intuitive insight knew it would not happen for one simple reason: the majority of human beings want human contact and sensory experiences.

There is a market for the online purchase because there are plenty of people who want to circumvent human contact for certain types of purchases, but technology has its intuitive limits. The online illusion reminds us of the entrepreneur who thought he came up with a great scheme when he decided to sell blue jeans in vending machines. He reasoned that most people know their size and would appreciate the convenience. He ignored one intuitive factor that controls the purchasing psyche, *affirmation*. Consumers want either a sales clerk or a three-way mirror to be present to tell them that they look great in those jeans!

Another important intuitive principle that comes into play in the relationship with a financial services professional is the more important the decision, the greater the intuitive leaning. People trust their intuitive instincts and lean heavily upon them when they are feeling confused or unsure. Intuition, according to Joyce Hall, founder of Hallmark Cards, is the "vapor of past experience." Intuition is measuring what you are seeing and hearing today with what you have seen in the past, and how those experiences played out in the long run. When the client has no prior experience by which to measure today's proposition, the intuitive function then relies on feelings associated with the person delivering the message. Can I trust this individual? Does this individual have my best interests in mind?

Many consumers have been led to believe that they don't need a full service advisor, yet they still don't have their financial acts together. Because both information about investments and the purchase of those investments have been commoditized, today's advisor has to bring greater value than information and execution to the table. This value-added benefit is largely intuitive in nature; to offer wisdom, insight, and coaching to help clients amalgamate their life goals with their financial behavior, to affirm investment strategies, and, ultimately, to develop a role that is akin to a personal CFO.

INTUITIVE RELEVANCE

The intuitive age is upon us. Prepare yourself by focusing on your people skills. In the intuitive age, clients will decide upon the advisor that asks clients and prospective clients the right questions (about their lives, not just their money) and demonstrates that she has truly listened to the answers. In the intuitive age, clients will look for advisors who can communicate in the subjective realm of emotion as lucidly as they do in the objective realm. In this age, clients place a higher premium on partnership than they do on processes. Financial advisors who prosper in the intuitive age will be those who discover how to make human contact and maintain that connection.

Until now, financial advice has been the most practical of professions. However, client expectations, technological advancements, and industry trends are forcing change. In the future, relevance will be defined not in terms of the products that advisors sell, or the way that they deliver service, but in the connection they make with each client's life. As Robert Veres, editor at large of the *Dow Jones Investment Advisor*, counsels: "Become a pioneer in the process of connecting financial affairs with deeper human values. . . . Until now, financial advice has become the most practical of professions . . . but that is going to change so quickly that if you blink you will miss it!" (*Getting Clients, Keeping Clients* newsletter, April 24, 2000.)

Where will your business be five to ten years from now? Who will your clients be at that time? What services will these clients ask for? What will their needs be, and who will you need to partner with to help you fill those needs?

REARRANGING THE FURNITURE

Many financial advisors are concerned about the long-term viability of their businesses. While most successful advisors understand that their business is always changing, many continue to believe that their main role, from the client's perspective, will remain the same. These advisors seek out ways to improve on the delivery of product, when, in fact, what clients want to purchase has changed. This is akin to rearranging the deck chairs on the Titanic. Let's face it, the financial advice industry knows it will have to change in order to meet the changing needs and wants of our twenty-first century clientele.

The issue is, however, the degree to which we will have to reinvent ourselves in order to maintain relevance in the lives of our clients.

THE REINVENTION OF
THE FINANCIAL ADVICE INDUSTRY

For the last 20 to 30 years, the financial services industry has made dramatic changes in response to consumer demand. On May 1, 1975, the commission structure was deregulated because Americans were growing increasingly interested in managing their own financial affairs. In the same year, industry giant Merrill Lynch commissioned the Stanford Research Institute to identify investor expectations for service delivery in the 1980s. That research identified two major demands.

First, clients wanted total access to their financial assets and to be more involved in the process of making their assets grow. Second, the research identified the desire for increased financial planning delivery. Again, this fit the profile of the "involved" investor who not only needed a financial planning process but also wanted to be an active participant.

The 1980s witnessed an explosion of new financial services products and a change in the way financial services were delivered. Banks no longer restricted themselves to traditional banking services, nor did wire houses focus solely on stock brokerage activity. To better meet the expectations of this new kind of client, companies began to offer one-stop shopping that hastened the demise of the four separate pillars of the industry—brokerage, bank, insurance, and accounting. By the end of the decade, financial supermarkets were beginning to emerge as the providers of financial planning information. Merrill Lynch chairman, John Steffens, referred to this move as the beginning of "being all things to all people"—a logical response by the industry-changing client expectations.

By the early 1990s, financial planning had become more mainstream and not simply the purvey of the rich. Clients were no longer compartmentalizing their financial affairs, and the financial services industry sought to provide total financial planning solutions such as insurance services, asset accumulation strategies, and tax advice. The great bull market that lasted through to the end of the century and created more wealth than any other phase in U.S. history not only increased the net worth of millions of North American investors, but also created a super industry that would meet their needs.

What were those needs? Long-term asset accumulation was, first and foremost, the marketing approach taken by most financial planners. In fact, asset accumulation became synonymous with retirement planning, creating a demand for long-term financial products such as mutual funds and variable annuities. Building a sufficient nest egg was the main objective.

Financial planning had also been redefined to mean creating strategies that would accumulate assets for the future. Financial planners moved away from such traditional areas as debt management, household budgeting, and a values-based understanding of what money means to the individual. Money management lost its connection with people's lives because of the long-term savings approach to financial planning drilled into the consciousness of boomers in their 30s and 40s.

It can be argued that one of the reasons for tremendous performance in equity markets over the past 15 years was the stability of the money that fueled North American equity markets. With trillions of dollars of retirement assets tied up in mutual funds, IRAs, RRSPs, group pension plans, and individual stock holdings earmarked for retirement, the core of the market didn't react as skittishly to the vagaries of stock market activity. Strong markets, a long-term approach to retirement savings by working baby boomers, and an asset accumulation focus by the financial services industry combined to create a wildly successful financial advice business.

"IF IT AIN'T BROKE, DON'T FIX IT!"

Today, we are no longer dealing with a simple, long-term asset accumulation strategy in a robust equity market. The relationship between advisor and client has also changed. A cover story in *Business Week* (February 22, 1999) asked the question "Who needs a broker?" when it examined the growth of do-it-yourself investing. In fact, the late '90s saw scores of investors run away from their traditional advisors and toward less expensive transaction facilitators. Ever quick to take advantage of investor trends, the major wire houses jumped on the Internet bandwagon. Some firms even competed with their own advisors for client business by performing "client triage," directing clients away from financial advisors and toward direct trading. Unfortunately, many clients who got caught up in the Internet trading frenzy should not have abandoned their advisors and the financial planning advice that they paid for through commissions. In the year 2000, $4 trillion in market value disappeared from the market. While not all of that money was earmarked for retirement, a significant portion of the retirement savings of North Americans was wiped out.

TESTING THE RELATIONSHIP

While many have suggested that investors were essentially playing with Monopoly money anyway, those approaching retirement have had to reevaluate the whole idea of playing the market. It is one thing for the value of an individual's IRA to decline because of market setbacks when he has 20 years to make up for losses. But for pre-retirees, the pain of declining markets and uncertainty about the future combine to create anxiety in their lives. In the past, many advisor-client relationships have been based on the client's need to generate higher returns on investments earmarked for retirement. Therefore, financial advice became as much a commodity as the financial products. When the inevitable change came to the performance of investment markets, those relationships lacked the sound foundation to sustain them.

While performance is not the key determinant of the success or longevity of an advisor-client relationship, lack of performance can bring to light the weaknesses that have been overlooked. Here is a good example of this principle.

> One of my advisors has always had a personality that bothered me. I don't know what it is, but I've always felt uncomfortable with him. When my portfolio was performing well, I wasn't as concerned. Now that my performance is in the tank, my personality clash with him is bothering me a whole lot more!
>
> —*J.L.*, *client*

Many financial advisors have relationships with their clients that are inadequate, but a strong bull market has a way of creating a state of ignorant bliss. The basic communication between client and advisor has too often been market related or accumulation-centered. Advisor-client communication is often based on nothing more than transaction facilitation, mutual fund performance, and asset accumulation. In this situation, the traditional advisor is in a precarious position. The financial advice community has created its own monster by focusing the financial planning discussion on facts, figures, numbers, and analysis. Because the human element can be removed from that discourse and be replaced by information and facilitation sources found on the Internet, the advisor is left trying to redefine his or her indispensable value.

YOU VERSUS THE MACHINE

A recent Canadian study conducted by a major provider of online investor information to online investors found that more than 70 percent of the survey respondents are "highly engaged investors," who describe themselves as needing to check the performance of their investments "as frequently as I can." ("Highly Engaged Investors Put Internet and Financial Advisors on Equal Footing." Canada Newswire via COMTEX, February 6, 2001.) The Internet has now become a significant source of information for active investors and worthy competitors for the services on which advisors have based their business. "The Internet's impact on investing is a revolution, not a fad," says David Keith, vice president of financial sites for Globe Interactive in Toronto. "Our site users are information collectors. They are taking in news, information, commentary, and research from a number of sources to put it to work for them with their overall investment strategy."

John Rekenthaler, director of research for *Morningstar*, notes the significant change that information technology has brought about in his business. Reviewing the impact of technology on financial advice, Rekenthaler noted that "in 1975 transactions were commoditized, as mainframes and regulatory changes opened the door to discount brokerages. In 1985, information was commoditized, as PCs allowed operations like *Morningstar* and *The Wall Street Journal* to make information available at low cost. And today, the Internet is commoditizing advice, proving asset allocation software, ongoing monitoring, and other sophisticated tools." ("Top Performers Conference." *Getting Clients, Keeping Clients* newsletter, April 24, 2000.) Figure 7.1 illustrates how the Internet has provided a low-cost, easy access alternative to financial or investment professionals for many investors.

Advisors who believe that the Internet will never replace them in the minds of clients will say, "That's all well and good, but the Internet can't give my clients the personal attention and caring that I can."

FIGURE 7.1   Advisor versus Internet

Service Need by Investors	Financial Advisor	Internet
Transaction facilitation	X	X
Access to asset accumulation products	X	X
Access to insurance products	X	X
Financial planning advice	X	X
Investment information	X	X
Portfolio reporting and analysis	X	X
Market commentary	X	X
Access to research	X	X
Tax planning advice	X	X
Consumer education	X	X

Many advisors are justified in that assertion. They long ago stopped selling the services listed in Figure 7.1 and concentrated on selling the actual service clients wanted from an advisor. For example, one advisor reported, "My clients look to me to help them make sense out of the tremendous amount of information available to them." Nancy Salk, director of research for J. D. Power and Associates in Aguoura Hills, California, agrees with this approach. She states, "With greater access to a plethora of financial material from the Internet and media, investors are in information overload. Investors are looking for a broker who will be an information disseminator."

This assertion is backed up by a survey that Salk's company recently conducted with investors who own more than $100,000 in investable assets. The findings revealed that information and education scored number one in importance, far outpacing broker performance and fees and commissions. A similar study conducted in 1997 by the International Association of Financial Planners (now the FPA) confirmed these results.

EXASPERATION

Has interpreter of facts and figures become the main role for financial advisors in the Internet age? Is redefining the relationship between advisor and client as simple as becoming an information disseminator, providing the client with education and even more information? With so much information available on the Internet, some advisors are trying to position themselves as the center of the investment information flow. That presents a problem that could be as harmful to the advisor-client relationship as focusing on products and transactions.

YOUR NEW JOB DESCRIPTION

If providing data, number crunching, rearranging portfolios, and performing transaction services are no longer the priority, how will you redefine your professional roles? How will you maintain a high relevance in the eyes of your clientele? The first step is to expand your vision and then to expand your clientele's vision of who you are and what you want to accomplish.

You can no longer simply be a facilitator of financial functions. You must become a fiscal and strategic partner in both life events and life preparation for your clients. You must help your clients anticipate their needs and transitions. You must help them to crystallize what is most important to them as individuals, determine what they want their money to accomplish in their lives, and develop a personalized strategy for reaching those goals. You must help your clients weather the storms of life and keep them on a steady course.

Members of our society are looking for meaning and purpose in their lives. They are realizing—from both a practical and philosophical perspective—that wealth alone is an unfulfilling goal. In this respect, when people are under the illusion that financial accumulation is the ultimate goal, they are less selective about whose services they will engage to that end. But when they awaken to the idea that a balanced and meaningful life is the goal, and that money is simply a tool to achieving that goal, they become more discriminating about who they will partner with in their personal financial processes. Herein lies the opportunity and the challenge for today's advisor.

Today's clients are demanding more. They are looking for a different kind of relationship with their financial advisors. They are demanding a partnership that revolves around their lives and not just around their money. Every stage of life requires financial preparation and adjustment, and your clients know that. As a result, clients are going to turn these matters over to someone who has gained a clear picture of where they've been, where they are, and where they want to go personally and professionally. They will turn to someone who they can relate to and who can help them *clarify* their vision for the future.

Your future is about teaching, coaching—strategically and inspirationally—and connecting with the lives of the clients. Your future is about their money and their lives, and the many ways money affects their quality of life. If you're willing to change your approach and develop the necessary relational skills, clients will find their way to you.

Chapter 8

Raising Your Value in the Eyes of the Client

The financial advice business is about to get very personal. Your relevance to your clients will be measured in terms of what you provide to help them live their lives rather than providing them with products and services to which they have little or no emotional attachment. That doesn't mean that you will not present products and services that you have presented in the past. It's the way that you present them that will change. Because the client is the ultimate driver of the kinds of information that advisors provide and will dictate how your business delivers its services in the future, it is important to take a close look at the needs, hopes, attributes, and expectations of an aging clientele.

PROVIDING VALUE TO TOMORROW'S CLIENT

Clients will seek out a new advisor if their current advisor does not meet their individual needs. One critical need that many people have is more knowledge about the relationship between their money and their lives. When we are in our 20s, 30s, and 40s, the knowledge that we need is most often associated with our investments, asset accumulation, and long-term financial planning strategies. In fact, the financial services industry has invested itself over the past 20 years to meet those needs and to provide that education.

However, as we near the numerous critical transitions in our lives, our thirst for new knowledge tends to move in a different direction. At some point, we start to realize that we are closer to retirement than we are to Woodstock; and that our parents are closer to the grave than our children are to the cradle. That changes our perspective on our lives and our money. It also changes the kind of help that we need from an advisor and the dynamics of the relationship that we have with them.

> As we approach our retirement, we are struck by the fact that we had never really thought about what retirement would be like. We were always conditioned by the idea that retirement meant "never having to work again." Following the advice of our financial planner, we put our money aside so that we could afford to live without having to work, and we have done a good job meeting that goal. Probably the biggest surprise to us, though, is that now that we are here, we are starting to realize that our retirement isn't just about the money. Sure, we don't have to work, but we are still young people. The thought of sitting around in a rocking chair doesn't have a lot of appeal.

—Jim and Glenda

Although retirement is just one of the significant transitions we can expect to face, it has been *the* transition that advisors pay the most attention to—almost monomaniacally. It will serve our purpose here to illustrate how our perspective on that particular transition must change to connect with the heart of today's client. The time has come for retirement planning to evolve into something other than saving for a day when we can become bored on a full-time basis. What's the point of building a nest egg if we're going to place it in a dying tree? Just as the definition of a meaningful and successful life varies from client to client, so does the definition of a meaningful and successful retirement. In fact, the ultimatum between the full-time working life and the fully retired is quickly dissolving.

There is not a template solution for retirement available into which we can squeeze each client's assets. The advisor's business must move toward the client's vision for life—instead of framing a client's assets around the advisor's vision for retirement. This fundamental shift is the beginning of a new partnership between advisor and client. Today's client is longing for this partnership with a financial life planner, and will not be satisfied with counterfeits.

Clients are reassessing their relationship with their financial advisor and the relevance of what an advisor provides. Even the best advisors are subject to this examination. The financial services industry has operated under the same assumptions for the past 20 years. Advisors have built their businesses based on:

- The need for clients to build up a retirement nest egg.
- Strong performance in equity markets that diverts both client and advisor attention from interpersonal interaction.
- Generalized solutions such as mutual funds and other packaged products in a "one size fits all" investment program.
- Marketing programs, advertising campaigns, and seminar topics that follow the same patterns as the competition.
- An emphasis on building very large books of affluent clients.

While strong market performance and accepting clients have made for successful advisor businesses in the past, there is now an undercurrent of change. As we enter the twenty-first century, two major changes have occurred exposing the fragile underpinnings of many financial advisor-client relationships.

First, a large segment of most advisors' client base is getting older, and thus, needs and expectations are changing. The baby boomer bulge that has greatly influenced how the financial services industry has evolved is now moving on to the next phase.

Second, investment performance shows every sign that it is returning to normal—or reverting to the mean. The long bull market of the '90s caused many investors (and many advisors!) to have false returns expectations for the long term. The inevitable downturn of the markets stunned investors and challenged the trust they held for the industry and their financial services providers. Craig Pickering, a registered rep in Hudson, Ohio, summed it up well in a *Registered Representative* article: "While research shows investment performance is not a primary factor in client defection, a volatile market can bring unresolved issues to a head. Unless you can justify that you're a value-added component to the equation, clients will perceive you as a commodity and may ultimately switch to brokers they believe will do more for them." (Michelle Gabriel, "Why Clients Leave." *Registered Representative,* February 1, 2001.)

It's time to lay a new foundation for the relationship between advisor and client. As always, clients will dictate the products and services that they expect their advisor to provide. Their interaction with their advisor will reflect the needs that they have as they move to the next stages of their lives. A key to success for advisors in the future will be the quality of their relationships with their clients and their understanding of each client's unique needs and circumstances and their life-directing priorities.

"IT'S THE RELATIONSHIP, STUPID!"

With so much of the interaction between advisor and client becoming commoditized or automated, the one truly personal element of the relationship that gains importance is the interaction between the two. Why else would you have an advisor? After all, the client no longer needs the advisor to buy product or to provide financial planning or investment information. The client can get much of that for free on the Internet or in the scores of books that have been published to help investors.

What the client can't get from any number of information sources is the heart and soul of the advisor who understands and cares about the client. As one advisor put it, "What my clients don't get from the Internet or online brokerage is me!"

Some advisors don't really understand what part of "me" the client really values. This is where the "disconnect" between advisor and client tends to reveal itself. Some advisors believe they are delivering value because of the products and services they provide. Some believe their value is the size and strength of their firms or their ability to pick the right investments. Still others think that their value lies in how smart they are. However, the truth is that clients overwhelmingly evaluate an advisor based on the degree of trust and confidence that exists in their relationship. It's not the "me" that the client is looking for—it's the "us."

Industry commentator Nick Murray summed it up when addressing financial advisors on why clients buy equity mutual funds, "People don't buy equity mutual funds from people whom they understand, they buy them from people they trust!"

REDEFINING THE TERM *CLIENT*

At a recent gathering of insurance professionals, the talk at the table turned to how many clients each of the agents had. "I have over

2,500 clients," boasted one seasoned veteran. "That's nothing. We now are managing over 3,000!" chimed in another. A rookie sitting at the table turned to us and said, "When I get big, I want to be just like them!"

Given the resources and the opportunity, we would have jumped at the chance to survey these clients to get their views on their advisor. How many would have actually admitted that they were the clients of these advisors? How many other advisors did these clients have? A study conducted in 1998 by Dan Richards of Marketing Solutions in Toronto, Canada, found that investors with over $100,000 in investable assets dealt with an average of three financial advisors. If you are only dealing with a portion of a client's financial situation, does that make them a "half-client" or less?

This is far from a mental gymnastics exercise. The perception of what a client is or is not will become increasingly important to both parties as each looks at the benefits of the relationship. Our definition of a client is someone who sees you as a personal chief advisor. We have a relationship with our clients that is based on two partners working together for a common cause. When you have a partnership, you truly have a client. The very idea of a relationship between client and advisor is that each has to get something out of the relationship or it doesn't work. There always has to be two sides.

MEETING CLIENT EXPECTATIONS

How do your clients score your relationship with them? What benefits do they get out of working with you? How bulletproof is the relationship? Who or what do they consider to be the primary source of financial planning information in their lives? Use the questions in Figure 8.1 to help your clients rate your relationship. For each question, have them assign a value from 1 to 10 (10 being the highest).

To properly answer the questions in Figure 8.1, your clients must understand what their expectations are of you and the value that you deliver. If you were a mind reader and were able to read your clients' thoughts whenever you talked to them, you might be able to discern what it is that they are looking for when they deal with you. You could then make sure that you always gave them what they wanted—even if it wasn't verbalized.

Do clients always know what they want from their advisors? Clearly, the answer is no. To illustrate this point, how often have you

---

FIGURE 8.1   Advisor Rating Profile

1. How well does your advisor understand your life needs and circumstances?

   1   2   3   4   5   6   7   8   9   10

2. How well does your advisor teach and communicate financial concepts and principles?

   1   2   3   4   5   6   7   8   9   10

3. How would you rate your advisor's investment performance?

   1   2   3   4   5   6   7   8   9   10

4. How in tune is your advisor to your life and retirement goals?

   1   2   3   4   5   6   7   8   9   10

5. How inclined would you be to entrust all your investable assets with your advisor?

   1   2   3   4   5   6   7   8   9   10

6. How inclined would you be to recommend this advisor to your close friends and loved ones?

   1   2   3   4   5   6   7   8   9   10

---

seen or heard of clients moving some or all of their business to a competitor because the competitor promised services that your client didn't know you offered? We know that clients want an advisor that understands them as well as they understand their own business. Clients want someone who can teach, advise, and guide as they pursue their goals and dreams.

THE CLIENT'S VALUE CYCLE

Your clients will develop trust in you when you bring value to your relationship with them. Clients who totally trust you will not hesitate to entrust most or all their investable assets with you. To a large degree, you could say that the amount or percentage they have invested with you indicates their level of trust. Clients may not always be aware of the various reasons *why* they value you. A lot of times it is the intangibles—the things at the margin that a client doesn't always think about—that determine whether a client finds value.

To be an effective financial life planner, you will have to redefine the product line that you offer in terms of life-oriented services rather than financial products. Take a look at your current marketing material. Does it reflect the products that you sell or the benefits that you provide?

Your products are not what you sell, but what those products *do* for your clients. It is important that each product or service description helps clients understand the benefits. Figure 8.2 illustrates some financial products and their benefits to your clients.

We have identified six areas in the value cycle on which clients gauge their expectations. The advisor's ability to deliver in these areas helps to cement the relationship. Figure 8.3 looks at how advisors have delivered value in the past in these six areas and how they might deliver value in the future.

The advisor doesn't have control of where clients are on the value cycle. Clients' needs change as their lives change. Therefore, the advisor not only has to keep on top of the life transitions that a client is experiencing but also has to ensure that the advice, information, and education delivered covers many different potential aspects of the client's life.

THE CLIENT VALUE EQUATIONS

If you could actually measure the value that your clients place on their relationship with you, it would look like a simple formula. The quality of your relationship is going to be a function of what a client finds valuable minus the negative aspects of the relationship.

On the plus side, you would place your ability to meet your clients' expectations plus the efficiency of the administration process. Quality of processing is seen as a positive because it is the way that your firm communicates with clients on the trades that they make, the performance of their investments, and the efficiency of your administrative staff. If you are in a position where this part of your relationship with the client is actually negative, you may have to assess the quality of your administrative support.

FIGURE 8.2   Financial Products and Their Benefits

Product	Benefit to Your Client's Life
Investment management	To help our clients manage their assets so that they will maximize the amount of money that they have to enjoy the lives that they want.
Tax planning	To maximize the amount of money available to our clients so that they are free to spend money on the things that they enjoy.
Estate planning	To provide our clients with plans to let them pass on as much of their assets as possible to those who are the most important to them.
Retirement planning vehicles	To give our clients access to vehicles that will let them build as much of a retirement nest egg as they can so that they can enjoy their futures.
Life insurance	To help our clients protect those who are the most important to them.
	To help our clients build assets for the future in ways that they may not be aware of.
Disability insurance	To help our clients ensure that their loved ones and their way of life is protected from some of life's challenges.
Critical illness insurance	To develop strategies that will give our clients peace of mind in the event that something happens to them that will make it difficult for them to provide for their families.
Critical care insurance	To work with our clients to make sure that they understand some of the challenges of getting older and that they plan ahead to ease the burden on those they love.

On the negative side of the equation, there are two main factors: the cost to the client of maintaining a relationship with you, and the presence of competition. Cost is much more than dollars and cents; it can also include subjective considerations such as opportunity cost or emotional cost. As your clients continually weigh the pros and

FIGURE 8.3   Delivering Value

Value Cycle	Advisors in the past	Advisors in the future
1. Education	Financial-oriented Product-specific Market information Rates of return Risk/reward	Life planning Career transition information Health/lifestyle-related Income strategies Financial coaching Family-oriented Goal setting

2. Communication	Left brain-oriented
	Performance-
	  oriented
	Cookie cutter,
	  generalized,
	  sporadic, and
	  reactive
	Advisor-friendly
		Right brain-oriented
		Life-oriented
		Specific, unique,
		  client-oriented,
		  systematic, and
		  proactive
		Client-friendly

3. Reporting	Performance-
	  oriented
	Meet minimum
	  requirements
		Life goal-oriented
		Online tracking
		On demand
		Customized to client
		  needs

4. Financial
   planning
	Accumulation
	  strategies
	Long-term
	  retirement
	Generalized
	Financial-oriented
	Individual planner
		Income strategies
		Lifestyle-related
		Customized
		Life-oriented
		Team approach

5. Investment
   advice
	Market related
	Short-term
	  performance
	Capital gains
	Long-term investing
		Asset management
		Overall safe returns
		Tax efficiency
		Shorter-term investing

6. Products	Mutual funds Individual stocks Variable annuities Whole and term life	Managed accounts Individual portfolios Lifestyle-oriented education

cons of working with you, they will mentally calculate the worth of maintaining a relationship with you. There are always plenty of alternatives available to your clients if you have failed to meet their expectations or satisfy their needs.

Steven Covey talks about "the emotional bank account" in his book, *7 Habits of Highly Effective People*. Every time we do well in a relationship with communication and interaction, it is equal to "making deposits." Each time we fail to communicate, show sufficient interest, or meet unspoken expectations, it is equal to "making withdrawals." Based on this concept, how many of our clients would say that our relationship with them is in overdraft or surviving month to month? Clearly, there is much more we can do to make better emotional connections with our clients.

Chapter 9

The Meaning of Money

What does money represent to your clients? What tangibles and intangibles do they hope to purchase with their assets? We will address the specifics of what today's clients say they want their money to buy. Their "shopping list" is equally filled with intangibles that they see affecting their quality of life and tangible items that most advisors are accustomed to and comfortable talking about. In one sense, much of what the financial life planning discussion is about for the advisor is expanding the conversation from the tangible product to the intangible product. In this chapter we will survey the following:

- Why people want to be millionaires
- How money or lack thereof affects major life decisions
- What matters to the wealthy
- What matters to the achiever

IS THAT YOUR FINAL ANSWER?

A majority of every demographic group except the WWII generation (born 1901–1935) express a desire to be wealthy, with the most decided groups being the generation-Xers (1965–1982) and the late boomers (1956–1964). But we must ask the question, Why do they want to be wealthy? According to the Money and the American Family study, it is not because they consider wealth to be the key measure of success in life. On the whole, people are measuring their success in life more on the quality of their personal relationships than on the quality of their possessions. Americans know what money can buy and are aware of its limits as well.

According to the study shown in Figure 9.1, Americans value self-fulfillment through family, friends, work, education, and religion more than they do from money. At the same time, these individuals understand the link between having money and being able to pursue the things they say are more important than money. For example, the respondents believe helping others is a greater measure of a suc-

---

FIGURE 9.1   How to Measure a Successful Life

Good relationship with your children	94%
Good friends	87%
Helping other people who are in need	87%
Becoming well educated	82%
Good marriage	81%
Interesting job	79%
Strong religious faith	74%
Living a long time	49%
Earning a lot of money	27%
Seeing a lot of the world	26%

■ % answering "absolutely necessary"

0% 10% 20% 30% 40% 50% 60% 70% 80% 90% 100%

Source: AARP/Modern Maturity Survey.

cessful life than earning a lot of money, but the connection between the two is well understood. Having money can put you in a better position to do the very thing by which you say you measure success (helping others).

It makes for an interesting mental exercise to view the items Americans say they use to measure a successful life and then ask yourself, "Does having money help or accelerate the pursuit of this goal?" You wouldn't have to earn a lot of money to be able to pursue good relationships with your children, spouse, and friends. Nor do you need to be wealthy to have strong religious faith or even to put yourself in a position to help others who have less. Nor will having a lot of money ensure that you will live a long life.

But read down this list and assess which goals are more accessible or can be accelerated with prosperity and you get a different perspective on why money is so critical to having a successful life to the average American—even if they refuse to put it in those terms. Some people feel that their relationships could be enhanced with the time and freedom to enhance them. These people harbor the hope that one day their money can buy them that time and freedom. There is no denying that earning a lot of money can afford you the ability to help others, get well educated, and see a lot of the world. Some people who do not find their work interesting would see a link between earning a lot of money and having an interesting job. Others, seeing the prospects for superior health care, would equate living a long time with earning a lot of money.

The bottom line is this, although Americans say they do not measure success by earnings, they do understand that having money accelerates the possibility of having the things that they do value. In every age group at least 40 to 50 percent said that money was somewhat important to being successful. It is not about having money for money's sake, it is about having money to attend to matters that they feel are important. The top reasons for having money include:

- *Being able to provide for family* (74 percent rate this as an extremely important reason for having money). This is the greatest concern of those with children under age 18.
- *Getting good medical attention when sick* (68 percent). This is more of an issue with women than men.
- *Staying healthy* (64 percent). This is most important to the WWII generation.
- *Being able to help family and friends* (50 percent)

- *Being able to have more free time* (34 percent)
- *Being able to contribute to worthy causes* (27 percent)
- *Having more things to enjoy* (18 percent)
- *Being able to travel* (18 percent)

From these responses a portrait begins to emerge that indicates what the intangible product mix is that people hope to have the money to buy. Their concerns are family, freedom, health, and the opportunity for charity. Meanwhile, what products are most financial service firms busily touting? Retirement by age *x*. If our conversation with clients centered around family and health concerns, freedom to pursue the ideal mix of work and leisure, and how to leave a legacy through charitable effort and giving, we would quickly establish a lifeline between asset management and the soul of the client. The time has come for the financial advice industry to move beyond helping people acquire money for the sake of acquiring money to helping people first establish why they want the money and then going about the business of acquiring and managing those assets. This is financial life planning in a nutshell.

HAVING MONEY DOESN'T MEAN YOU'LL HAVE A LIFE

What are the intangibles that people believe in and want their money to buy? It is important to know because when advisors are fully tuned to the specifics of these intangibles they can facilitate a conversation that goes below the surface of clients' fiscal statements. Clients then begin to see the advisor as the bridge between their intangible hopes and the tangible means to realizing those hopes. The chart in Figure 9.2, from AARP's *Modern Maturity* magazine, illustrates the various intangibles people expect their money to purchase. The number at the top of the bar represents the percentage of respondents that felt their money could purchase each particular intangible.

The intuitive advisor will look at this chart and realize that it is a great entrée into the life and psyche of the client, a veritable shopping list of intangibles. What sort of intriguing (and differentiating) conversations can you initiate with your clients using this window into their fiscal soul? Many interesting conversations emerge from this list.

FIGURE 9.2   What Can Money Buy?

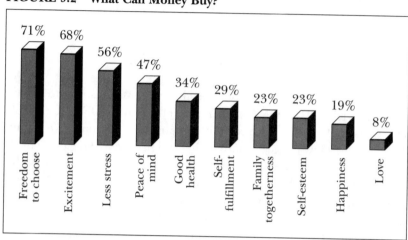

Source: Modern Maturity, July/August 2000.

- *Freedom.* Seventy percent of people believe that money can buy the freedom to choose. If you had money what choices would you make?
- *Excitement.* What exciting experiences have you dreamed of or been putting off until you have the money?
- *Stress.* How much of your stress is coming from money and work issues?
- *Peace of mind.* How much better would you sleep knowing you had a plan in place that takes care of the people you care about and covers the major transitions you will face in life?
- *Good health.* Are financial issues causing you stress? Do you think the amount of money you have when you are older affects the quality of health care you receive? Do you have all your health bases covered with asset protection and estate planning?
- *Self-fulfillment.* If the financial bridge was built what pursuits would you take up? Have you thought of a different career? What contributions would you like to make to with your abilities and assets?

All the intangibles that clients say they want their money to buy are available *if* they initiate the financial processes necessary for realization. This is where the advisor can partner with the client in an effective and lasting manner. Every aspect of a person's life—tangible and intangible—can be affected by money. One thing we know for sure is that many lives are adversely affected by a lack of money.

ROOT OF ALL EVIL

I remember hearing a radio preacher who would shout to his audience, "THE LACK OF MONEY IS THE ROOT OF ALL EVIL!" This message was then followed with a litany of pleas to relieve his audience of whatever spare change they might have. The preacher's message was an adulteration of the verse "the *love* of money is the root of all evil," but he seemed to have no trouble finding a ready audience for his material message. When you look at the decisions Americans have made because of a lack of money, there is no doubt he could find plenty of followers today.

The Money and the American Family study surveyed how Americans would adjust their lifestyles if they had more money, and discovered the following.

- One in three would stay home with their children instead of working outside the home.
- One in four would have gone to college.
- Almost one in four would not have foregone health care they needed.
- Almost one in four would have lived alone instead of sharing a domicile.
- One in five would have sent their children to a different school.
- One in four would have changed their marital status.

When you view the compromises people were forced to make because of financial necessity, it's easy to see why the feeling that the lack of money is the root of all evil has such a hold on the psyche of the modern client. Destinies are often affected by the lack of income or savings. Maybe this helps to explain why the number one intangible people say their money can buy is the freedom to choose. Perhaps they have been forced to make choices for themselves and family members that they regret because of lack of sufficient financial resources.

Ponder the fact that 18 percent of people say they decided to stay married instead of getting a divorce because of money, and 8 percent said they decided to get divorced or separated because of a lack of money. You now have over a quarter of the population whose personal lives are being greatly influenced by their financial state. Divorce has a monumental impact on fiscal well-being—most notably for women. According to an article by Susan Jacoby in *Modern Maturity* ("The Allure of Money," July–August, 2000), 70 percent of divorced or separated men said they were able to save money out of their current incomes, while only 59 percent of divorced or separated women said they managed to do so. Divorced or separated women are twice as likely as men to rate themselves as below average financially. No advisor would want to bring up such statistics in front of married clients, but it is helpful to realize that helping clients organize their financial picture may have a profound impact on their life picture as well.

THE RICH AND ACHIEVING

All financial service firms and professionals have their scopes set on building a client base of affluent and high-achieving individuals who continue to amass assets. Let's take a look at the life needs and desires of these individuals as they relate to money. In the Phoenix Wealth Management Survey conducted by Yankelovich Partners, Inc., a picture emerges of the new affluent in our society that reveals their need for some financial life planning dialogues. The mark for affluence in this study was set at $1 million in assets not including one's primary residence. This group voiced the following concerns:

- 76 percent want to spend money on experiences that will enrich their lives, such as travel and vacations. Are they going to enter into a relationship with an advisor whom they perceive will lobby against such expenditures in favor of retirement savings?
- Two-thirds feel they are overly busy and feel that no matter how hard they try they can't find enough time to do all the things they need or want to do. Does this sound like a need for prioritization and planning? Less than half of this high net worth group had a plan, and of those who did, less than 40 percent had fully implemented their plans!
- High net worth individuals feel they have an obligation to contribute both time and money to charitable organizations; 83 percent stated that everyone should give time and 90 percent give money with a third giving away at least $5,000 annually. How can you the advisor help to facilitate this desire and sense of obligation on an ongoing basis?

- 81 percent of the affluent expect to pay for their children's college costs, 36 percent expect to contribute toward graduate school costs, and 25 percent plan to provide support after college. Have they calculated the costs, made arrangements, and followed through? The advisor who can automate this process will lift a burden off of their parental shoulders. (It is ironic to note that over 40 percent of the affluent parents are concerned that their children will be spoiled and will not share their work ethic.)
- Only 32 percent feel "very knowledgeable" about financial matters and just 20 percent feel the same about the stock market. A ripe harvest field for the advisor who is willing to play both educator and coach.

CONNECTING WITH HIGH ACHIEVERS

What needs do you think you will find with the already wealthy executive? According to the Phoenix study, there are plenty of issues the advisor can address. Despite having achieved millionaire status, senior corporate executives are more stressed and feel less secure about their financial futures than other high net worth individuals. It seems that their wealth has come at a great cost to them. Seventy-four percent of these executives say they need to find ways of reducing stress in their lives, and 64 percent say they are looking for ways to gain control of their lives. What lifestyle change do they think will help them regain the steering wheel in their lives? Becoming a free agent.

Two percent said they want to 'retire' early but not in the traditional sense of retirement. Over 90 percent of these executives want to segue to a life of consulting or some other work where they have more control over their time. The advisor who can initiate this conversation and follow through by partnering in the development of a plan that can make this shift a reality will have no trouble winning the allegiance of the high achiever.

Forty-five percent of high achievers also said they spend too much time making money and not enough time enjoying it. Eighty-eight percent say they have an obligation to make a community contribution. This sounds like a group of people that has achieved material success but not fulfillment. They are also a group that feels it has paid too high a price at times for the material success it has achieved. These people are ready for a conversation about using their money to make a life.

LIFE AT THE CENTER

All that is indicated with the various groups mentioned in this chapter is that in the mind of the client *life* is the central concern. For the advisor to connect, life must become the axis around which the financial discussion revolves. People see money as a means to building the lives they want—and avoiding lives they will regret. They quickly connect with the individual who possesses the skill to draw out his vision for his life and can help facilitate the materialization of that vision. Your clients' money has meaning. Their money promises the fulfillment of a sense of purpose. That money was obtained with a defined set of values and has within it the seeds of a legacy they intend to leave. To make the life connection, the advisor needs to draw out the purpose of the money, the values that created the assets, and the legacy the clients intend to leave with it.

No professional is better positioned for this role than the financial advisor. Participating in this conversation does not change the traditional role of the advisor, it simply shifts the context of the discussion into the arena where the clients have the most invested—their lives.

Chapter **10**

The Paradox of Plenty

People say they want to be wealthy, but do they? People say if they had a little more than what they have now they would be content, but will they? People say money cannot buy the things that matter most, but do they really believe it? Suffice it to say people are conflicted on matters of money. At times we all have a hard time reconciling our beliefs and behaviors regarding our handling of money. We want wealth, but down deep, many of us fear that having wealth will negatively affect our attitudes and relationships. Some people have a terrible time finding contentment even as their assets grow. We say money can't buy the things that bring true happiness, but down deep we wonder. What we are facing is *the paradox of plenty*.

It is as if our spirits and wallets are in a perpetual wrestling match for dominance of our minds. There are questions people must bring to the table and attempt to address if they hope to bring philosophical clarity to the meaning of money in their lives.

- Will the achievement of wealth change me? If so, how will it change me?
- Will wealth bring me contentment? Why or why not?
- Am I being honest with myself when I describe what money can and cannot buy? Am I chasing money to buy (tangible and intangible) things I could have right now?

Because people are sometimes conflicted on money matters, their behaviors often fail to align with their intentions. This situation ends up confounding their mates, their advisors, and themselves. In order to bring clarity to the financial life planning process, it is important for the advisor to understand that these conflicts are universal. In this chapter, we will reveal where these money conflicts are most obvious and help to frame a conversation with clients in which both advisor and client will be comfortable participating.

A paradox is a tension between two opposing ideas. Both ideas contain truth, hence the tension. People today face internal tension regarding the quest for wealth. This may be because they live in a culture that publishes scores of business books every year that detail how ordinary people became wealthy (and so can you) and at the same time publishes scores of self-help books admonishing us to be content and care for our souls.

These paradoxical truths form a foundation for confusion, ambivalence, and discontentment. In our culture, these internal conflicts cause some to give up the idea of contentment and chase wealth. There are other individuals, however, who have learned to strive for balance in their lives—a point somewhere in the middle of these two tensions. They are attempting to pursue wealth in a manner that does not topple contentment. They are pursuing a more well-rounded sense of wealth, what they might call "true wealth." It seems important that people learn to recognize this paradox of plenty for the simple reason that, until they do, they will continue to sabotage either their fiscal well-being or their psychological well-being.

In this chapter, we will address three conflicting thought patterns.

1. Will I like who I am if and when I achieve wealth?
2. Will I really be content when I reach my financial goals?
3. Do I really believe that money can't buy happiness?

DR. JEKYL AND MR. GREED

Will the achievement of wealth contribute to making me someone that I won't like? Is there a monster in me that prosperity will unleash? A study commissioned by the AARP entitled Money and the American Family revealed this first pattern of the paradox playing out within members of our society. When asked what they would do with their money if they became millionaires overnight, respondents stated that they would help family and friends, save for their own future, and donate to charity. But, in a response that illustrates the duality of many Americans views toward the wealthy, respondents overwhelmingly stated that they believe that wealth is likely to make people insensitive and greedy, and give them a feeling of superiority over others. If you read between the lines, what Americans are saying is that although they want to become millionaires, they do not want to be given the stigma of other wealthy people. This paradox possibly is one of the reasons for the commercial success of books on how ordinary people became wealthy. Maybe people want wealth with the assurance that they can maintain their values and attitudes toward others. They also want others to view them as unchanged.

Many people fear that too much money will unleash superiority, insensitivity, unkindness, and greed. Do people question the affect of plenty because of what they have seen in others or is it because of what they have seen in themselves at times? If people are afraid of feeling superior to others, is it because they have felt the brunt of conceit, or because they have at times felt superior toward those below their stations in life? If they fear being less kind after they have money, is it because an insensitive rich person bullied them or made them feel inferior, or is it because they have, at times, been kind toward others only for the purpose of getting something? If greed is perceived to be a problem that comes with wealth, is it not also a problem now? Is greed not a ubiquitous temptation at any income level?

Many people have at some time or another felt the bitter sting of condescension at the hands of a successful individual who was dismissive or rude toward them. As badly as they want the comfort that wealth brings, they loathe the idea of anyone seeing in them the character that they saw in the individual that looked down upon them. Consequently, not every person desires to be wealthy. In fact, the AARP study revealed that one-third of Americans say they do not want to be wealthy. This is especially true in the mature crowd where roughly 60 percent said they do not desire to be wealthy. Is this because they have experienced more of the wealth-induced condescension in their lifetimes? Or, is it possibly because they have learned to be more content with simpler means? Or, is it a combination of both these ideas?

Some advisors may draw the conclusion that the only people who say they do not want to become wealthy are those who have no chance of doing so. We would expect that some of the people fit that characterization—but not all people do. An advisor's job is to optimize

the clients' earning potential within their parameters of risk tolerance. It is not the *plenty* that these people are so uncomfortable with
as it is the characterization that goes with it. No rational person
would turn away additional income, because he or she could always
give it away. It may merely be a matter of you choosing the description of prosperity that your clients are most comfortable with, or
even better, let them choose it for you.

No matter where clients place their goals, they have indicated
the definitions of prosperity that they are comfortable with, and have
offered you a springboard for developing a plan to meet their goals.
Each answer leads to a question of "How much will it take to get you
to this place?" If a client is conflicted about having too much, he or
she is best working that conflict out in a counselor's office, not yours.
Your efforts simply need to assume a context and description of prosperity that will connect you with the client. If you are on the same
page, you will have a better chance of working with their entire financial picture and maintaining lasting relationships.

Quite possibly, clients who have an aversion to the concept of
wealth need to be reminded that much of that thinking could be
based on myths and stereotypes. The spoiled, silver-spoon-fed, handed-
down-from-daddy rich is hardly the case with the modern wealthy set.
According to Thomas Stanley and William Danko in *The Millionaire
Next Door,* 80 percent of America's millionaires are first generation
wealthy—they are regular people who went out and EARNED IT.

Caveat: I have a doctor friend who will tell you he has no desire
to be rich, even though he makes over $250,000 per year. This indi-
vidual lives a relatively simple lifestyle and gives over 80 percent of
his income to various charities. It would be a poor assumption on an
advisor's part to think that every person who indicates that he or she
doesn't want to be wealthy, lacks the assets or the potential for becoming wealthy. If an individual's assets have greater potential than
his or her lifestyle requires, the advisor can simply segue the conversation toward charitable planning. In the case of this doctor, he chose
a definition of wealth that differed greatly from the crowd.

I CAN'T GET NO SATISFACTION

The second pattern of the paradox of plenty is that the more
people get, the more discontent they often become. Ask your clients
at what income level they would be comfortable, and they will likely

tell you a figure that is just a notch above where they are today. The person earning $50,000 will be content earning $75,000. The person earning $100,000 will be content earning $150,000, and so on. One cannot help but conclude that the marker for wealth is always moving forward in the mind of the client. Maybe it has something to do with the first paradox of not wanting to be characterized as rich, or maybe it has to do with the fact that the figures they pictured bringing wealth was an illusion. Does this progression of discontentment ever end? Apparently not. A recent study of the wealthy (with assets of $1 million plus) demonstrated that once a person reaches the million plus threshold, their sights are immediately set higher.

HOW RICH IS RICH?

According to the 2000 Phoenix Wealth Management Survey, individuals typically define wealth as a step or two above their current status. Approximately half of the individuals with a net worth between $1 million and $4 million do not believe they will be wealthy until they cross the $5 million dollar plus plateau. Tell that to your clients making $75,000 per year! If you do, they will scoff and say how ridiculous such a thought is, yet they are experiencing the same discontentment phenomenon at a different income level. We are no doubt pointing out the obvious when we say that prosperity in the minds of many is perpetually one step away. It is not so much the state of the account as it is the state of mind. How many people are living in the highly taxed state of discontentment? It is not as many as you might think.

The aforementioned study by AARP divided respondents into the following five attitudinal groups.

1. *Left Out.* These are people who have little and want much (6 percent of the population).
2. *American Dreamers.* These people have some and want more (21 percent of the population).
3. *High Achievers.* These have much and want more (24 percent of the population).
4. *Settled and Satisfied.* These are comfortable and do not desire more (38 percent of the population).
5. *Wealth Averse.* These have little and are reluctant to want more (11 percent of the population).

You could lump the first three groups together (51 percent) as the "want more" crowd. They vary in income levels with the left out having the least and the High Achievers having the most. The left out group possessed the strongest faith in the value of money yet did not possess the money they valued so highly, nor did they seem to have education or youth on their side. This group seemed to feel both discontent and disenfranchised.

The American Dreamers are the youngest group (two-thirds under the age of 45, with a high proportion of minorities) and are trying to save but are saddled with high levels of credit card debt.

Of all the groups, it was noted that the High Achievers had clearly embraced wealth and believed it to be an important facet to a successful life. But we find it surprising that together these three groups comprise only 51 percent of the population. We expected to find higher numbers in the want more crowd.

Forty-nine percent of the respondents fell into the satisfied category. The Settled and Satisfied group were highly satisfied with their financial situation and they hesitated to want more wealth. These middle-income, married homeowners place little value on money as a measure of success and were quite uncertain as to whether they wanted to be wealthy.

The last group, the Wealth Averse, were decidedly nonmaterialistic and yet the effects of lacking money were felt in their lives. They had low incomes and high debt (nonmaterialistic?!) and many had to forego education, medical care, and retirement because of a lack of money.

MAKE UP YOUR MIND

When you closely study the features of these attitudinal groups, the money conflicts quickly rise to the surface. You will soon realize that all the groups, to some degree, demonstrate inconsistent attitudes and behaviors that reflect elements of the paradox of plenty.

- 70 percent of the Left Out group believes that earning a lot of money is absolutely necessary for a successful life, yet most (90 percent) have no college education and earn less than $30,000 per year.
- The American Dreamers group wants more than its current means will allow. They hold high rates of credit card debt

and many invest more in lottery tickets than in retirement programs.

- The High Achievers (98 percent) work hard for the lifestyle they say they are content with, but would probably be the first group to tell you they wish they had more time and less stress.
- More than any group, the Settled and Satisfied (80 percent) say they are saving and investing for their future, yet this group says it places little importance on obtaining and having more money.
- The Wealth Averse may just have a denial problem, as in if you don't have it, just say you don't want it. There is a definite conflict here between espousing nonmaterialism and carrying disparate amounts of credit card debt.

Of all the groups, the settled and satisfied might be the happiest. They earn between $30,000 and $75,000, but it seems that a sense of practicality and gratitude is the key to their contentment level. Seventy-two percent describe themselves as just average financially— but average is fine with them. Ninety percent say they are happy with the lifestyle they can afford. They have learned to live within their means. Over three-quarters of this crowd describes themselves as better off than their parents.

MONEY CAN'T BUY ME LOVE

There are many clichés that people are quick to quote like money can't buy love, health, friends, etc., but one has to wonder if people really believe these aphorisms or if they just like the way they sound. Another aspect of the paradox of plenty is the disconnect between what people say money can and cannot do and the underlying motivations for how they spend their money. Let's examine what people say money can and cannot buy, and the underlying contradictions become clear.

Money Can Buy

When you ask today's clients what they expect their money to buy, they will talk of many things, but four expectations are most often cited: freedom, security, excitement, and less stress. While there is no denying that the right amount of money can deliver the opportunity to do as you choose, there are far too many people whose lives are so intent on acquiring money that they have surrendered all freedom and have become slaves to the process. They have surrendered in the present what they hope to have in the future. They have placed entirely too much faith in money. If and when they get the money they expected to relieve their stress, they discover other areas of their lives out of kilter, and may no longer know how to relax. Money, to a degree, can purchase freedom, exciting experiences, and relief from stress; however, the world is full of people who have had all these features in their lives before they ever had a million dollars. It is hard to enjoy the destination if you haven't also been able to savor and enjoy the journey.

Money Can't Buy

People are also quick to tell you that money can't buy the emotional payoffs in life, but a perusal of our society reveals contradictions. They will tell you money can't buy love, but when was the last time you saw a *poor,* bald, overweight, middle-aged man with a trophy wife? What is the prospect that motivates millions to "invest" in plastic surgeries?

People say that money can't buy self-esteem and self-fulfillment, yet many say money makes them feel successful and affords them the opportunity to pursue the goals that will give them self-fulfillment.

People will say that money can't buy family togetherness, but how many people wish they had more money for the simple reason that they could have more time with their families? Lack of time with people they care about is one of the greatest stressors in our society today.

People will say that money can't buy good health, but have you ever had to make a living arrangement for an aging relative? Once you do, you quickly realize how important the relationship is between the money you have and the quality of care you receive. Millions do not have access to the prescriptions and medical care and services they need because they cannot afford it.

Finally, people will say that money can't buy peace of mind. But those with adequate financial resources can pay high fees for psychologists, career coaches, and other contentment gurus. The actions of these individuals will tell you they are expecting their money to liberate them from the stress, pressures, and constraints in their lives.

Money won't make you happy but neither will poverty.

—Anon

We do not mean to say we do not see the truth in the idea that money can't buy love or health or quality relationships. We do intend to point out, however, that many people simply pay lip service to these ideas and down deep believe that somehow, someway, money will answer all.

One inescapable and undeniable conclusion we can draw about people and money is that, for most, there is a constant wrestling match going on in their relationship with money. There will always be inconsistencies. There will always be uncertainty and tension between paradoxical truths. People want plenty but do not do the things they should to get it. They say they don't want it but down deep yearn for it. They say they will be content when they reach their financial goals and then they aren't. They can't fully decide if money is good or evil. They have seen some of the things that money can do and they've seen some of the things the lack of money can do. Consequently, most people hold inner conflicts regarding money.

Although your clients may be somewhat ambivalent about what they expect from money, they are more likely to be decisive about what they expect from life. Whether they like it or not, there is a price tag attached to almost everything people want in life.

Chapter *11*

Redefining Today's Retirement

Imagine being a blacksmith 100 years ago. As a blacksmith you prospered in your business for many years because you provided an indispensable service to the community's chief transportation system. One day you look up and see a loud contraption coming down the main street that people are calling the horseless carriage. "Huh?" You think, "That will be the day," and go back to work. Ten years later your business is half of what it once was and 20 years later it no longer exists. You, the blacksmith, failed to recognize one psychological key in succeeding with consumers, *if there is a more efficient way to live our lives, we will choose it even if it presents a whole new set of challenges.* Many a blacksmith probably discounted the motorized contraption as too complicated, academic, and unproven for the majority of consumers to adopt.

Markets for popular products don't dry up overnight. The shift starts as a slow trickle, gains current slowly, reaches a rushing torrent years later, and eventually settles into a predictable stream. Successful merchants keep a fluid mind-set as they watch the trends develop and adapt their goods and services to these trends. The wise merchant 100 years ago would have expanded his business to include repairing horseless carriages as well as shoeing horses. This expansion would also be accompanied by a new learning curve on the workings of gasoline engines. Those who simply kept their noses to the grindstone with the same offering of goods and services were one day replaced by a new breed of mechanic.

Are the goods and services you sell today as progressive sounding as they were 10 or 15 years ago? Do your goods and services resonate with the way people want to live their lives? As the demands of your clientele change, the answers to these questions become crucial to your business success.

The old life model followed a simple pattern.

- The first part of your life you spent learning.
- The second part of your life you spent working and earning.
- The last part of your life (retirement) you spent in leisure or travel.

This model for living life is being rejected and rearranged for a more tailor-made design on life. Consider current trends that are evidence of this paradigm shift in life course navigation.

- Trend 1: Senior citizens are going back to college in record numbers. Thousands are "retiring" to university towns instead of the traditional snowbird destinations.
- Trend 2: Many retirees are becoming entrepreneurs and reviving shelved dreams and passions.
- Trend 3: Many people in their prime earning years are taking steps *back* in order to spend more time with their children in their formative years. These individuals are no longer willing to sacrifice parental influence for immediate material advancement. They feel they can make up for lost earnings when the children are grown.
- Trend 4: Many people are rearranging their living circumstances in order to shift into more meaningful and fulfilling forms of work and less hectic lifestyles.
- Trend 5: Over 50 percent of retirees are going back to work after becoming bored with the prospects of full-time leisure.
- Trend 6: The idea of periodical sabbaticals from work are gaining popularity with high achievers and earners. They view these periods as necessary to rejuvenate and to reflect on their life direction.
- Trend 7: Adventure travel and learning vacations are popular with all age groups—especially the 50-plus crowd.
- Trend 8: The migration to the Sunbelt is declining and more people are retiring (and becoming involved) in their own communities.

Next, add up the following demographic and societal changes and ask yourself what they mean to your future business.

- The average median age in the United States is 35 and is getting older every year.
- The workplace is facing a looming brain drain of managers and executives and is beginning to offer phased retirement packages. ("Brain Drain," *Business Week*, September 20, 1999, 113–124)
- Reversing a 50-year trend, the number of Americans working past age 65 is now rising. (*New York Times,* February 26, 2001)
- With companies reducing pensions and health benefits, many aging workers will not be able to afford to fully retire.
- With the repeal of the Social Security earnings restrictions, a major economic disincentive to working past age 65 has been removed.
- Many baby boomers continue their expensive indulgences not wanting to wait until they are older to enjoy them.
- 80 percent of baby boomers say they intend to continue working in some form in their retirement. (Roper Starch Worldwide press release. Commissioned by the AARP. "Baby Boomers Look toward Retirement." June 2, 1998, 1–5.)
- Two-thirds of Americans say they feel stressed from working too much. (Hilton Generational Time Survey, January 2001, reported in *USA Today*)

What conclusions can you draw from the preceding facts and findings? What impact do you foresee in relationship to the products and services you are selling and the manner in which you market or promote them? One question that begs asking is, "Is the traditional retirement planning process on the road to extinction?" If your business focuses on traditional retirement planning, is it also on the same road?

THE TIMES ARE A CHANGIN'

Many people feel the concept of traditional retirement is hopelessly outdated and no longer applies to their lives. Many also feel that the times have so radically changed that even the term *retirement* is no longer appropriate. If people no longer connect with the concept or even the term, how long will it take before they reject the process that leads to a concept they no longer embrace?

The extended working life is being made possible by a number of factors that are physical, psychological, and intellectual in nature.

- People live longer today and are healthier and more active at older ages.
- People are beginning to view early retirement years as a "middle-escent" stage where they can chase dreams in a sort of child-hood without supervision.
- Knowledge capital rather than physical labor is our chief form of earning.
- Studies demonstrate the importance of intellectual stimula-tion and purposeful pursuits in successful aging.
- Many retirees desire "re-creation" as much as recreation in their retirement years. They see retirement as an opportunity to redefine themselves and to explore their potential.

None of these factors have escaped the attention of the 77-million-strong baby boom constituency. This is a group that has often frustrated the financial services industry with their free-spending, live-now men-tality. But this group, by and large, has looked traditional retirement in the eye and has seen it for what it is—an outdated concept that no longer fits.

The book *The New Retirementality* gives a succinct history of where the idea of retirement got its start and how it established a foothold in American culture. The idea was invented in Germany in 1875 by Chancellor Otto Von Bismarck. At that time, the average male lived to age 46 and the retirement age was set at 65. The idea was imported by the FDR administration in 1935 as a way to remove old men from the labor force and put young men to work during the Great De-pression. It was an appropriate idea in an industrial society where age had a significant bearing on output. Also motivating FDR was the fact that similar employment struggles in Italy and Germany had led to the rise in power of both Mussolini and Hitler. In 1935, the aver-age male lived to the age of 63 and the retirement age was set at 65.

It is clear in viewing the genesis of the traditional retirement model that the retirement journey was designed to last for two to three years, not for 20 to 30 years. If a person only expected to live to the age of 63 or so and retired at age 62, it might make sense to fully indulge in a life of leisure and rest. But such full-time pursuits make no sense when faced with 20 to 30 years of retirement living. How about the individual that retires at 55 and lives to 100. That is a whopping 45 years in retirement! Society is struggling for a new term to describe this period of life because many sense that the traditional concept is no longer relevant or valid.

How much longer then can the retirement savings industry continue to approach clients with the same old plans and approaches? The time may be short according to Jacqueline Quinn in her article "The Metamorphosis of Retirement" (*Journal of Financial Planning*, April 2001). She writes:

> Because it is inevitable that the vision of retirement will continue to undergo a metamorphosis, some would argue that it behooves today's planners to adopt an entirely fresh approach to retirement planning, to reinvent retirement planning itself. Out are the old parameters of solely planning for a client's retirement, bearing in mind life expectancy increases. It is a much broader picture of retirement planning, the dimensions of which not only encompass the finances of retirement but the dimensions of the client's lifestyle (with its myriad nonfinancial issues). Planners are now helping clients plan not only for retirement, but how they are going to live in retirement.

FINANCING LIFE

If your retirement planning process is simply about having x dollars at x age, then you are doing nothing more than helping clients prepare for what Mitch Anthony has called "the artificial finish line." Life does not end or begin at age 62. Many clients are working in careers that they don't particularly enjoy with the hope that they can put away enough money to do what they want at age 62. These people must believe that life begins at age 62. Others are preparing only in fiscal terms for retirement from their work at age 62 and are making no plans for how they will utilize their time, knowledge, and energies past that point. These people are grossly underprepared for life past the age of 62. The retirement planning process can and must adapt to the reality that there is a lot of life left to live for today's retiree, and then begin using processes and services that better attend to this reality.

Michael Stein, author of *The Prosperous Retirement*, suggests that retirement is a "time in life where an individual shifts from earning a living for the sake of economics to contributing to society with the goal of self-realization in mind." Retirement for baby boomers will become a classic animation of Maslow's "Hierarchy of Needs" as people move their minds and money up the pyramid toward self-actualization. Tomorrow's planner will be found engaging in conversations with two types of self-aware clients: (1) those who want meaning and balance in their lives and can afford to retire; and (2) those who want meaning and balance in their lives and cannot afford to retire.

In the next chapter, we will talk about the place that work will hold in the lives of both these types of clients. Just because one client *can* afford to fully retire does not mean that he *should* fully retire. It is important for everyone to consider all that is gained from work beyond the paycheck if they are interested in pursuing meaning and achieving balance with their lives. For many people who have the means to retire, engagement in work (paid or unpaid, part-time or full-time) that challenges and energizes them will be the key to a happy, rewarding, and satisfying retirement period. Those who cannot afford retirement will need help exploring a work-life situation that will help them find the expression of meaning and attainment of balance they desire, while also providing the necessary income for the lifestyle they desire.

The conversation clearly needs to move from how much money we will need to reach the artificial finish line to how do we design the kind of lives our clients hope to live once they reach that line. Even better is the conversation that helps clients remove the artificial finish line and starts to work on transitioning to a life that works now. This will help the clients pursue interests they love at a pace they can live with. Research indicates that only 15 percent of preretirees are interested in the traditional retirement experience. How are you going to help the other 85 percent redefine retirement for themselves? (Roper Starch Worldwide press release. Commissioned by the AARP. "Baby Boomers Look toward Retirement." 2 June 1998, 1–5.) Tomorrow's retiree will have no interest in being finished.

For the conversation to move past a pot of gold at the end of the artificial finish line, clients must be made aware of the differences between the retirement model of yesterday and that of today. The conversation between the advisor and client needs to move to the realm of self-actualization, which is how the majority of prospective retirees are beginning to view the period of retirement. However, it is important to keep in mind that this redefinition of retirement as a time for self-actualization is not restricted to the 60-plus crowd. Self-actualization seems to be a driving force for baby boomers and also foundation for the career decisions of the generation X population.

The redefinition of retirement raises a number of issues for both advisor and client to establish a dialogue around. Consider the questions in Figure 11.1.

FIGURE 11.1   Thinking It Through

Exercise 1—My Views about Retirement

□ Yes   □ No   *I'm counting the days until I can retire.*

□ Yes   □ No   *I expect my retirement to be very different from what my parents experienced.*

□ Yes   □ No   *I don't want to retire "cold turkey."*

□ Yes   □ No   *I worry about not having enough money when I retire.*

□ Yes   □ No   *I wonder what I am going to do with my time when I retire.*

□ Yes   □ No   *I worry that Social Security will not be available when I retire.*

□ Yes   □ No   *I haven't thought much about what I want to do when I retire.*

□ Yes   □ No   *I like being productive and would like to continue working after I retire.*

□ Yes   □ No   *I'm worried that my health will fail when I retire.*

□ Yes   □ No   *I have a clear vision of how I will invest my time and energy when I retire from my current position.*

Exercise 2—Personal Reflections

1. What I most look forward to about retirement:_____

_____

_____

_____

_____

2. What I am most concerned about in retirement:

_____

_____

_____

_____

_____

The list of issues raised because of the redefinition of retirement is expansive. We covered these more comprehensively in Chapter 6. What is important is to realize that redefining retirement ultimately forces the redefinition of our products and services and how we interface with the client.

Ross Levin, CFP, of Accredited Investors, Inc. in Edina, Minnesota, relates a retirement transition story that fits quite well with the model of self-actualization as the target rather than just attaining a set amount of money at a certain age. Ross tells of a 53-year-old client who sold his business, but had concerns about his investment assets supporting his lifestyle. Rather than going back to work in the same industry, Ross's dialogue with this client led to this man taking a position in the public service sector, which was something he had always wanted to do. Despite the cut in salary, he is "in the black" both at the income and self-actualization levels. When faced with this scenario, how many advisors would simply tell the client the number of additional years he would have to work to build his retirement nest egg?

The above client is entering phase one of what may be a 40-year retirement journey. It is vital that the client work with an advisor who understands this model of retirement living and offers as many options for self-actualization and personal fulfillment as possible. The goal is more than monetary. Tomorrow's clients will measure their progress in life more by their self-worth than their net worth, and more by what they contribute than by what they keep.

TOO YOUNG TO RETIRE

If you examine closely how retirement is being redefined and reinvented, you will be better equipped to connect and resonate with today's client, especially the 77 million baby boomers who are quickly approaching traditional retirement age. The Web site Too Young to Retire <www.2young2retire.com> lists ways to reinvent retirement. Some of them are:

- Retire the word *retirement*—in the traditional sense—from your vocabulary.
- Understand that retirement is a relatively new concept in human evolution. Until the past 100 years our elders not only remained active but also were relied upon for their wisdom, insight, and skills.

- Organize your life priorities around what is most important to you, like enhancing relationships with loved ones.
- Become a student again. Begin to address intellectual hunger and look for new and stimulating challenges.
- Surround yourself with positive people who are growing, rather than those who have been there, done that.
- Start taking risks. If you try something new and it succeeds, celebrate the discovery. If it doesn't, you have gained a valuable experience.
- Respond to new opportunities. You may just now be realizing your full potential.
- Re-energize your system daily with your preferred form of exercise.
- Revisit some of your childhood dreams and believe that you can live them now, if they still feel right for you.
- Put passion first. This is a time to act on wisdom gained and follow your true passion.

These ideas are indicators of how your clients currently view—or are at least beginning to view—the concept of retirement. Too Young to Retire sponsored a contest in which visitors to the Web site were challenged to come up with a word to replace the term *retirement*. Some of the ideas submitted were:

- Renaissance
- Graduation
- Entirement
- Redeployment
- Refirement
- Keenagers
- Refinement
- Regeneration

The advisor who wants to stay in step with the times should provide the opportunity for clients to offer their own definition of retirement. The New Retirementality workshop by Money Quotient, Inc., offers advisors a client seminar for that purpose. The workshop helps clients bring a personal definition to retirement and subsequently defines and designs the work, play, relationships, and legacy they want to pursue with their lives. When the workshop is over, clients then bring their life maps to the advisor for the financial services and arrangements that will be necessary to bring their plans to fruition.

If you look up the word *retire* in the dictionary, you will see that it means to withdraw. Suffice it to say that today's retiree is not the withdrawing type. They aim to squeeze everything they can out of life. In the late 1960s, labor economist Seymour Wolfbein wrote that people of the baby boom generation would have at least five distinct careers— not jobs, but careers (from "The Reggies Are Coming" by Stephen Kindel and Raymond Goydon <2young2retire.com>). Wolfbein prognosticated a time of retraining and reinvention and he placed no upper limit to when and where that training would end. It would seem that Wolfbein's crystal ball was crystal clear regarding the revolutionary approach of baby boomers. The years previously set aside for reclining will be used for redefining; some of the time reserved for recreation will be used for personal re-creation.

Consider the popular Silicon Valley myth that all the Internet startups were the invention of 22-year-old Stanford business school students. Ian Greenberg writes in the June 12, 2000, issue of *Industry Standard:* "The pervasive image is of a startup founder straight out of business school or still living in a college dorm. Only 9 percent of those who have founded Internet firms are 29 or younger. People in their 40s and 50s make up nearly half of all startup founders." Add in the founders who were over 60 and the percentage of founders aged 40 to 60 plus goes to 58 percent."

As much as this generation desires challenge, they also now crave more balance between their work and personal lives. It is the convergence of self-actualization and the realization of what truly brings happiness that has forced the razing of traditional retirement models and redefining this phase of life on a more personal level. Advisors who understand this paradigm shift and begin the redefinition dialogue with their clients will find themselves connecting with clients in a new and dynamic manner. Begin today to redefine your services and approach with the new retirement realities.

Chapter *12*

Working It Out:
The Role and Significance
of Work in Our Lives

> The leading edge baby boomers are likely to work at least 20 hours a week. They'll be returning for second careers, they'll be going back to school.

—*Charles Longino, Jr., Professor of Gerontology, Wake Forest University*

In the year 1900, the average life expectancy was 49 years of age, and only one in 25 Americans reached 65 years of age. Today, one in eight Americans is over 65, and by the year 2030, it will be one in five. In 1937, the first applicant for Social Security, Ernest Ackerman, a streetcar motorman from Cleveland, received a lump sum payment of 17 cents—enough possibly for a cup of coffee and a donut. In those days, a retiree could only expect to live another year or two, so the only concern was for some economic security in that year or two of work-less living. Today, the average 65-year-old can expect to live an additional 18 years. Those age 65 to 74 is the most prosperous group in our country with a median net worth of $190,000. Seventy-two percent of these individuals say they are in good or excellent health. Consequently, their concerns have expanded beyond economic security.

When surveyed on retirement fears and disappointments, there is a stark difference between the nonretired individual's concerns about retirement and the actual disappointments faced by the retiree.

FIGURE 12.1   Concerns Before and After Retirement

BEFORE	AFTER
1. Health	1. Alienation
2. Money	2. Health
3. Boredom	3. Money
4. Alienation	4. Boredom

In the chart in Figure 12.1, prospective retirees list their biggest concerns as poor health and financial worries; however, actual retirees rated alienation as the biggest disappointment. By alienation, these retirees are referring to being lonely; being cut off from former colleagues, groups, and organizations; missing their jobs; and feeling behind the times. It is interesting to note that the biggest discrepancy between preretirement concerns and postretirement realities is the issue of financial worries.

Could this realization be due in part to the fact that many retirees come to learn that much of the propaganda regarding financial shortfalls and gaps coming from retirement product vendors has been overblown? Could it also be due to the fact that retirees—more than any group—learn to simplify their living costs and adjust to their income streams? Add to this the fact that we are now seeing books and articles explaining to potential retirees that they can live comfortably and even luxuriously on under $20,000 per year. Financial columnist Paul B. Farrell recently documented how many well-heeled retirees attending a Berkshire-Hathaway gathering shared how they were living quite comfortably on $15,000 to $20,000 a year (CBS.MarketWatch .com, "Yes, You Can Retire on $22,000 a Year: Don't Buy Wall Street's Scare Tactics, Self-Promotion," February 7, 2001, p. 2).

This trend in thinking serves to amplify the point that the financial services industry has placed such a monomaniacal spotlight on having more than enough money for retirement that it has painted a picture of retirement as exclusively an economic event. When that event actually happens, however, the retiree soon finds financial concerns being superceded by life concerns, most notably the issue of alienation from the people and productive activities that caused them to experience a sense of significance and purpose in this world.

Retirement has always been defined as work versus no work. In fact, many financial advisors assume that the ultimate goal of retirement planning is freedom from work.

However, work performs several important functions in our lives. Preretirees must continually keep in mind that not only does work provide an income stream, but it also is a source of much of their social lives, their self-esteem or status in the community, their life structure and their sense of utility. A key element in the new "retirement mentality," therefore, is the strategy needed to replace these work functions in the next stage of life.

Today's retirees voice much more interest in an active life—including the continuation of work—than their parents' generation. Those people looking ahead to retirement, which includes the group of 77 million baby boomers, are viewing retirement as an opportunity to start a new life, explore their potential, reignite old dreams, and make a mark upon the world. Marc Freedman, president of Civic Ventures, thinks that this new perspective will be a potentially profound phenomenon that will impact American society both economically and socially for the next two to three decades. "This aging society presents us with a massive opportunity," says Freedman, author of *Prime Time—How Baby Boomers will Revolutionize Retirement and Transform America*. He continues, "This current transitional generation is actually reinventing retirement. The baby boomers will just do some fine-tuning."

It is important to note Mr. Freedman's distinction between the currently retired group who are in the process of redefining retirement but do not carry a well-publicized socio-label and the baby boomers. Borrowing a European characterization, some refer to the current group of 56- to 70-year-olds as the "third-agers." It is actually these third-agers, not the baby boomers, who are setting the trends for working and active retirements that baby boomers will capitalize on in their own retirement experiences. The relevance of this trend to the financial advice community is summed up in the words of Thomas Riehle of the Peter Hart research organization who said, "Future retirees expect a better life in retirement. They are convinced they will have more diverse sources of income and will lead a more active retired life."

A BETTER LIFE

It is important for today's financial advisor to engage in a discussion with clients about what that better life looks like and what those more diverse sources of income might be. The old model of looking forward to a life of leisure with three sources of income (Social Security, pension, and investment savings) is being supplanted by a model where the retiree pursues interests and dreams and adds a fourth income stream (wages) that might be more substantial than all the others combined. Retirement has evolved from reclining to redefining.

Dave Cryden, CFP and radio personality in the central coastal region of California, recently shared this story with me:

> At our last family reunion on the East Coast, a couple of conversations stood out which seem to be indicators of a great trend in our society. The first was with four cousins of mine who were all turning 60 and were sitting around talking about it. None of these people looked or acted like what we traditionally have been taught to expect from a 60-year-old. They were all in good health and nearing their retirements, but none of them were anywhere near wanting to "hang it up" regarding work. They all felt they had plenty to offer and were plotting how they would stay engaged and continue to contribute. The second conversation was with my uncle Max who is 91 years old, and with his wife who is 89, who still go to work everyday in Manhattan. Max is still sought after in his field of expertise. Someone asked him and his wife when they were going to retire like everyone else their age, and their answer was, "Why would we do that? This is our life. We love it!"

The better life that today's retiree—or potential retiree—envisions is one of integrated rather than compartmentalized living. In Figure 12.2, we see the distinction between tomorrow's mind-set and the aging paradigm of how we live the latter years of our lives. In the old model, education was crammed into the early years, work in the middle years, and leisure in the later years. I describe this model as the "binge design of life." This model is being replaced with an age-integrated model of life where education, work, and leisure are all balanced in day-to-day living. Mature people seem to better recognize

FIGURE 12.2   Compartmentalized Living

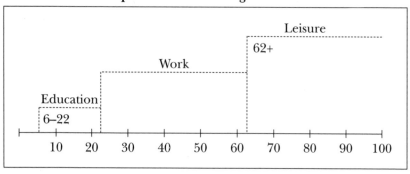

the unhealthy aspects of a myopic focus on either work or leisure. What is one without the other? Does leisure maintain its meaning without the contrast of work? To paraphrase Shakespeare, if holiday and sport are all we have, then all too soon our holiday and sport become toil.

Today's retirees are as interested in engagement as they are in playing golf. They feel healthy and many have the material means to do what they wish, but they want to feel useful and still have a great desire to exercise their skills and talents in meaningful ways. Many feel that they have gifts that have been lying latent throughout their adult lives. For these retirees, the old model of retirement is not working. Dave, a retired surgeon put it this way, "I saved my whole life so I could someday do as I wanted. Now that I have it, I want to do things I've never done before, and yet much of society is trying to tell me what I should be doing."

You can be sure that whatever it is that your clients in this age group imagine doing, it will most likely have a positive effect on their financial picture. In fact, many will be earning enough to live on so that their investments can continue to grow further or be applied to other interests. We will discuss these other interests in Chapter 15, "Leaving a Legacy." Philanthropy will become an increasingly important topic to future retirees. Planners who can help simplify the charitable processes will find themselves with a windfall of clientele.

I had a client that I began a conversation with regarding the possibility of a "working retirement" because I noted that he didn't seem like the reclining type. I asked him what kind of work, maybe on a part-time basis, that he thought he could do until his dying day. He said that one aspect of his work was particularly satisfying and he felt he could do that "forever." We started calculating what might happen if we plugged potential earnings from part-time work in that area into his retirement scenario, and found that if he were to arrange such employment with his employer as a consultant, he would be able to "retire" earlier than previously planned. He was ecstatic at the prospect. He went to his employer, who was receptive to the idea because the business did not want to lose his expertise to their competition, and an arrangement was struck. My client ended up retiring six years ahead of schedule, and he never stops telling me how happy he is that we had that conversation.

—*Jack T., CPA*

For many third-agers, this is the better life that will make their retirement a more fulfilling experience than what their predecessors experienced. For 80 percent of the baby boomers, this retirement design will be a must—simply from the aspect of psychological fulfillment. For others, it will be a must for both economic and psychological reasons. Even for potential retirees who are looking ahead and realizing that they will have to work, most will find that being engaged keeps them healthier and more vibrant than those peers who live out idle and bored retirements. Financial advisors need to discuss the possibilities of a working retirement with their clients. This discussion is not just reserved for those close to retirement.

A 45-year-old client may be close to the place where a change in cash flow planning and a reconfigured work schedule could make retirement or emancipation a prospect for the near future. We use the redefinition *emancipation* because in this sort of scenario it is a more accurate description of what the client is looking for. Instead of looking at every client and asking "When do you want to retire?" we could start asking "What kind of life do you desire?" and work toward that objective.

PHASED RETIREMENTS

What are the ramifications of the boomers wanting work in their retirement years coupled with the fact that many corporations are beginning to feel the crunch of mature managers walking out the door? With a growing shortage of talented and experienced workers, we now have an environment where many will be able to negotiate part-time, flexible working scenarios for their retirement years.

Demographics show that corporate America is just now beginning to feel the effects of a brain drain that will continue for the next decade as baby boomers approach retirement age. The baby-bust generation (1964–1980) lacks the human capacity to supply the necessary numbers to replace them. The pain will be most notable in the managerial and executive positions that are typically occupied by experienced workers aged 35 to 55. In Figure 12.3, you can see that as the country gets grayer and as the workforce ages, the talent shortage will continue to get worse.

The baby boom generation could not have planned a better scenario for themselves. They want to work in retirement on a part-time basis and the workplace badly needs their expertise. (Score a point for boomers!) They will have unprecedented negotiating power regarding their working responsibilities and schedules.

Will it be difficult for the 62-year-old to find a new position? The experts say no. An unemployment fact of life is that there is more demand for experience in many areas than there are qualified workers. Another point is that baby boomers won't discontinue being consumers just because they retire, therefore, their consumerism will help sustain economic growth and a strong job market.

The other piece of good news that accompanies phased retirement is that it gives individuals (who didn't save enough) time to work out their finances while entering a less hectic and stressful working lifestyle. One of the easiest ways to keep from depleting savings early in retirement is to retire in stages instead of all at once. Within the next 15 years, the old work or retire ultimatum will be supplanted by the more flexible, attractive, and practical phased retirement proposition.

In an article titled "Reinventing Retirement, Baby-Boomer Style," online reporter, Sage, described the phased retirement experience in these terms:

> The emerging model looks something like this. When you retire from your old job, you find another position, possibly part time, doing something you enjoy. This can be anything from consulting in the industry you just left to teaching at a community college, to working in an antique shop or

FIGURE 12.3   The Graying Workplace

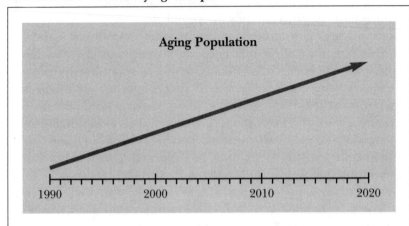

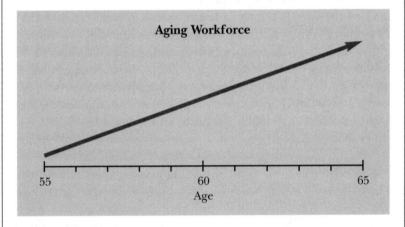

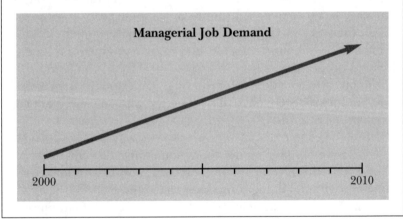

bookstore. You probably won't make as much money as you're used to, and this is a good time to learn to streamline expenses and pay off any remaining debt. You probably won't be able to save any money at this point but, but the longer you can leave your existing savings alone, the better. This gives your portfolio time to grow while you still escape the rat race in favor of a more relaxing lifestyle. Eventually, you'll be ready to quit working completely, and by then, you should have accumulated enough money to last through the rest of your retirement.

Growing numbers of workers will be able to negotiate such agreements as more and more companies begin to embrace the phased retirement concept. Currently about 10 to 15 percent of companies offer some sort of phased retirement arrangement, but hundreds of others, recognizing the demographic threat, are looking at developing this sort of program. There will be trade-offs, as many employers will see a phased retirement package as a way out of paying for benefits such as health coverage. If a client desires a phased approach to retirement, it will be incumbent on the advisor to help that client financially navigate this novel path.

It will also be necessary for advisors to discover the type of working retirement that their clients are looking for. A study conducted by Gallup and PaineWebber titled Retirement Revisited sheds some light on what the new retiree wants to do in retirement years. In this study, 85 percent of the respondents said they wanted to continue work in some form. Respondents' answers fell into the following five categories:

1. I want to work as long as I can doing what I do now. (15 percent)
2. I want to become an entrepreneur. (26 percent)
3. I want to find a new job. (34 percent)
4. I want to find some balance between work and life. (10 percent)
5. I want the traditional retirement. (15 percent)

One group wants to die with their boots on. Another group wants to do their own thing. Another group just wants a change of scenery and to try different things. And another group has come to the point where just making money isn't doing it any more. Many of these people desiring to travel an unfamiliar route will need to gain a realistic picture of how it will all work out for them financially. They will need the advisor to illustrate where the tradeoffs will be and how their assets should be managed to make such a life possible.

COLLECTING A *PLAY*CHECK

> When people talk to me about retiring from my work it just doesn't strike a chord with me. I must be a very blessed person because I feel like I've hardly worked a day in my life with the work that I do—I love it that much. I always told myself that if it ever felt like work then I would quit it. So far that hasn't happened.
>
> —*Ray, age 52*

Linus Pauling, a Nobel prize-winning researcher and a professor into his mid-90s used to tell his students, "Try to decide what you like to do best—what you enjoy doing—and then check up and see if it's possible for you to earn a living doing it." This is the life that so many wish they had. They want a vocation rather than a job, and desire to pursue a sense of calling in their working life. They want work that is fun—work that makes them want to get out of bed in the morning. They want to collect a *play*check. According to a study by a the AARP, of the 80 percent of boomers who said they want a working retirement, only one-third said it was for economic reasons. Sixty-seven percent said they want to continue working simply because they enjoy work.

These people know that the old paradigm of a work or retire ultimatum at age 62 is dead. Intellectual capital doesn't turn off at age 62. Today's worker is a "knowledge worker" and is highly adaptable having exercised these skills in many arenas. Some jobs they have enjoyed more than others and maybe some jobs they have hated. Through it all, many have formed an opinion of a vocation they might enter for the love of it—a job where they are rewarded as much psychologically as they are materially. This focus is not just pertinent to those clients nearing retirement but for any clients who have been in the workforce long enough to have a feel for what it is they want and do not want.

There are clients who are 40 years old with visions of being and doing something else with their lives. There are clients in this age group who are burning the candle at both ends and are lamenting how much of their children's lives they are missing. They have flirted with changes and compromises in their minds but are not sure how these changes might play out in their financial future.

A good advisor can help people in these situations determine what their options are. Maybe they could sacrifice some earning power for a few years to spend more time influencing and interacting with their young children. Maybe they could negotiate an independent contracting position or telecommute one or two days a week. Maybe one of the wage earners could go part time during an important period in a child's or other loved one's life. Clearly the discussion must move past doing everything in our power and sacrificing everything important in our lives just to make sure we have a pot of gold at the end of the rainbow at age 62.

According to Michelle Conlin, who writes about workplace trends in an article entitled "9 to 5 Isn't Working Anymore," the things that are not working are workplace childcare and the Family Leave Act. The things that are working are independent contracting and work arrangement flexibility. IBM, the company that once forbade floral neckties, now allows key managers to work from home to balance personal and professional lives, and these managers are *more* productive from their homes because they have more peace and balance. Regarding independent contracting, Conlin writes, *"One in four workers are saying adios to corporate America. And what a happy lot; they are twice as likely as W-2s to earn more than $75,000 per year and half as likely to work more than 40 hours per week."*

The dominant goals in the minds of today's workers are doing something they'll love doing and having a sense of balance in their lives. There are many people over 40 who have just now decided what they want to be when they grow up. There are many that are feeling stressed from the unproportionate place work plays in their lives. If an advisor can ascertain what kind of working life the client desires and put together a plan that shows how such an arrangement might work, this advisor will have a grateful client—a client for life.

Chapter *13*

Designing Your Life in Retirement

> I wasn't ready to wrap my arms around my money and die.

—Howard, former retiree, age 74

Michael Stein, author of *The Prosperous Retirement: Guide to the New Reality*, stated, "I have come to the conclusion that more retirements will fail for nonfinancial reasons than for financial reasons." In this modern society, there are countless messages reminding people to plan *now* and be ready for their retirement years. There have been so many reminders that one would think that the only thing a person has to do to be ready for retirement is save enough money. Retirees learn very quickly, however, that while having enough is important, it is far from enough to guarantee a happy retirement.

RETIREMENT'S DIRTY LAUNDRY

What difference will all our financial planning for the future make if we have no idea what kind of life we want to purchase with the financial assets we acquire? Money has no value in and of itself. Money is only valuable in the way we use it—to improve our quality of life. Millions of people run full speed into retirement with great anticipation only to have their expectations break down in various ways because they failed to anticipate the nonfinancial challenges such as boredom, alienation, disillusionment, and loss of direction. If unresolved, these problems can lead to drunkenness, divorce, and even premature death. While researching for *The New Retirementality,* I ran into a multitude of stories of retirees who got less joy out of traditional retirement than they had bargained for. There were those who died within a year of retiring because they lacked purpose in their lives. There were those who developed extraordinary prowess at the 19th hole of the golf course because they lacked purpose in their lives. Then there were others whose happy retirements were quickly spoiled by tension at home. As one wife of a retiree put it, "I married him for better or for worse but not for lunch. I didn't need him around the house telling me how to organize the closet."

Most of these and other retirement disappointments can be anticipated and avoided if clients have the opportunity to view their retirement through a more holistic lens. Clients have heard plenty about investing their money properly for retirement but have heard little about investing their time, energy, and skills. John Wasik, author of *The Late-Start Investor,* wrote:

> Instead of absorbing an obsolete view of retirement, we should consider what I call your New Prosperity. This includes a flexible life plan that provides for your financial, vocational, physical, emotional, and spiritual needs. Unless you look at your future holistically, merely saving up a pile of money will be a meaningless act.

The Wheel of Life chart in Figure 13.1 delineates the aspects that contribute to a contented life in retirement. Which of the nine categories is the average client sufficiently prepared for? Have you ever seen a retiree who had plenty of money, but allowed his physical health regimen to soften because he was unchallenged? How many fail to obviate the lack of psychological satisfaction equated to leaving work behind? How many are realistic about where they want to live in retirement? How many have thought about the important relationships they will leave behind if they move to a new location or the new relationships they will have to form in their new environments? All nine aspects contribute to a fulfilled retirement for retirees and their spouses. If one party is not happy in retirement, chances are that this discontentment will taint the visions their partner had of retirement living as well. Advisors have told us of a number of not-

FIGURE 13.1   Wheel of Life

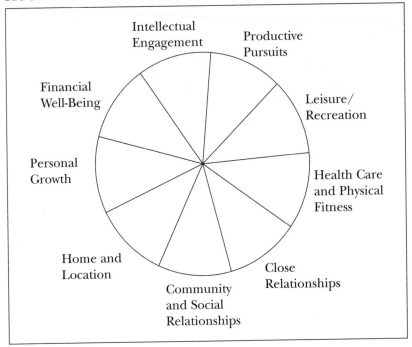

so-happy commentaries from clients who were struggling to adjust to the nonfinancial aspects of retirement. Here are some examples.

- An advisor heard a 67-year-old retired executive lamenting about his boredom and subsequent disillusionment with not being needed anymore. The advisor commented that this scenario struck him as sadder than the person nearing retirement with an insufficient nest egg. It is one thing to lack money, it is altogether another to lack purpose.
- The wife of a retiree confided to her advisor that her husband was driving her nuts sitting around the house all day. She also feared that his health was declining.
- A retiree commented that his dream of retirement life in a warmer climate was souring due to the difficulty his partner was having adjusting to a different social and cultural environment.
- A retiree took early retirement to start a business that ended up as a psychological and financial nightmare for her family.

The stories are manifold, but the underlying theme is the same: many people are entering their retirement years with too narrow a focus. A person's fulfillment with retirement living will not hinge simply on investment account balances. The Wheel of Life chart in Figure 13.1, borrowed from Carol Anderson's *Designing Your Life in Retirement* seminar, illustrates how quality of life requires a plan and a strategy for all nine areas of life.

1. Intellectual engagement
2. Productive pursuits (paid and/or unpaid work)
3. Leisure/recreation
4. Health care and physical fitness
5. Close relationships
6. Community and social relationships
7. Home and location
8. Personal growth
9. Financial well-being

When approaching retirement, clients analyze their portfolios of retirement income sources, double-check their companies' retirement benefits, reevaluate their insurance needs, and so on. Their satisfaction in retirement, however, ends up being derailed by factors other than financial circumstances. In retirement preparation, money was treated as the end all instead of being used as a tool for achieving goals in all other areas of life. The most satisfied retirees have anticipated their lives in retirement and not just their cash flows. Consequently, they are living the best years of their lives—instead of being disappointed by a modern day mirage.

FREUD'S COUCH

We can almost hear the thoughts buzzing through the minds of many advisors reading this chapter, "So now you're telling me that when I talk to my clients about retirement planning, I need to address their health, homes, intellectual and personal growth, and relationships as well as their money? Maybe I should get rid of my calculator and just get a couch installed in my office." We are not suggesting that advisors need to engage in dialogues about any matters outside of the financial planning context—only on matters directly impacting the financial life of the client. For example, discussing where a client plans to live will have a direct impact on fiscal well-being. Discussing whether or not a client wants to engage in post-retirement work will have a direct impact on his sources of retirement income. Discussing leisure goals and associated expenses are relevant to the client's financial picture as well. Talking about relationships is also fair game, especially when there is a financial link, such as helping to support an aging parent or the goal of contributing to a college fund for a grandchild.

In addition, many midlife and older adults buy into the concept of life-long learning and long to return to college or graduate school to continue their educations. In addition to tuition, what would be other associated costs? In more abstract matters, such as physical, emotional, and spiritual well-being, many advisors have found they can simply act as catalysts for proactive thinking, conduits for relevant information, and referrals to trusted professionals within their network.

With all this said, each advisor needs to stay within his own conversational comfort zone. Advisors seem to fall into three categories regarding the type of material they are comfortable with in advisor-client dialogue.

1. Those who desire exclusively transaction and financial services dialogue
2. Those who are comfortable in financial and life dialogues, and desire to provide information only on peripheral issues
3. Those who are comfortable in advice-giving/counseling dialogues

In our conversations within the industry, we have concluded that advisors who prefer categories 1 and 3 are in the minority, and advisors who prefer category 2 make up the majority of advisors. Most financial services professionals understand that they need to provide a more comprehensive suite of services to be competitive today—and that a wider suite of services naturally leads to a broader dialogue into the life of the client.

The New Retirementality workshop materials developed by Money Quotient, Inc., provide another vehicle for having a more holistic retirement planning dialogue with clients. This workshop is designed to encourage participants to reject the outdated "retiremyths" and to adopt a new attitude about the opportunities of life after 50.

Both client seminars, *Designing Your Life in Retirement* and *The New Retirementality,* provide an effective means to broaching a more comprehensive life dialogue with your clients. Money Quotient, Inc. licenses and trains advisors to deliver public seminars and consults with them on how to market a more life-oriented advisory practice. The service is popular with advisors because of its ease of implementation. Money Quotient customizes a financial life planning newsletter for each advisory firm and provides tools for helping clients recognize the financial implications of each life event and transition.

The tools are available to advisors who desire to help their clients develop a more comprehensive approach to their retirement years. Your audience is more than ready—many are demanding a personalized, individualized approach to their lives and their money. Clients who take the time to plan for their physical, intellectual, and personal well-being will enjoy healthier retirement living. Those who plan where they want to live, how they want to participate socially and vocationally, and how they want to contribute to others will certainly increase their chances of having a fulfilling retirement experience. The advisor who helps to facilitate this process with an individual stands a much better chance of earning the client's loyalty. Not to mention the opportunity to manage the client's full complement of assets than the competition.

WHO'S ZOOMIN' WHOM?

The much-hyped and ballyhooed baby boom will be taking a much more holistic view of retirement living, and chances are this more enlightened perspective will be called something other than retirement living. For the most part, they are going to view this period as the "middlescent" stage of life—a kind of second adolescence without parental supervision. If there is one word that describes the boomer approach to retirement and life as a whole, it is the word *individuality.* It is a big mistake to categorize all baby boomers into one sociological description or behavioral pattern, and to try to treat every baby boomer client with a cookie cutter approach. According to demographer, William Frey, "Despite attempts by marketers and the media to brand them as one, perhaps the most common trait of the generation born between 1946 and 1964 is its individuality." (Tim Smart, "Not Acting Their Age." *U.S. News and World Report,* June 4, 2001.) Advisors who are helping baby boomers design their lives in retirement must keep this fact front and center in their minds as boomers are quickly put off with the one-size-fits-all approach. For many baby boomers, their retirement years will be the most exciting, adventurous, thrilling, and fulfilling years of their lives. It will be a period of *carpe diem*.

Many modern clients entering retirement will be better recognized as "zoomers" because the lifestyles they lead will defy traditional laid-back retirement stereotypes. In the article cited above, Tim Smart described them as

> . . . independent, youthful, with prospects of a long life ahead, and well off. Their bank accounts fattened with years of appreciation in their primary homes and their company-sponsored retirement accounts, their bodies strengthened by years of exercise, their minds stimulated by college and sometimes postgraduate education, boomers are generally far better equipped for retirement than their parents were. Many will be in households where there is not just one but two earners, with multiple retirement savings accounts gathered over the years at different jobs.

While this sounds like a blissful picture, there may be a black lining to this silver cloud. According to Smart there is.

> Most of these aging baby boomers are blissfully unaware—or maybe just unwilling to acknowledge—what it might mean to live 30 to 40 years beyond the day they quit their day jobs. This will be a time when they may be caring for adolescent children and aging parents at the same moment because they delayed having children, and because their own parents are living longer. There is tremendous denial about the issues of aging.

THE IDEAL WEEK

Two questions asked in *The New Retirementality* workshop are "What would your perfect week in retirement look like?" and "How do you want to invest your time between work, leisure, relationships, and social involvement?" We use the analogy that your portfolio is a snapshot of how you invest your money, but your calendar is a snapshot of how you invest your life. Not planning how you might invest your time is "equal to putting your life in a passbook savings account earning 2 percent."

To help clients begin to visualize what life in retirement might look like, we ask them to first list how they will invest time in developing each spoke of the retirement life wheel. In order to help clients prioritize, we ask them to complete the scenario planning exercise shown in Figure 13.2.

FIGURE 13.2   Scenario Planning

Question 1: If you could be assured of having all the money you or your family would ever need, would you make changes on your Weekly Calendar in the way you propose to invest your personal resources (time, energy, skills, and money)?

Intellectual Engagement	Productive Pursuits (paid and/or unpaid work)	Leisure/Recreation
Relationships	Personal & Spiritual Growth	Community Activities
Physical Health & Fitness	Financial	Home/Location

Question 2: If your doctor told you that you had a maximum of five productive years to live, would you make changes on your Weekly Calendar in the way you propose to invest your personal resources (time, energy, skills, and money)?

Intellectual Engagement	Productive Pursuits (paid and/or unpaid work)	Leisure/Recreation
Relationships	Personal & Spiritual Growth	Community Activities
Physical Health & Fitness	Financial	Home/Location

FIGURE 13.3   An Ideal Week in Retirement

DAY	MORNING	AFTERNOON	NIGHT
Sunday			
Monday			
Tuesday			
Wednesday			
Thursday			
Friday			
Saturday			

After clients make a speculative allocation of how they might invest their time in retirement, they chart it on the Ideal Week in Retirement calendar shown in Figure 13.3.

In the example shown in Figure 13.4, we see the calendar of Ed S. who is 57 and estimates he is three years away from his emancipation. This exercise forced Ed to see that his vision was originally too narrow in focus. He originally stated that he was going to golf and play cards, and the hardest work he planned on was mowing the lawn. By the time Ed completed the exercise, he realized that he wanted to spend 10 to15 hours of work a week to keep his skills and his mind sharp. He wanted to get involved with a high school program that helped students develop business skills. In addition, he decided that

FIGURE 13.4 Ed's Life—An Ideal Week in Retirement

DAY	MORNING	AFTERNOON	NIGHT
Sunday	Church	Family time	Family time
Monday	Read, consult	Golf	Board meeting
Tuesday	Read, consult	Run errands, misc.	Off
Wednesday	Read, consult	Golf	Church
Thursday	Read, consult	Run errands, misc.	Care center visit
Friday	Volunteer in school	Golf	Dinner date
Saturday	Open	Time with grandkids	Open

he wanted to spend time each week visiting people in a care center and wanted to help his church in a project to expand its building.

With these goals in mind, Ed experienced a new sense of purpose for his retirement years. He gained a greater and more gratifying anticipation of retirement living than before he had completed these exercises. This holistic retirement planning process helped Ed to realize how much he had left to contribute and how important it was to his well-being to remain active in productive pursuits.

Success in retirement involves balancing all facets of life into a state of stability or equilibrium. People that focus on only one or two areas may find that this will work for a while but eventually their lives will feel out of kilter and, ultimately, spin out of control. The retirement stage—as well as all stages of life—should be met with a balanced approach to planning. *Retirement should not be viewed as a single life event, but rather as one of many transitions in a continuum of life experiences.* Those who navigate well through other life transitions will likely have the same experience with retirement. The skills, values, interests, and attitudes they have accumulated in life's journey will continue to serve them well in retirement.

Because choices made today impact our future, it is important to seek growth and development in all areas of life throughout adulthood. Those who do so will more likely find retirement to be a rich and rewarding experience. That is because all along the way, they have been preparing for *life,* and not just preparing for retirement. Their plan for retirement will be comprehensive—a blueprint for life that allocates all of their personal resources: time, energy, skills, and money, in ways that are most meaningful to them as individuals.

Chapter 14

Offering Guidance in Times of Career and Retirement Transitions

The cost of a thing is the amount of what I will call life which is required to be exchanged for it, immediately or in the long run.

—*Henry David Thoreau*

A recent survey (Richard Leider, "People Describe Their Workplace," *USA Today,* June 27, 2001) asked retirees about their greatest regrets in retrospect to their working years. Their top three responses were:

1. They wished they had risked more.
2. They wished they had reflected more.
3. They wished they had focused more on a *raison d'être* as opposed to just collecting a paycheck.

The regrets of these retirees are not lost on their progeny. They hear their parents lamenting the fact that they fell into a working rut and were too afraid to break out—or too busy to even think about it. As a result, they are assessing their quality about life and forming an opinion about what they want their futures to look like.

Many of these next generation retirees are seeing the same pattern unfold in their own lives and desire to somehow break the pattern.

The collective mood of our culture and civilization could be characterized as *stressed out*. In a survey conducted by the Nierenberg Group and New York University Management Institute, professionals were asked, "If you had to describe your office environment as a type of television show, which would it be?" (Shannon Reilly and Quin Tian, "People Describe Their Workplace." *USA Today,* June 27, 2001, B-1.) Their answers were:

- Real life survivors (38 percent)
- Soap opera (27 percent)
- Medical emergency (18 percent)
- Courtroom drama (10 percent)
- Science fiction (7 percent)

Aside from the entertainment value it brings, today's workplace provides more than its fair share of stress. Such circumstances, coupled with the cloud of job insecurity, place a premium on the well-being of the average worker. A recent survey in the 2001 *Farmer's Almanac* (p. 30) revealed that:

- Forty-four percent of Americans call themselves workaholics.
- Since 1995, the number of people calling in sick due to stress has tripled.
- People entertain less often; they don't have time.
- Parents complain that teachers overload their kids with homework (stressed out parents now get to come home to stressed out kids).

A recent poll conducted by the National Sleep Foundation demonstrated that instead of working to live, Americans were living to work. Participants in the study reported that they spent more time working and less time sleeping, engaging in social and leisure activities, and having sex than they did just five years ago. A secondary effect of long working hours is the sleepiness people feel during the hours they intend to be awake. One in five adults reported being so sleepy during the day that it interfered with their activities at least three times a week. In addition, many suffer from sleep problems. (Source: "Less Fun, Less Sleep, More Work," Executive Summary of the National Sleep Foundation Study, March 2001.)

The stressed and frazzled are finding ways to fight back the stress in their lives. Spa visits are up. Many are taking advantage of flex time and sabbatical policies at work. Old-fashioned, hands-on activities like knitting and crocheting are popular again with four million new people taking up those hobbies in 2000. Home schooling is booming, thanks in large part to online instruction. Telecommuting has become more of an acceptable alternative to working 9 to 5 in a cubicle. In search of ways to reduce stress, many people in this society are wondering if there are steps they can take—short of a radical career shift—that will bring more balance to their lives. This is where the financial advisor can act as a valued guide. A solid positioning statement for today's advisor would be:

> My work is based on what is going on in your life at this moment or changes you are considering—not just building a nest egg for *x* years down the road. Many of my clients face unexpected transitions such as job loss, personal disability, or illness in the family, and I try to help them navigate financially through those times. Other clients want to make transitions in their work lives, either to a different career or a modified version of their current career, and I can play the same role in those transitions as well.

Let us assume that today's worker wants more out of life than 40 years in the workforce, a gold watch, and a condo in Florida. Let us assume also that these people have witnessed their parents' retirement regrets and would like to take more risks, reflect more, find greater purpose, and connect with ways to explore their potential. To attain these life qualities, they will need an astute and holistic-thinking financial guide. In this chapter, we will discuss the types of transitions many wish to make and transitions that they are often forced to make. The financial life planner understands that life does not always move in a linear track, and that adjustments are necessary when life plans meet with unexpected challenges or opportunities.

Most career transitions require financial analysis and planning as they center on work issues and impact an individual's earning power. A cursory glance at reasons for early retirement indicates that the majority of early retirements were not planned. Forty percent of retirees were forced into early retirement because of health issues. Layoffs are the second highest factor leading to early retirement. Those experiencing health issues and layoffs often find themselves in situations of involuntary and unplanned retirement—for which they are emotionally unprepared. Because their retirement came sooner than expected, many have not reflected on how they would spend and contribute their time.

Many others in their 30s, 40s, and 50s are questioning work routines which are increasingly imposing upon the quality of life they desire. For some, this contemplation will be fleeting; for others, it will turn out to be a pivotal reflection as they determine a life-altering course. We should be careful not to underestimate the number of people who long for satisfying work as opposed to a "good job." Retirees seem to have a good grasp of this concept and desire to engage in satisfying work—even if they no longer have a paying job.

In *The Power of Purpose*, Richard Leider points out the crucial distinction between one's work and one's job. According to Leider, a job is what you do to earn money, whereas work is the actions you take to have purpose—to make a difference. Retirement may be the end of one's job, but not the end of one's life work.

The formula Leider prescribes for working on purpose is $(T + P + E) \times V$, which translates as follows.

- *T* stands for *talent*. This is the launching point for considering a career or career change.
- *P* stands for *passion* or *purpose*. As Aristotle stated long ago, "Where the needs of the world and your talent cross, there lies your vocation."
- *E* stands for *environment*. What work environment best suits your temperament, style, and working values?
- *V* stands for *vision*. How do you envision your life playing out in regard to life, location, wealth, relationships, and health?

Leider's ideas resonate with today's workers and prospective retirees who are not always sure what they want, but realize when they get it.

WORKING TRANSITIONS

In the financial life planning model, advisors are attuned to their clients' career goals and work-life transitions not only because of the direct impact on cash flow planning, but also because of their clients' sense of life satisfaction. The advisor actually can play the bridge builder between where the client currently is and where the client wants to go. Because most advisors do not want to play the role of career coach, we suggest finding a credible career coach in your community to refer clients to when the topic of a career transition is raised. Advisors can readily define the role they want to play in laying the financial groundwork for changes their clients are contemplating. The advisor would do well, however, to be better equipped to facilitate the working transition's dialogue.

The working transition's dialogue could be opened in facile fashion by asking, "Are you contemplating any changes in your work life?" If the answer is *yes,* we then ask, "What sorts of changes are you contemplating?" Common transitions range from making a radical career shift (entrepreneurial pursuits, free agency, consultation) to rearranging the work situation (moving into new responsibilities in the same company, partial or full-time telecommuting) to downshifting (simplifying) to taking a sabbatical to reassess everything.

Following are examples of each of these types of working transitions and how the advisor was able to guide in the transition process. The scenarios we will share here include:

- A client who felt consumed by her work but who concluded she was addicted to the pace and action.
- A client who negotiated a change in his working situation to care for a terminally ill wife and their children.
- Clients who have decided to drop out of the rat race—at least for awhile.
- A client who quit a secure, high-paying job to pursue an entrepreneurial dream.
- Clients who retired on less than $22,000 per year.

RAMPING DOWN

An advisor told us the story of Mike and Andrea, a young professional couple in their mid-30s who expressed their desire to make some sort of change so they could have a less stressful lifestyle. They were both good savers and had a few hundred thousand dollars each in 401(k)s, IRAs, and personal investment and savings accounts.

As they discussed all the possibilities regarding work scenarios, Andrea admitted that she was addicted to the corporate life and pace, and frankly loved the adrenaline rush of it all. She was upwardly mobile and still had higher aspirations. Andrea came to the conclusion that an annual week-long "Caribbean catharsis" would help alleviate her stress. The advisor suggested setting up a special travel account to ensure that possibility each year and she loved the idea. She was most concerned about Mike, who, in her words, "was beyond burn-out."

As the discussion regarding work turned to him, Mike felt he needed a change but didn't know exactly what kind. The advisor referred him to a career coach and suggested that they revisit the issue when he had a clearer sense of direction. The advisor assured him that whatever direction he chose, there were sufficient resources to build a bridge to get him to where he wanted to go. The couple seemed comforted by this approach and agreed to revisit the situation after consulting with a career coach.

Following the consultation, Mike decided to work six more months in his high-paying position in order to save toward a period where he might not be earning. This would also give him time to explore the possibilities of consulting part time and going back to school to get a master's degree in another field.

When Mike brought these ideas back to his advisor, the advisor demonstrated how he could tap some investments during that period without any serious impact on his retirement savings. The advisor also demonstrated how he could draw a small-annuitized income off part of his investments to help make up the difference between the reduced income he would have in the near future and the income he currently had. Knowing that they had a number of options available to them raised their spirits and gave them a glimpse of a less stressful existence.

ILLNESS AND MONEY

After Joe lost his wife to cancer, he knew he wanted to spend more time with his three grown sons, and also spend more time fishing and hunting. Joe felt like his opportunity had come when his company offered him a buyout of either a $500,000 lump sum or an annuity worth $2,000 a month for the rest of his life. He was 54 at the time. Yet wherever Joe turned for professional advice, they told him he was too young to retire. These advisors told him the chief impediment to his plan was the fact that rolling the half-million dollar buyout into an IRA would lock up the money until he was $59\frac{1}{2}$. What would he live on in the interim period? Fortunately, Joe found an advisor who was creative enough to navigate around this challenge.

This advisor informed him that, although tapping an IRA early normally results in a 10 percent penalty, individuals can avoid the problem by setting up substantially equal payments based on life expectancy. As long as the payment stream lasted for at least five years, there was no penalty on the payments. Joe and his advisor set up a plan where he would work part time until he was 58, and then start withdrawing from his IRA until he was 63 to satisfy the five-year rule. Joe was thrilled by this solution! The part-time work schedule freed him to pursue the more meaningful goals that became so apparent through the loss of his wife.

Chuck had a different situation brought on by the diagnosis of his wife's breast cancer. Her struggle is currently at six years and counting—during which time Chuck has been working out of his home in order to be the primary caregiver to his children, ages 8 and 11. When Chuck told his advisor of his dilemma, they agreed that they would deplete his savings only as a last resort, as Chuck is only in his mid-40s. Chuck decided to ask his company to change his job responsibilities to a position that required less road time, which would allow him to be more productive at home. Chuck knew of such a position in his company.

Chuck's advisor helped him sort through the cash flow issues and available options for bridging some months should he need to find another company that would allow this working arrangement. Fortunately, for Chuck and his family, his company agreed to the new working arrangement, and he has been able to care for his wife and children while continuing to be the family's sole source of income. Recently, because his company has become a takeover target, Chuck and his advisor are revisiting his financial situation, in case the new company is not as sympathetic as his present employer. Chuck has commented repeatedly how helpful and comforting he has found his advisor's partnership during this difficult period in his life. Although the prospect of his wife's health does not look good, Chuck feels that he has a valued guide to help look out for his family's financial well-being.

THE DAY OF REST

According to a *Washington Post* article entitled "After the Layoff, Time Off," many layoffs are being used as an opportunity to drop out of the rat race, at least on a temporary basis. Workplace and human resource experts are confirming that this is indeed a trend in the making as those in midlife reexamine how much "life blood" they want to donate to the corporation.

Those who have a larger severance package are more likely to take a sabbatical, especially those living through a second career downsizing. Brita Askey, an outplacement expert in Washington, D.C., says: "The stigma once attached to unemployment has diminished as people become more accustomed to downsizings. People think differently now. They are taking more risks. People are getting more focused on quality of life issues now; they want to combine something they really enjoy with the reality of needing to make money with it." (Quoted in the *Washington Post*, "After the Layoff, Time Off." August 15, 2001.)

A theme we see developing in our culture is one of people moving away from a life that is totally dedicated to career. Those who have gone down that path and have been burned by companies that do not reciprocate that loyalty are deciding that they do not want that kind of life anymore. After 20 to 30 years in the workforce, many individuals feel emotionally and physically drained. They worry because they know their creativity, as well as their enthusiasm, is waning. Because their work is no longer fulfilling, many think that early retirement will be their escape route to a more satisfying life. In actuality, however, most of these individuals wouldn't choose an early retirement if they had a chance to take time off to rest, reflect, and rejuvenate.

As the labor shortage expands and growing numbers of baby boomers reach retirement eligibility, more companies are looking for ways to retain valued older employees. While only 10 to 15 percent of corporations currently offer sabbaticals, studies show that employees who have this opportunity will return to work with a deeper commitment to their employers. Other benefits include improved morale and increased productivity. Most human resource specialists agree that sabbaticals are an expensive employee benefit, but well worth the investment. ("Sabbatical Programs Becoming Valuable Way to Retain Employees," by Michael Bradford, *Business Insurance*, June 25, 2001 and "Taking a Sabbatical from Work," by Jim Owen, <www.careerbuilder.com>.)

If your client's company is not hip to the idea of sabbaticals, they still might be able to negotiate time away from work. David Sharp, coauthor of *Six Months Off*, recommends using the terminology *leave of absence* instead of the often-misunderstood term *sabbatical*. In addition, a well-prepared and thoughtful proposal to management may win over objections.

Many people desiring a sabbatical period hold high-level positions in corporations as managers, chief officers, vice presidents, and even presidents. We are seeing that the higher one has climbed the corporate totem pole, the greater the possibility that they have contemplated a sabbatical period to regain their sanity.

Many in the downsized predicament desire to enter a sabbatical to contemplate how to move from having a successful career to having a successful life. They are seeking work that leverages the skills they have and are less concerned about the size and structure of the company they work for. In the words of Pat, a high-level executive who took a sabbatical bridge to freelance in her career, "It's finding the one or two opportunities that really make your heart sing and you really feel suitable and a good fit."

For many, a sabbatical period will be a path to working out of their homes, freelancing, becoming an entrepreneur, or changing the type of work they do within the same industry. As one manager who went to freelancing said, "What I love about my life is that I stopped being Dilbert." What advisors need to recognize about these people is that many of them have come to the point where they are willing to give up some money and prestige in exchange for some quality of life because all too often, quality of life is what they traded in to get the money and the prestige. Thousands who have been through the corporate grinder are deciding that they no longer want to live the unexamined life.

What if a client is burned out, stressed out, or simply out of energy and fresh ideas, and a leave of absence is out of the question? In that case, give the client a copy of Pamela Ammondson's book *Clarity Quest: How to Take a Sabbatical without More than a Week*. Ammondson will guide your clients through a process to recharge their batteries, assess what is genuinely important to them in life, and rediscover who they are and what they really want.

All indications point to a rise in sabbatical periods in the next decade. It is becoming enough of an issue that workplaces are now taking a close look at forming or modifying sabbatical policies for key personnel. It is certainly worth bringing up with clients when inquiring about their most desired working scenario. If advisors can assist in making the financial arrangements and preparations for a desired sabbatical period, their clients will be most indebted.

RESTRAINING JUDGEMENT

The financial planning experience needs to improve the quality of our clients' lives today, not for some unforeseen tomorrow.

—*Ross Levin*

As financial life planners, our purpose is to partner with, guide, and educate our clients. Our jobs should be directed toward facilitating our clients' dreams rather than trying to plug everyone into the same retirement model. Heretofore, most retirement planning has hinged on calculating the financial gap between each client's age and investable assets, and each client's retirement age and the amount of assets necessary to draw at least 70 to 80 percent of that income. This conventional wisdom permeates retirement planning. Practically every advisor and retirement calculator on the Internet is using the same 70 percent rule. This rule is being challenged by many from both sides of the argument.

Some are saying that the retirement baby boomers will require at least 100 percent or more of current income levels, while others are proving that you can make arrangements to live on much less than 70 percent. As facilitators, our role is to help our clients by playing out, in financial terms, the fiscal realities of the goals they hope to pursue, not to cast judgements on the fiscal prudence of pursuing those goals.

THE END OF THE 70 PERCENT RULE?

Recently, there has been a proliferation of books and articles telling people that they can do more with less and not to worry about the old 70 percent rule. This is due, in part, to the market downturn and to people's sense of exasperation with saving enough to provide the 70 to 80 percent they are told they need for retirement. This sense of exasperation only grows when these same people are told of the eroding effect of inflation on their nest eggs over time. One example is a recent article that warned that individuals under 40 with one million dollars in savings would actually need three million to maintain their standard of living in retirement. While hoping to spur more savings, this advice instead has stimulated a backlash.

If a person with a million dollars can't retire comfortably, what hope could the average person possibly have? "Plenty," according to columnist Paul Farrell in a Marketwatch.com column entitled "Yes, You Can Retire on $22,000 a Year." Farrell reports on people enjoying ribs and corn at Warren Buffett's annual Omaha barbecue—many of whom are living comfortably on $15,000 to $30,000 a year, and still saving lots of money. Of course, these people have little debt, but there are many examples of multimillionaires living on as little as $15,000 a year. As one semi-retired client told us, "Money tends to lose its meaning as you age, and you find yourself being content with the basics—good health, good friends, shelter, and food. If you have enough or a little more than enough, you take pleasure in that."

Ralph Warner, author of *Get a Life, You Don't Need a Million to Retire Well*, found that when he asked retirees why they were happy, money wasn't high on their list of concerns. Instead, Warner found a direct correlation between a midlife obsession with work and savings, and an unhappy retirement. Warner also discovered that content "seniors spent their middle years investing in themselves—acquiring the skills, connections, and an outlook that made the free time of retirement a good time." Warner advises: "Think about the kinds of work that you'd do for the sheer joy of it if money ceased to be the main motivator, and start planning now to make the transition to part-time work in that field. In short, the more interesting you find yourself, the more interesting you'll find retirement."

It is precisely this idea that may render the 70 percent rule obsolete in the lives of future retirees—if that 70 percent is based only upon Social Security, pension, and investment incomes. Many will retire early, engage in interesting part-time work, and make up any possible shortfall from investment income. Some of these people will aim for modern retirement when they have enough to draw 30 percent of their current income off of investments—not 70 percent. It is important for advisors to learn what their clients want, and to be flexible when it comes to creating a patchwork of finance solutions to help clients get the lives they desire.

We have heard many clients bemoan the fact that when they told their advisor of their plans, for instance, to change to a lower-paying, slower-paced career, that they sensed a tacit disapproval coming from their advisor. As one client put it: "I felt like he was looking at me thinking, 'How could you leave this kind of money?' I just wanted to move on and have a life. I wanted help in rearranging my money to make that life possible." To facilitate the needs and wants of the modern client, advisors must—to borrow a worn out phrase—think out of the box. The rule of the box is to keep doing what you're doing to earn as much as you can to be able to do what you want at retirement age. The new rule for the age we live in is do whatever you can to have the highest quality of life *now* while also preparing for the future.

Yes, today's clients really do want to have it both ways. They want to enjoy the present and the future. While the old model exhorts us to sacrifice the present for the sake of our future, today's clients feel uncomfortable deferring all the pleasures of life to an uncertain future. Today's advisor must possess the flexibility to allow clients to define what they want out of the present and the future, and facilitate the financial processes to make it happen. This will require loosening our grip on old retirement "gap" models and restraining judgment and biases based on outdated ideas regarding retirement.

The goal of financial life planning is to help the client achieve quality of life in a resourceful manner—and as soon as possible. This ethos will inevitably supplant previous planning models such as having x dollars by age y, as such a goal may in fact be an impediment to achieving true wealth in one's life. Life is unpredictable. Vicissitudes visit with no warning flares. Life continually offers us opportunities to examine the roads we are traveling and to change our course.

Advisors who can demonstrate that they can think out of the box and possess the necessary flexibility to help clients who want or need to change courses will gain reputations as financial partners and guides, as opposed to conventional brokers or planners. Just as one size does not fit all, neither does one plan fit all lives. The public is waiting for a group of advisors to step forward and tailor their services to individual lives, instead of trying to stuff individual lives into prefabricated career and retirement models. This will require that we know the transitions our clients are contemplating and do whatever we can to help them make those transitions. Anyone can tell them, "It can't be done." It takes creativity and genuine interest in the clients's well-being to help them find that quality of life now as well as in the future.

In the next chapter, we will examine how you can help your clients, retired or preretired, move from making a living to making a difference.

Chapter 15

Leaving a Legacy

The last stage of life is either spent in integrity or despair. You will not despair if you believe your life has meaning.

—Erik Erikson

We cannot live the afternoon of life according to the program of life's morning.

—Carl Jung

Bill is a senior level executive at a *Fortune* 500 company. After reading *The New Retirementality,* he shared his vision of retirement with me. Because both he and his wife had saved well, he will be able to "retire" in his mid to late 50s. He has also embarked on a three-year course to receive the Certified Financial Planner (CFP) designation. His plan, once he receives his CFP, is to open up a practice that caters to those who typically cannot afford such services. He related an incident that set his mind upon this unusual career transition.

Bill was helping a young single mother with her taxes when she told him of a breakthrough in her life. This young lady, who earned no more than $15,000 a year, had told him with great pride how she had just paid off her last debt and how free she now felt to be able to pursue her dreams. Bill said this story touched him in a deep and meaningful way. It helped him to grasp how relative numbers were and how meaningful it was to gain complete control of one's financial life—whether you earned $150,000 or $15,000. He immediately recognized the dilemma that accompanies lower wage earners: these individuals can hardly afford financial advice, and few advisors are willing to work with individuals with such meager assets.

From this experience and realization, Bill's dream of becoming a "charitable advisor" was born. He plans on working on a sliding scale for those who can afford to pay so the individuals have something invested in the process. He also plans to provide services to those who need help but have no payment to offer. Bill has always been interested in financial matters and his faith has always been important to him. He is interested in having a positive and meaningful impact in our society. Now he has set on a course that will integrate these goals and values. Bill has found a way to leave a legacy.

INVESTING OURSELVES

Bill's story represents the highest goal of the financial life planning perspective: finding a way to invest all we are, all we know, and all we have in a cause that is bigger than ourselves. It is about leaving an idiosyncratic signature upon the world that only we can bring. It transcends rote tasks of volunteerism or keeping busy just to stay busy. It is a way for people, especially those making the retirement transition, to reinvest what they have gathered—both in material and spiritual terms.

The desire of retirees to make a difference is a trend that is well underway and will pay dividends not only for society at large, but also in the lives of the retirees themselves. Many of today's retirees are suffering unnecessarily under a dark cloud of insignificance. Many have gone from a who's who in their community to who's he?—and this transition takes a terrible toll on their spirits. One retired physician summed it up when he said, "I didn't realize what retirement had done to me until a woman walked up to me and said, "You used to be Dr. Wilson, didn't you?" He walked away feeling like society saw him as a has-been—an obsolete contributor resigned to count out his days and relive old memories. This is a definition of retirement that will not stand the acid tests of meaning and significance with the "down-agers" that are now entering retirement.

Down-aging is the term used to explain the idea that a person of, say 65 years today, is not the same as a person of 65 years living 20 or

30 years ago. People at retirement age today surpass the previous generation in their level of vigor and expectations of an active lifestyle. A generation ago, a person of 65 was sitting in a rocker waiting to die. Today, we lament how young they were if they pass on before reaching the age of 80.

Today, the average person over 50 says he feels 19 years younger than his driver's license says he is. Combine this new perspective on aging with the burgeoning boomer ethos of making a difference, and you have the makings of a renaissance movement in innovation, social contribution, and altruism among the over-50 set. A person of 65 years today still has considerable reserves of time, energy, and creativity left to invest. The question that individuals have to answer for themselves is how to best go about making such an investment.

ENLIGHTENED SELF-INTEREST

According to James Gambione, author of *Refirement—A Boomer's Guide To Life After 50,* a key value of the maturing and soon-to-enter-retirement baby boomer is giving something back. Many are reawakening a social consciousness that may have been sidetracked during the years of work and material acquisition. Along with the leading edge of the baby boomers entering retirement are the current third-agers (those born before 1946), who comprise a growing population of older Americans willing and able to invest themselves in redeeming many of the ills in our society.

Marc Freedman, author of *Prime Time—How Baby Boomers Will Revolutionize Retirement and Transform America,* is challenging our country to create and publicize meaningful activities for our older citizens— not simply giving them busy work like stuffing envelopes. "Most of the opportunities available to senior citizens were designed for a former generation of older adults, to get them out of the rocking chair. But this is not the retirement of their parents. We need activities that capture people's imagination, use their skills, and give them a sense of purpose," says Freedman.

Freedman gives the following as examples of groups that have mobilized retirees with a sense of purpose.

- *Experience Corps.* This group provides schools and other youth organizations with older adults who help improve academic performance.

- *National Senior Service Corps.* This group operates the Foster Grandparent Program, the Senior Companion Program, and the Retired and Senior Volunteer Program.
- *Care-a-vanners.* These are retirees who travel in Winnebagos building houses for Habitat for Humanity in projects that involve teenagers whom they mentor.

Many more benevolent, educational, mentoring, and altruistic causes will result as future retirees rise to the challenge of meeting the many specialized needs in our society and environment. Freedman tells the story of Marv Welt of Portland, Oregon, who, upon retiring from management consulting, decided to build a legacy by following his passion—fishing.

Unlike many retirees who simply sit on the dock trying out new lures, Mr. Welt, in his early 70s, decided to parlay his passion for fishing into an environmental experience for children in poor neighborhoods. The resulting program, the WaterWorld Program, is now operating in a number of public schools. When it started, Welt simply taught kids from the projects how to fish.

At the same time, Welt went back to school himself to take biology courses. As a result, he now takes groups of kids on field trips and gives them lessons on the environment. Welt's feelings about spending his retirement years in this way characterize the importance of living with a sense of purpose in later years. "Before I started I had no idea I would be doing any of this. But it gives a purpose to life that I think everybody needs. Sitting out in your RV contemplating your navel is, to me, a total waste."

This is a time in life where people can rethink how they want to invest their lives. Michael Stein wrote, "It's a time in life where people switch the primary focus of their lives from earning a living to chasing their dreams." For many of those retirees and future retirees, their dreams do not necessarily revolve around the old retirement image of self-absorption.

A good barometer of a shifting paradigm within any demographic group is the content of advertising from the financial services community. These companies spend enormous amounts of money researching the emotional "triggers" of the marketplace through focus groups and studies. It is interesting to note the evolution of advertising in the last five years as it has moved its scope from self-absorption to meaningful living.

For example, in the mid-1990s, there was a TV ad from ITT/ Hartford that showed a well-dressed, 60-something couple dancing on the deck of a boat, kicking up their heels, and acting like adolescents. The caption underneath read, "One day you'll get to act like a kid again but for now let's discuss your allowance." Within just a few years, however, a new, more significant theme was evolving in financial services advertising. This change is typified by an American Express ad that depicts three attractive people in their 60s wearing hard hats and jeans huddled together with wide grins as they discuss some aspect of a Habitat for Humanity project. The tag line on this particular advertisement is, "Do more." This is the satisfaction that future generations of retirees will want—to know they have done something.

People like former president Jimmy Carter have been trailblazers in setting an example and in writing about how people can best invest their lives once their careers are over. The need for meaningful pursuits does not dissipate in an individual's psyche once sufficient assets to retire are acquired. In fact, the financial freedom that liberates one to engage in leisure on a full-time basis only serves to intensify the deep longing to build some sort of meaningful legacy. This longing is amplified again by the ever-growing consciousness of one's own mortality, which intensifies as we grow older.

Marc Freedman wrote about retirees who were attempting to do more in a cause called the Work Connection. "In many ways The Work Connection offered [the volunteers] a second chance every bit as much as it did for the kids—the chance to redeem themselves from past failings, to be the father they hadn't been before, to reaffirm the value of their own life experience. It was an opportunity for finding new purpose, for leaving the land and the world a little better than they found it. They were doing something that mattered to themselves and to the community. In short, the success of The Work Connection program wasn't dependent on the shaky soil of idealism but rather was anchored in the much sturdier ground of enlightened self-interest."

Enlightened self-interest is Freedman's view of the rallying cry of new retirees. Rather than engaging in generic charity busywork, the next generation will want to play out the vision of a better world and society that resonates in their souls, and the solutions they imagine and create will be as unique as each individual. Today's advisors would do well to help their clients discover and articulate how they want to invest their lives in this way and to help create the financial tools necessary to fulfill this pursuit of enlightened self-interest. Millions of financially liberated retirees will find that their greatest joy will come through benefiting others. Many are ready now for the conversation that helps them determine how to build a legacy through the purposeful investment of their time, knowledge, energy, and financial assets.

GENERATIVITY

This idea of transferring a lifetime of acquired values and knowledge in later years is what famed psychologist Erik Erikson called "generativity." According to Erikson, the hallmark of successful late-life development is the capacity to be generative—passing on to future generations what one has learned from previous work and involvement. Erikson encapsulated this ideal in the phrase, "I am what survives of me."

Generativity involves the desire to leave a meaningful legacy. Legacy is often thought of as an inheritance, but can be much more than that. A legacy can be a sum of money that is designated for some special purpose to help younger generations. Leaving a legacy can also mean passing down your values and stories, and being a role model for success and fulfillment in life. These issues are best dealt with in the context of an ethical will. Before we discuss the concept of an ethical will and how you might introduce such an idea to clients, let us deal with the practical and fiscal aspects of leaving a legacy. To set up this conversation with clients you may say:

> Mr. and Mrs. Client, for many, an important facet of a comprehensive financial plan is deciding how to invest charitably in our communities, churches, schools, or particular causes we feel strongly about. First, I would like to get an idea about the types of causes you hope to support, and second, talk about some creative ways of leaving a financial legacy toward helping those causes. This could involve setting up a charitable fund or a scholarship fund, developing a benevolence plan, including charitable causes in your estate planning, or setting up an automated giving program for someone or some cause.

To help your clients define their feelings on this topic, have them complete the benevolence survey in Figure 15.1.

FIGURE 15.1 Benevolence Survey—Designing a Financial Legacy

1. In what charities or causes do you feel impressed to invest your time and energy?

2. What charities or causes do you currently contribute toward?

3. In what charities or causes would you like to invest financially?

4. Are there causes that you would like to support on a perpetual basis? On an annual basis?

5. Are there any family members for which you would like to develop an ongoing income stream (i.e., college fund for children, parental pension, funding for a disabled child or sibling, etc.)?

6. Are there any causes into which you would like us to look to make sure they are using charitable funds responsibly?

7. How often would you like to review your benevolence plan?

For some people, developing a benevolence plan for leaving a financial legacy is as important as managing their investments. Many people feel a sense of stewardship regarding the wealth they possess. As one client put it, "This money is just passing through my hands. I'm the conduit, not the possessor, but I have a responsibility to make sure it flows in the right direction." You will be able to quickly gauge the importance of charitable giving when asking your clients about their plans for benevolence. For some it is a nonissue; for others it is a priority—the motivating factor for earning more. For those who have not pondered charitable possibilities, you may spark an interest in charitable giving by bringing up the issue. For those who place a high value upon benevolence, you have communicated that you share their values and will partner with them to create the most responsible and effective means of giving.

Chapter 16

The New Philanthropy

It is important to be aware of the fact that for many, charity starts at home. Their definition of charity may include college funds, wedding gifts, or down payments on homes for children or grandchildren. It may also include setting up a pension for aging parents who could greatly benefit from a few hundred extra dollars per month. Advisor Bruce Bruinsma tells us that most people would be amazed at how much breathing room is created for retired parents with an additional $300 to $400 per month. Many prosperous baby boomers are looking for creative means of blessing their parents who may be experiencing some financial pressure in their autumn years.

The term *philanthropist* tends to conjure images of society's elite who bequeath a portion of their tremendous wealth to large institutions such as hospitals, universities, and museums. However, current trends show that a growing number of philanthropists are ordinary people who share an extraordinary desire to give back and make a difference. The new philanthropist is also interested in a more hands-on approach to giving. (Sources: "The New Face of Giving," by Lisa Fichenscher, *Family Money,* November/December 2000, and "Charity Gets Personal," by Ronaleen R. Roha, *Kiplingers Personal Finance,* September 2000.)

Instead of inherited assets, these new philanthropists are likely to bring their own earned income to their favorite causes and to give generously while still living. Another trend is to support human services and community-based organizations rather than the larger, more prominent charities. In addition, this new generation of donors is demonstrating personal involvement by also contributing their time, energy, and expertise.

Likewise, the new philanthropists tend to be more results-oriented. They carefully scrutinize their charities because they want to know how their gifts will be used. They expect measurable results from their philanthropic "investments," and are also willing to donate their skills to improve such areas as management, accounting, and fund raising.

Philanthropists are also choosing nontraditional channels for giving, such as giving circles, which operate somewhat like investment clubs in that members pool their money. The pooled funds help members have a greater impact on the causes they support and often allow more say in how those funds are used. Members of giving circles typically contribute a predetermined amount each year and vote on how to dole out the pooled funds. In contrast, traditional foundations build up endowments and donate the interest.

Another tool favored by the new philanthropist is the donor-advised fund. Like giving circles, this is inexpensive to set up and allows a great deal of creativity. But unlike giving circles, this type of fund can be set up by an individual—somewhat akin to running a philanthropic foundation. Funds such as the Fidelity Charitable Gift Fund or the Schwab Fund for Charitable Giving allow tax deductible donations to be deposited into the account from which the fund then issues checks (grants) to particular charities as directed. The administration fee for supervising donations and handling bookkeeping varies, but generally ranges from .45 to 1.00 percent of the assets.

PURPOSEFUL PHILANTHROPY

Those who wish to help clients develop a benevolence plan as part of their legacy design may find these useful tips to pass along to their clients.

- *Find your passion and focus your giving.* Think about two or three areas or causes you want to support and make these the focus of your philanthropic mission. Not only will your gifts have more impact, but you will also find your giving more satisfying.
- *Know your charity.* Charities have an obligation to provide detailed information to interested donors. Request written liter-

ature and a copy of the charity's latest annual report which should include a list of the board of directors, a mission statement, and the most recent audited financial statements.

- *Find out where your dollars go.* The American Institute of Philanthropy recommends that 60 percent or more of your charitable donation should go to program services. Less than 40 percent should be spent on general administration and fund raising costs.

- *Check out the leadership of the organization.* A key question to ask is, "What percentage of board members have made a contribution to the group in the last year?" The reply should be 80 percent or better. If those in the know are not involved, you may not want to be either.

- *Develop a "giving" budget.* Determine a percentage amount of your annual income to dedicate to your philanthropic interests. Start small, if necessary, and strive to increase your percentage of giving every year.

- *Create a legacy of giving.* Teach the art of philanthropy to the next generation through your example. Share your values with your children, grandchildren, and other young people and demonstrate your commitment to support those values. Developing an ethical will is a way of passing along these values.

(Carol Anderson and Joyce Cohen, *Unconventional Wisdom,* Fall 2000.)

THE ETHICAL WILL

An inheritance is usually thought of in terms of property, real estate, financial assets, jewelry, automobiles, and antiques. Wills are drawn to help with the dispersing of property at the owner's death. In some families, certain items are passed from generation to generation and bestow to each new "owner" a sense of connection to the individual's heritage.

Even more important than the tangible items that are willed to descendents are the intangibles that comprise a lasting legacy. Richard W. Bowers, an editorial columnist, recently wrote that a good legacy is a valuable asset. "It is that 'property' which is handed down from the past generation that helps to shape life. It is rooted in solid values, teachings, pride of accomplishment, and goals." He further explained that unlike physical property that can rust, decay, or disappear (as in money slipping through the fingers!), a legacy of love, compassion, determination, optimism, and respect can never be destroyed.

Ross Levin, CFP, also recognizes the overriding importance of a moral legacy. "We challenge clients, especially in retirement, to consider what they value and how their actions are congruent with their values." In addition to the traditional form of estate planning, Levin assists his clients in drafting an ethical will. "In an ethical will, rather than talking about distributing your financial aspects, you talk about what kind of personal legacy you would like to leave for your children and other important people in your life, and what you would want to be remembered for."

An ethical will is not a legally binding document, but is one that tells the client's personal story, including dreams, goals, successes, and failures. The ethical will explains to those for whom it was written, what has been important and why. "If I had to do it all over again, would I have made the same choices?" Many choose to include hopes and dreams for future generations, not to dictate what their choices should be, but rather the moral and ethical principles that they hope their heirs will follow.

A FRESH MAP OF LIFE

If Carl Jung was correct and we cannot live the afternoon of life according to the program of the morning, then we must address how we will define success for those who have many retirement years ahead of them. That definition must consider what it is they want to leave to others, to their families, to their communities, and to their lasting memory. Modern retirees need what Peter Laslett refers to as a fresh map of life. This fresh map of life will not be filled with self-absorption but must strike the necessary balance between seeking personal fulfillment and responsibility to others.

Yes, we want leisure. Yes, learning and growth are good. But we must ask ourselves, "To what end?" What are we resting for? For what objective do we seek learning and growth? At some point, retirees must be challenged to contribute what they have gathered toward the societal good and to the cause of the future. Our concern at some point must transcend our personal well-being. Author Betty Freidan, in *The Fountain Of Age,* writes, "It's only by continuing to work on the problems confronting our society right now with whatever wisdom and generativity we have attained over our lifetimes that we leave a legacy to our grandchildren."

F. Scott Fitzerald's proclamation that "there are no second acts in American lives" has largely been interpreted to mean that our lives lose their relevance once the first act (work) ends. Not so in the new retirementality. The mentality of possessing a second childhood must be balanced and eventually superceded by the ideal of having a second adulthood—a time in which we can do much to improve the world around us which will be passed on to the next generation.

Marc Freedman summed it up this way: "Much of our intellectual energy goes into simply denying the prospect of aging . . . face-lifts are a multibillion dollar business . . . the predominant outlook is the 'second childhood' ideal offering up the chance of endless play—often at playgrounds with names like Sun City and Leisure World. This perspective does not constitute a compelling ideal of how we might spend the new one-third of life we've been granted. Despite the great gift of longevity, this third stage remains, in the words of cultural historians, Harry Moody and Thomas Cole, *'a season in search of a purpose.'*"

The fresh map of life in the new retirementality depicts the balance and purpose needed for this season of life: work with a purpose; play to stay fresh; take time to build meaningful relationships with those you love; and finally, focus your time, experience, knowledge, and resources on leaving a legacy larger and broader than your own efforts could produce. This means we invest our life energy in people and causes that can cause our legacy to multiply. This is how we ensure that our impact outlives our days. This noble sentiment exists within clients sitting across the desk from you. With your skills and expertise, you can help facilitate, nourish, encourage, and distribute these visions of doing well by doing good.

RESOURCES FOR GIVING

The following are some resources you may find helpful for educating clients and for assisting you as you work with clients to develop their benevolence plans.

- *Don't Just Give It Away: How to Make the Most of Your Charitable Giving*. This book by Renata J. Rafferty with foreword by Paul

Newman was written for individuals of all income levels who are interested in social change and charitable giving. No matter how much we can give and how often, we should all be concerned with where our money goes and how it is used.

- *Women's Philanthropy Institute.* The role of volunteer and giver is a traditional one for women, yet few people think of women as philanthropists. This national organization is dedicated to helping women discover their capacity to transform themselves and the world through philanthropic leadership. For information, call 608-270-5205 or check the WPI Web site at <www.women-philanthropy.org>.
- *GuideStar.* The goal of this Web site, <www.guidestar.org>, is to promote philanthropy by providing information that will help donors, institutional funders, and charities become more informed, effective, and efficient. Each of the more than 640,000 nonprofit organizations in the database has a GuideStar Report that summarizes its mission and programs, goals and results, finances, and leadership. Many reports also contain financial reports, newsletters, and press releases.
- *Giving circles.* Joining or forming a giving circle will provide clients with a hands-on opportunity to collaborate with others and practice giving in a supportive environment. Giving circles vary in structure, size, and charitable focus. For more information and guidelines for starting a giving circle, check <www.nwgiving.org> or <www.newenglandgiving.org>.

Chapter *17*

Building a Resource and Referral Network

How do you guide your clients in domains that are outside your field of expertise? The financial life planning approach is holistic in nature and acknowledges both the financial and nonfinancial implications of life transitions. Usually the main concern of advisors who want to integrate this perspective into their practices is how to deal with issues outside their comfort zones.

In Chapters 9 through 16, we have discussed many important concepts: the meaning of money, the paradox of plenty, and the significance of work in our lives. We have also discussed the importance of addressing the nonfinancial aspects of retirement and coming to grips with new retirement realities. And how about those new perspectives on legacy and philanthropy?

By now, you may be asking yourself, "How can I possibly address all these areas of need in my clients' lives?" Although you see the value of the financial life planning approach, you may be concerned that you will be required to be all things to all people or to delve into matters for which you are not qualified. On the contrary, as a financial life planner, you will not be required to be all things to all people or to offer advice and provide services in areas in which you do not feel qualified.

As a financial life planner, your most important role will be to identify life issues that have financial implications. Therefore, your focus will be on refining your inquiry skill set and learning to identify your clients' needs in all areas of life. You'll take care of the action steps you are qualified to address and then guide your clients to other qualified professionals who can handle the other aspects of their needs. One of the most effective ways to distinguish yourself as a financial life planner is to enter into a referral arrangement with other professionals who can enhance the services that you provide. This will serve to set you apart from your peers and will help you brand the service that you provide to your clients.

It is a mistake to believe that a financial life planner needs to become a sociologist, psychologist, or personal coach all wrapped up in a financial planning practice. In fact, the most common concern that many advisors express about moving to the life planning approach is that they don't feel comfortable in areas outside of their financial planning expertise. While recognizing the need to help clients understand their life issues, these advisors don't feel that it is their place to go beyond providing financial planning or investment information. Susan Bradley, president of the Sudden Money Institute in Florida, confirms the validity of this approach: "There are some financial advisors who have a natural inclination to become a mentor or a coach for clients. They fall into the role because of their own personalities. If you are not comfortable doing that and you still feel that you want to help your client understand their life, you may have to call upon outside professionals to augment your services."

In addition, some advisors utilize outside experts to answer specific questions they might have that they later can pass on to their clients when needed. For example, Cicily Carson Maton, president of Aequus Wealth Management in Chicago, has a psychologist as part of her team. This individual is contracted by Maton to provide her team with focused information and is considered an integral part of the services that she offers through her practice. The psychologist is also available to work with clients and will conduct workshops. Other advisors have formed relationships with personal coaches, fitness trainers, nutritionists, and other professionals in the community who can either work directly with clients or simply act as sources of information. Your clients will come to see you as a valuable resource for referrals to well-qualified professionals in many fields.

Financial advisors have routinely sought strategic alliances or collaboration with other financial specialists such as tax accountants, estate planners, and lawyers. Financial life planners have extended their referral network to include those people in their community who focus on the nonfinancial aspects of life planning and can support and enhance the advisors' service to their clientele. In that way, the advisors avoid taking on the role of being an expert in all areas, and instead leverage the knowledge of other professionals.

ENHANCING YOUR ROLE AS GUIDE

Among the financial professionals that you will want to include in your referral network are insurance agents, mortgage bankers, loan officers, accountants, and attorneys. In addition, there will be a number of other professionals that can assist with major life decisions such as buying and selling a home, family business succession, career transitions, and arranging long-term care for a loved one. There are also professionals who can help your clients with the emotional side of major life events such as bereavement counselors and divorce specialists. You may also want to network with personal coaches for clients that are seeking career transitions.

To build your referral network, you will want to identify experts in their respective fields who are client-centered, highly qualified, dedicated to professional growth and development, and who maintain the highest ethical standards. The first individuals you are likely to include in your referral network will be those you have worked with who have impressed you with their level of knowledge and quality of service. To become acquainted with other well-qualified professionals, you can join and participate in organizations such as Rotary Club, Kiwanis, or the local chamber of commerce. You can also ask your friends and colleagues for recommendations. When you identify professionals you think would provide value to your clients, meet with them to get to know them better. Ask questions to help you determine their business philosophy.

After you make referrals, it is wise to follow up with your clients and make sure they are satisfied with the advice and service they received. You will only want to retain those professionals in your referral network that you know will provide the same quality of client care that you do.

A strategic alliance is a different kind of professional relationship than a referral network. Usually there is a formal agreement regarding service and compensation expectations. For example, two professionals may team up to provide a well-rounded approach to money and life. Charles Haines, president of Haines Financial Advisors, first got involved with the softer side of financial planning several years ago by hiring a part-time counselor who helped family members communicate their deep feelings related to money and happiness. (Source: "More Planners Using both Couch and Caluculator," by James B. Arndorfer, *Investment News,* February 7, 2000.)

DEVELOPING A LIFE PLANNING TEAM

Most advisors have an unofficial list of people that they call on when they need answers to help a client. There is an opportunity, however, to create a more formalized life planning team with a group of professionals and use that association to extend your branding as a financial life planner. Note that you aren't necessarily offering the services of a psychologist or personal coach in your practice. Instead, you are offering your ability to provide a meaningful referral to a professional who has expertise in a particular area. You will have helped your client by doing the legwork to find someone knowledgeable and you will have demonstrated that you are interested in a holistic approach to your client's life by recognizing the need for outside assistance in areas not directly related to financial planning.

Finally, by creating the concept of a life planning team of outside professionals for your clients, you have shifted your role from being the expert to becoming the "point of entry" from which a client can launch an understanding of the key issues associated with a life plan. In other words, you don't have to be the expert. You just have to know where the experts are!

YOU ARE KNOWN BY
THE COMPANY YOU KEEP

Regardless of the kind of referral arrangement you strike, you want to make sure your clients are well served. The trust that your clients have in you will be tested each time you recommend an outside expert. If the professionals who comprise your referral network don't maintain the same high standards that you do, your reputation could suffer. For that reason, here is a list of criteria that can help you evaluate the other professionals you choose to recommend.

- Their reputation in their field and in their community
- How they service their own clients

- Whether or not they share your same values in the area of life planning
- Their ability to communicate effectively
- Their views on confidentiality
- Their level of efficiency and timeliness in completing projects and services

Ideally, you will want to network with professionals who share your ideology. A good example of professionals who are beginning to embrace the life planning versus transaction only model is a group of estate planning attorneys who belong to the National Network of Estate Planning Attorneys. According to Brad Wievel, an estate planning attorney in Dallas, there are approximately 400 attorneys in this network who have adopted a life planning process called, "The Three Step Strategy." The steps are:

1. *More counseling.* "The majority of estate planning is simply word processing," Wievel says, "and there is a great need for personal counseling." Issues like remarriage, protecting children's inheritances, revocable living trusts, and ethical wills are discussed in depth in an average of nine to ten hours spent with the client. (This period of conseling includes a three-hour client education workshop at the outset.)
2. *Formal updating system.* Clients' assets are often not coordinated with their trusts. Attorneys like Wievel coordinate with other financial professionals to ensure that all assets are channeled into one stream and flow properly with estate plans. Each client goes through one update per year.
3. *Assure your successors utilize fixed fees on death.* Wievel says that clients' assets are like icebergs. The issues the client is aware of are only a portion of what lies under the surface and everything that lies under the surface will have costs attached to it. These life planning attorneys offer clients an upfront fee option that reduces their estate settlement costs and allows associated expenses to be more predictable.

THE PERSONAL COACH

Another strategic referral for many advisors is a personal coach. We talked to one advisor who has negotiated a fee with a personal coach that he pays each month to talk to clients who need assistance and coaching in formulating a life plan or handling a specific life situation. The fee that they have agreed on covers a set number of hours that the coach provides for clients. The coach is available if and when the advisor needs services, and the advisor advertises in a brochure available to clients.

According to recent statistics, the increasing popularity of life coaches does not appear to be a fad. The International Coach Federation in Washington, D.C., states that there are now about 10,000 full-time and part-time life coaches working in the United States. Personal life coaching is safe and convenient (with no stigmas attached) and most of the work is done by phone.

USING OUTSIDE PROFESSIONALS IN CLIENT WORKSHOPS

Many advisors are moving toward financial workshops that take a holistic or life planning view rather than being financial product events. If you are reticent to talk to your clients about certain life issues, yet you believe that there is a good level of interest in your clientele, this is an opportune time to bring in an outside expert to speak on the subject. Not only do you show your clients that you are interested in all aspects of life planning, but you also reinforce your role as a point of entry or guide in the life planning process.

KEYS TO DEVELOPING SOLID REFERRAL RELATIONSHIPS

Following are some practical tips we have gathered from advisors who have done an admirable job of networking within their community. The win-win arrangements you make with other professionals begin with some simple steps where you show the other party that you are willing to help their business as a part of the referral arrangement.

In any referral relationship, you have to give something to get something. A relationship is a two-way street and if you are going to ask a professional to enter into a strategic alliance with you, you want to make sure that you give something back. The simplest way is to refer clients to them. However, if you aren't in a position to do that immediately, here are some immediate shows of good faith that can help get the relationship off to a good start.

- Ask for a supply of business cards or brochures that you can use in your office and give to clients.
- Invite the professional to write a brief article to post on your Web site or include in your newsletter. Make sure that it is an information piece and not a selling piece.
- Offer to write an article for the professional's Web site or newsletter.
- Create a joint education seminar or workshop—inviting both your clients and your client's client—and focus on a topic that combines everyone's expertise.
- Create a breakfast club or strategic alliance group with other professionals and work on joint marketing opportunities.

The professional referral market represents far more than a group of professionals to whom you can refer customers. It also represents exposure for your service through those professionals who get to know and understand the approach that you take.

Everyone in business is interested in developing new customers. The key to building successful referral networks is to remember that you have to give before you can expect to receive. If you can find ways to direct business to your strategic alliances, you will find them much more willing to assist you in the same way.

Relationships work if both parties continue to receive benefit. When you have a strategic alliance with other professionals, you receive the benefit of their knowledge and reputation, access to their clients, and enhancement of the services that you provide. What do they receive in return? Chances are that they are looking for the same kind of payback in dealing with you. Keep in mind that you will have to continually make your side of the relationship work for your referral partners if the alliance will have any longevity.

A referral is an extension of your own reputation that is out of your control once it is made. For this reason, be doubly sure of the people to whom you refer your clients. A well-developed referral network is a wise method for introducing your services and branding yourself as a different kind of advisor.

Chapter 18

Addressing
Financial Intelligence

Can clients improve their prospects for wealth by becoming more educated on financial issues? We think it depends on the type of education they receive. There are an awful lot of very smart people who make very stupid choices with their money—so stupid that many have never told anyone what they did and how much they lost. In examining financial education today, we have seen a need to present consumers with the basics of financial literacy and teach them to recognize how their behavior, attitudes, beliefs, and patterns are either accelerating or sabotaging their wealth-building prospects. Most financial advisors are keenly aware of the fact that their clients' financial knowledge can be quickly offset by a lack of emotional awareness regarding their financial behavior.

According to Mark Riepe, CFA, and senior vice president for Investment Products and Research at Charles Schwab & Company, "Psychology and behavioral finance show us that there are some very strong decision-making patterns that influence people. Advisors can do a better job to ensure a successful plan if they take these into account." (Shelley A. Lee, "Why Do Financial Plans Fail?" *Journal of Financial Planning*, June 2001, p. 66–67.) Most financial education approaches have failed to adequately address this pivotal aspect of financial literacy; i.e., how your emotions, attitudes, and behavioral patterns will affect your wealth-building process and ability to reach your goals. Riepe goes on to say, "The education of clients must be nonstop. It's not just the client's financial capital that will be expanded, it's their intellectual capital that will go way up." We are learning that smarter investors become better clients and are less likely to fail in their plans.

This idea of amalgamating logical and emotional financial education has led to the development of a new, more holistic approach to financial education that we call "raising your Money Quotient™" (MQ). Money Quotient is the crossroads where financial knowledge meets emotional intelligence. It is a balanced approach of learning helpful facts and personal insights and examining our behaviors in light of that information. In order to help people assess on which areas of financial intelligence they should focus, we have developed the Money Quotient Self-Assessment. This profile is a subjective tool designed to help clients grade their personal grasp of the knowledge and habits that contribute to wealth and living a "rich" life.

Here are the principles of emotional intelligence, as they affect an individual's financial well-being.

- Emotional intelligence (EQ) will have more bearing on a client's financial success than the intelligence quotient (IQ).
- A person makes poor financial decisions when the logical part of his or her brain is hijacked by the emotional part of the brain.
- A person who lacks emotional intelligence will choose the wrong reasons and motivations for financial decisions and, therefore, sabotage financial goals.

> When an archer misses the mark, he turns and looks for the fault within himself. Failure to hit the bull's-eye is never the fault of the target. To improve your aim, improve yourself.
>
> —*Gilbert Arland*

Current research shows that IQ influences at best 25 percent of people's success in their careers. A careful analysis suggests a more accurate figure may be no higher than 10 percent and perhaps as low as 4 percent. (*Successful Intelligence,* by R. Sternberg, Plume: 1996.) Recent studies in emotional intelligence demonstrate that EQ is a far greater predictor of success (80 to 85 percent) in the workplace and life in general. The following story tells of the genesis of the study of emotional intelligence.

In 1960, psychologist Walter Mishel conducted a psychological test involving marshmallows and four-year-olds. At a Stanford preschool, the children were given a marshmallow and told that the teacher had to run an errand. If they waited until the teacher got back, they could have two marshmallows. If they couldn't wait, they would only receive one marshmallow. Some of the four-year-olds were able to wait what must have seemed an endless 15 to 20 minutes for the teacher to return. Those who waited used various techniques to survive the waiting period. They covered their eyes so they wouldn't have to view the temptation, rested their heads in their arms, sang songs, talked to themselves, counted their toes and fingers, and even tried to go to sleep. Others swallowed their marshmallows as soon as the teacher left the room and some even taunted those who restrained.

As a part of this study, all these four-year-olds were subsequently tracked down as adolescents and later as they graduated from high school. The emotional and social differences between the eat-it-now crowd and the gratification delayers were quite dramatic. Those who had resisted the temptation at four years of age were more socially competent, personally effective, self-assertive, self-reliant, composed under stress and frustration, likely to embrace challenges, confident, trustworthy, dependable, and self-initiating as adolescents—and they were still able to delay gratification in pursuit of their goals. Even the SAT test scores of these waiters surpassed the grabbers by over 20 percent.

Systems based on IQ have many positives; however, they cannot predict unerringly who will succeed in life. This fact is one of psychology's long-held secrets and industry's frustrations. Students with high intelligence are not necessarily going to become the most successful in their personal or professional lives. Put another way, can you think of someone who is really smart but really *stupid?* I often ask this question to my audiences and, of course, everyone knows someone who fits this description. When I inquire further into how they define "really smart but really stupid," I hear answers like "They lack common sense" or "They don't see the big picture" or "They lack people smarts" or "They just don't get it." Although their answers may seem a bit vague, when you distill them to their most basic level, you are left with a picture of someone who is intellectually astute and emotionally backward, out of touch, or even dangerous.

People who fit this description seem to alienate others and have trouble controlling their emotional impulses. As a result, they cause offense to others and sabotage their plans for success because of their lack of emotional smarts. (*The Financial Professional's Guide to Persuading 1 or 1,000,* by Mitch Anthony and Gary DeMoss, Dearborn Trade Publishing, 2001, pp. 137–138.)

These same principles hold true in the realm of financial intelligence. In the arena of financial literacy, the average approach has been to focus on the intellectual aspects of money management to the unwitting neglect of the emotional facts that can influence one's financial success to a disproportionate degree.

These individuals are likely to be successful in other endeavors while their financial lives are out of kilter. Here are a few examples.

- Joan has a great job and earns a six-figure salary. Even though she gets a generous raise each year, she can't seem to save and invest for her future.
- Three years ago, John received a large inheritance from his grandmother. If well managed, her generous gift could provide John financial security for the rest of his life. However, he feels anything but secure. The responsibility of financial stewardship has challenged his self-confidence and has triggered anxiety attacks and depression.
- Tina recently graduated from law school and landed a position in a top firm in San Francisco. Though she was offered a generous starting salary, she finds that it is inadequate to meet her living expenses, car payments, and student loan payments. After all the sacrifices she has made to reach this career goal, she is angry and frightened about her financial problems.
- Tim wants to micromanage the family budget and it is driving Karen crazy. They have been married five years, and Tim's attention to their money matters is becoming increasingly obsessive. To assert her independence in this relationship, Karen frequently goes on shopping sprees.
- Single and 50 years old, Linda finds financial matters to be boring and confusing. Her dad, retired and with time on his hands, is all too eager to relieve Linda of any task she finds onerous. He oversees all of her accounts and makes all her investment decisions for her.

You can probably relate to one of these descriptions because nearly everyone has or has had a complex and difficult relationship with money. As these examples illustrate, financial wellness is not exclusively dependent on how much money people have, but on how well they integrate money into all areas of their lives. Clearly, money can't buy happiness, but it is important for clients to understand how their money beliefs and attitudes can affect the quality of their lives and relationships.

Learning the basics of money management and financial planning will increase your clients' confidence and equip them with the tools they need to make good financial decisions. In addition, understanding the underlying emotional motivators of their financial attitudes and behaviors will give clients the extra edge they need to achieve life goals. When clients earn, spend, and invest their money in ways that are compatible with their values and priorities, they will experience a sense of purpose and satisfaction.

For everyone, self-knowledge is an essential ingredient to understanding and improving their relationship with money. The Money Quotient Self-Assessment is designed to focus your clients' thinking on both the *fact* and *feeling* aspects of their financial lives. This tool will guide advisors in evaluating five key areas that contribute to a client's successful and satisfying financial life: recognition, resilience, resourcefulness, relationships, and wisdom. Figure 18.1 provides an outline of the logical and emotional building blocks that constitute financial intelligence.

All of the building blocks listed in Figure 18.1 are evaluated in the MQ Self-Assessment. The sections of the assessment in which clients rate themselves low can be addressed by focusing on the educational building blocks associated with it. Figure 18.2 is a copy of Part One of the MQ Self-Assessment, a tool that is available for use with your clients. This instrument will help you facilitate the conversation regarding both the rational and emotional facets of financial well-being.

FIGURE 18.1   Five Key Factors to Financial Success

1. **Recognition:** understanding the roles of practical knowledge and emotional awareness in achieving financial well-being. (Section 1, Statements 1–8 of the Money Quotient Self-Assessment)

   Building Blocks:
   - Reflect on money history, beliefs, and patterns.
   - Clarify financial goals and priorities.
   - Assess risk tolerance.
   - Evaluate satisfaction with financial life.

   (continued)

FIGURE 18.1 Continued

2. **Resilience:** ability to navigate transitions and to bounce back from financial setbacks (Section 2, Statements 9–16)

   Building Blocks:

   • Build a foundation of financial protection.
   • Expand income earning options.
   • Gain a sense of control of financial destiny.
   • Increase financial skills and knowledge.

3. **Resourcefulness:** motivation and ability to maximize resources for achieving financial well-being and life satisfaction (Section 3, Statements 17–24)

   Building Blocks:

   • Organize financial records and activities.
   • Set financial goals based on life goals and values.
   • Develop a money management strategy that includes debt reduction and a spending plan.
   • Take a proactive approach to reaching financial goals and building financial independence.

4. **Relationships:** connections with others that affect financial well-being and life satisfaction (Section 4, Statements 25–32)

   Building Blocks:

   • Improve communication skills and relationship dynamics regarding money issues.
   • Evaluate financial responsibilities across generations.
   • Build good working relationships with financial professionals.
   • Participate in giving and philanthropy.

5. **Wisdom:** linking financial goals to values and to life as a whole (Section 5, Statements 33–40)

   Building Blocks:

   • Engage in meaningful "work."
   • Seek to understand and achieve true "wealth."
   • Pursue a balanced and meaningful life.
   • Make a lifelong commitment to raising your MQ.

FIGURE 18.2   Money Quotient Self-Assessment (Part One)

Directions: For each of the 40 statements, quickly choose the response that best reflects your feelings or behavior (your first reaction is what you should record). Write the number of your selection in the right-hand column. When you have completed all 40 statements, add together the numbers in each section and record the subtotal in the space provided. At the end, add the subtotal figures together for your MQ score.

Section 1	**Number**
1. My financial life is a source of frustration and inner conflict. 1. Always agree 2. 3. Halfway agree 4. 5. Never agree	
2. Financial matters are of no interest to me. 1. Always agree 2. 3. Halfway agree 4. 5. Never agree	
3. I have identified specific financial goals. 1. Not at all like me 2. 3. Halfway like me 4. 5. Exactly like me	
4. I have a good understanding of the important financial issues that need to be addressed at this stage of my life. 1. Not at all like me 2. 3. Halfway like me 4. 5. Exactly like me	
5. I will consider an investment only when I'm guaranteed not to lose any money. 1. Exactly like me 2. 3. Halfway like me 4. 5. Not at all like me	
6. I am attracted to "get rich quick" tips and ideas. 1. Exactly like me 2. 3. Halfway like me 4. 5. Not at all like me	

7. I feel that at this point in my life,
   1. I am way behind where I expected to be financially
   2. I am somewhat behind where I expected to be financially
   3. I am about where I expected to be financially
   4. I am ahead of where I expected to be financially
   5. I am way ahead where I expected to be financially	

8. I worry about not having enough money in later life. 1. Exactly like me 2. 3. Halfway like me 4. 5. Not at all like me	

Section 1 Subtotal _____

(continued)

FIGURE 18.2 Continued

Section 2	Number
9. I am well-protected against major financial loss caused by extended illness, disability, long-term care, or downturn in the stock market. 1. Not at all like me 2. 3. Halfway like me 4. 5. Exactly like me	
10. If I were to miss a month's pay, I would experience serious financial problems. 1. Exactly like me 2. 3. Halfway like me 4. 5. Not at all like me	
11. I have skills, knowledge, and/or talents that are transferable and in demand in the job market. 1. Not at all like me 2. 3. Halfway like me 4. 5. Exactly like me	
12. In the past, I have been creative in finding ways to earn extra income when I have needed or wanted it. 1. Not at all like me 2. 3. Halfway like me 4. 5. Exactly like me	
13. I feel defeated when I think about my financial future. 1. Always agree 2. 3. Halfway agree 4. 5. Never agree	
14. If I were to lose half of my income, I could successfully navigate the transition. 1. Not at all like me 2. 3. Halfway like me 4. 5. Exactly like me	
15. I feel I have the skills and knowledge needed to build financial security. 1. Not at all like me 2. 3. Halfway like me 4. 5. Exactly like me	
16. I'm easily confused or intimidated by financial terminology or jargon. 1. Always agree 2. 3. Halfway agree 4. 5. Never agree	

Section 2 Subtotal _____

Section 3	Number
17. My financial records are well organized. 1. Not at all like me 2. 3. Halfway like me 4. 5. Exactly like me	
18. I have gotten the help I need to assess my financial picture. 1. Not at all like me 2. 3. Halfway like me 4. 5. Exactly like me	
19. The way I manage money is in agreement with my priorities in life. 1. Never agree 2. 3. Halfway agree 4. 5. Always agree	

FIGURE 18.2   Continued

Section 3 continued	Number
20. This is how long I estimate it will take before I will be able to live the life I want: 1. I have no idea 2. Over 10 years 3. 6–10 years 4. 1–5 years 5. I'm there now	
21. In regard to my saving habits, 1. I overspend and have too much debt to save 2. I spend what I earn and there is none left over to save 3. I save when I can 4. I save regularly, but not enough 5. I save regularly and adequately to meet my goals	
22. I frequently make purchases spontaneously. 1. Exactly like me 2. 3. Halfway like me 4. 5. Not at all like me	
23. I am taking full advantage of my tax-advantaged retirement plan opportunities such as IRAs, 401(k)s, deferred compensation, etc. 1. Not at all like me 2. 3. Halfway like me 4. 5. Exactly like me	
24. I check my progress toward meeting my financial goals on a regular basis. 1. Not at all like me 2. 3. Halfway like me 4. 5. Exactly like me	

Section 3 Subtotal _____

Section 4	Number
25. Financial issues cause a lot of tension in a relationship that is important to me. 1. Always agree 2. 3. Halfway agree 4. 5. Never agree	
26. I experience a lot of tension and frustration when discussing financial matters with certain family members. 1. Always agree 2. 3. Halfway agree 4. 5. Never agree	
27. I am concerned about the impact of meeting the costs of higher education. 1. Exactly like me 2. 3. Halfway like me 4. 5. Not at all like me	
28. I often feel squeezed between the competing financial needs and wants of family members (spouse/partner, children, parents, etc.). 1. Always agree 2. 3. Halfway agree 4. 5. Never agree	

(continued)

FIGURE 18.2 Continued

Section 4 continued	Number
29. I feel comfortable talking with financial professionals (i.e., accountants, bankers, investment representatives, etc.) about my financial matters. 1. Never agree 2. 3. Halfway agree 4. 5. Always agree	
30. I feel confident in my ability to evaluate the accuracy and appropriateness of the financial advice I receive. 1. Not at all like me 2. 3. Halfway like me 4. 5. Exactly like me	
31. A major goal for my money is helping others and/or supporting causes. 1. Not at all like me 2. 3. Halfway like me 4. 5. Exactly like me	
32. Charitable giving is currently an essential element of my financial plan. 1. Not at all like me 2. 3. Halfway like me 4. 5. Exactly like me	

Section 4 Subtotal _____

Section 5	Number
33. If I could, I would change the kind of work I do. 1. Always agree 2. 3. Halfway agree 4. 5. Never agree	
34. I engage in paid or unpaid "work" that gives my life a sense of purpose. 1. Never agree 2. 3. Halfway agree 4. 5. Always agree	
35. I have a difficult time clarifying what is most important to *me.* 1. Exactly like me 2. 3. Halfway like me 4. 5. Not at all like me	
36. I've spent a lot of money trying to find happiness. 1. Exactly like me 2. 3. Halfway like me 4. 5. Not at all like me	
37. I feel I do not spend adequate time with the people I love. 1. Always agree 2. 3. Halfway agree 4. 5. Never agree	
38. I feel like my life revolves around making money. 1. Always agree 2. 3. Halfway agree 4. 5. Never agree	
39. I am motivated to take charge of my financial life. 1. Never agree 2. 3. Halfway agree 4. 5. Always agree	
40. I am committed to discovering my emotional roadblocks to achieving financial well-being. 1. Not at all like me 2. 3. Halfway like me 4. 5. Exactly like me	

Section 5 Subtotal _____

FIGURE 18.2   Continued

Now, write the subtotal figures in the grid below and add them together to determine your MQ score.

Section 1 Subtotal	
Section 2 Subtotal	
Section 3 Subtotal	
Section 4 Subtotal	
Section 5 Subtotal	
Money Quotient Score	

RAISE YOUR MQ

Self-knowledge is an essential ingredient to understanding and improving your relationship with money. Part One of the Money Quotient Self-Assessment measured five key factors of a client's financial well-being: recognition, resilience, resourcefulness, relationships, and wisdom. The next step is to act on this information. Part Two of the Money Quotient Self-Assessment focuses on ways to help clients raise their MQ in each of these areas.

In the next five chapters, we will address the five components of financial intelligence: recognition, resilience, resourcefulness, relationships, and wisdom, and give an overview of the process of raising your MQ that clients can participate in to bring success and harmony to their financial lives.

Chapter *19*

Recognition of Personal Financial Issues

When I was growing up, my father would make me feel I had committed a crime every time I spent money. He bought nothing outside of the category of "necessary for life" and questioned all our purchases under a tight scrutiny that would end with a not-so-subtle condemnation of, "Well, it's your money. Just don't come crying to me when you run short." Later in life, in my 30s, someone asked me about how money was dealt with in my home, and it dawned upon me that I was still rebelling against my father's tightness. I made good money, saved nothing, and denied myself no material good—whether I could afford it or not. In the process, I sabotaged my own financial success. I'm now in the process of turning that around.

—*Cindy H., client, age 41*

Although the preceding sounds like something that you might expect to be volunteered by the client of a psychologist, it was, in fact, spoken by the client of an advisor. The client offered this response when the advisor inquired how disciplined she had been about saving in the past. The client's response indicates how out of touch clients can be with the undertow of personal history, beliefs, and behavior patterns that have a direct bearing upon their financial well-being.

Financial intelligence is a broader topic than simply knowing how to explain a PE ratio, max out on tax-advantaged investment opportunities, or bring some semblance of balance to financial portfolios. The fact that smart people make foolish decisions with their money reveals a fundamental lack of awareness on the part of investors of their own vulnerabilities and frailties. One could hypothetically become a walking encyclopedia of financial jargon and continue to throw hard-earned money down a sinkhole of ill-advised risks as a result of such unawareness. Many people do.

The primary component of financial intelligence that acts as a catapult to the other components is *recognition*. The Money Quotient approach to recognition—as in all the MQ components—is to blend the hard science of information and logic with the soft science of understanding the role of emotion in the process.

The four building blocks necessary for financial recognition are:

1. Reflect on money history, beliefs, and patterns
2. Clarify financial goals and priorities
3. Assess risk tolerance
4. Evaluate satisfaction with financial life

Recognition involves understanding the significant roles of both practical knowledge and emotional awareness in achieving financial well-being. This fundamental component requires introspection and honesty on the part of clients regarding the elements that have shaped their current relationship with money. Once a client walks through this process, recognition acts as a powerful catalyst for growth in money maturity.

BUILDING BLOCK 1: REFLECT ON MONEY HISTORY, BELIEFS, AND PATTERNS

In the money quotient approach, clients are guided in the process of looking for clues in their past that will help them to understand their current financial lives. Starting with their early years, clients discover what experiences have shaped their underlying beliefs and attitudes about money. Lifetime patterns of earning, saving, investing, and giving begin to emerge. The questionnaire in Figure 19.1 helps to clarify the linkage between past experience and current financial reality. In a workshop setting these questions become great tools of self-discovery and conversation between couples and participants.

FIGURE 19.1   Reflect on Your Money History, Beliefs, and Patterns

The following questions help guide clients in the process of looking for clues in their past that will help them understand their current financial life.

1. Growing up in your family, was money mainly used to reward, punish, survive, impress, control, help others, have fun, buy love, reach goals, or _____?
2. What were the spending/saving patterns of your mother? Of your father?
3. When you were young, did you consider your family to be rich, poor, or _____?
4. What were you taught about money when you were growing up?
5. In your family, was money an "issue"? A source of conflicts? A tool for achieving goals?
6. When did you first start earning your own spending money?
7. As a child, what was the most important lesson you learned about money?
8. As an adult, what has been the most important lesson you have learned about money?
9. In your current financial life, are you more of a spender or a saver?
10. In your current financial life, are you more of an avoider or a worrier?
11. In your heart of hearts, what do you want money to give you?
12. Has money been an "issue" or source of conflict in your important relationships?
13. What money habits have brought you closer to your life goals?
14. What money habits have been obstacles to reaching your life goals?
15. What or who has most influenced your financial philosophy? How and why?

BUILDING BLOCK 2: CLARIFY FINANCIAL GOALS AND PRIORITIES

I once went to a workshop on goal setting and came to the rude realization that I was nothing more than a day dreamer. I had never researched the process of getting to where I said I wanted to go. There was not the vaguest hint of a plan and absolutely no agreement between my hopes and my checkbook. The simple process of articulating in exact terms what it was I wanted and when I hoped to achieve it gave me the impetus to start aligning all aspects of my life—especially the monetary—in line with this vision.

—*Reggie O., client, age 44*

The hopes of many clients are swimming in a mind of turbulent intentions, pipe dreams, longings, and a vision of life they wish they had. The turbulence is due to disorganization. Rare is the individual that has sat down and clearly articulated his or her goals for the short-term and long-term, and developed a plan and time line for reaching those goals. The great need that must be recognized is for an organizational process that points clients in the direction of their dreams.

In the Money Quotient approach to clarifying goals and priorities, clients learn to go beyond simply jotting down their goals. They are taught to answer the following.

- What is your goal?
- Why do you want to achieve this goal?
- What is the price tag of this goal?
- How great a priority is this goal at this stage of life?

The answers to these questions can be brought back to the advisor for the purpose of developing a financial plan and time line for accomplishing the objectives. Many people, upon discerning their reasons for wanting what they think they want, will reassess the goal and move it up or down in their priority list. Others are discouraged or encouraged when they investigate the price tag of their goals. Some will give up the idea for a more appropriate time, while others will become more resolute, focused, and optimistic once they see the price tag of success posted in front of them. Others realize that although their goal is noble and feasible, the timing may not be right with other events and transitions that are concurrent in their life, and place a more appropriate chronological expectation on that particular goal.

To facilitate this process, clients are invited to list their goals in the chart shown in Figure 19.2, whether it is earning an MBA, building an addition to the house, touring France, or having long-term health security. They are invited to list what they consider pipe dreams as well as what they consider to be essential accomplishments. After they complete the list. they are required to assign a priority status of A, B, or C to each of their financial life goals.

FIGURE 19.2   Clarifying Your Goals

Short-term goals and priorities (1–3 years)

Life Goal	Reasons	Price Tag	Priority

Mid-term goals and priorities (3–5 years)

Life Goal	Reasons	Price Tag	Priority

Long-term goals and priorities (5 years and longer)

Life Goal	Reasons	Price Tag	Priority

BUILDING BLOCK 3:
ASSESS RISK TOLERANCE

In the dictum of "know thy client," assessing risk is debatably the most fundamental need of discovery between client and advisor. Advisors are aware of this but this part of client discovery often slips through the orientation process. How else can we explain the panicked and manic stream of phone calls that many advisors receive when major world or economic news comes to the fore? If clients are calling in a panic and are uncomfortable with their exposure to risk, then either the client or the advisor—or both—is not in recognition of his or her true level of risk tolerance.

This observation could be balanced by the suggestion that some clients won't know for sure what their risk tolerance is until a real threat of risk knocks on their door. Some would contend it is then— and only then—that risk tolerance is established.

Such reasoning, however, does not excuse the lack of inquiry that often leads to panicked clients in disquieting times. Every effort can and should be made with each investment sold to make clients aware of a realistic definition of the downside probabilities as well as upside possibilities.

As one advisor told us after the terrorist attack on New York, "I wasn't a bit surprised that not one of our clients called in a panic after the attacks. We have long and detailed discussions with our clients about the inherent risks of each investment they enter. We do our best, at the outset, to dissuade those who display the slightest signal of being faint of heart from investments that stir uncertainty in them. We let them know that we must balance the objectives of investment return with getting a good night's sleep in troubling times."

Defining Risk

Risk is defined as the chance of experiencing loss. In regard to financial decision making, we all mentally calculate the risks and rewards we are likely to experience. Some of us focus more on the potential losses (risks), and some of us focus more on the potential gains (rewards). Here is an example.

When Karla got a promotion at the large architectural firm she works for, she gave serious consideration to buying a new car. She thought about the rewards of having a new car such as having a dependable means of transportation, getting better gas mileage, portraying a successful image to her clients, and the emotional high of having a new car. She also pondered the risks such as increased insurance premiums, car payments that would reduce the amount she could afford to invest in her retirement plan, unknown gas and maintenance costs, and the emotional weight of greater financial obligations.

When making a financial decision, do your clients intentionally weigh the potential risks and rewards? Is weighing that balance more of a rational or emotional process? In other words, do they tend to rely more on facts or on feelings?

In regard to investing, when we ask clients about their risk tolerance, we are really asking about their emotional response to the possibility of loss and the possibility of gain. At one end of the continuum are those who are risk adverse and focus on the loss part of the equation. For them, risk is anxiety producing. They value stability of their money above all else and are willing to sacrifice higher returns to achieve that sense of guarantee.

At the opposite end of the continuum, are those who are risk-addicted and focus on the gain part of the equation. In order to get rich quick, they are willing to take a gamble with their money. For them, the potential for gain is exciting and the associated risk is adrenaline-producing.

Individuals at either end of the risk continuum operate more on feeling than on facts. Those who are either adverse or addicted to financial risks are operating in economic "danger zones." Both types are jeopardizing their long-term financial security by viewing money more as a commodity than as a tool.

It is interesting to note that financial education can cure both the risk avoider and the risk exploiter. Knowledge is the antidote for overcoming the emotional responses that can sabotage sound investment decisions.

Understanding Risk

Risk knowledge means clients must understand that there is risk inherent in *every* investment. Money that is conservatively parked in

CDs or money market accounts risks not keeping pace with inflation. Stocks that rise quickly risk meteoric falls. Finding appropriate risk can only be decided in the context of personal goals, comfort level, and time frame. All three factors must coalesce for a risk to "feel" right. If you don't feel right initially, that feeling will be exacerbated in a downdraft and may lead to more foolish financial behavior.

Risk knowledge refers to a client's grasp of risk and return with each investment decision. The greater the comprehension of risk, the greater the likelihood that decisions will be made that are consistent with personal goals and appropriate timelines.

Because there is no accepted measurement device to evaluate risk knowledge, advisors have used subjective judgment to evaluate the client's relative level of risk knowledge. This judgment can become more concrete only by advisors increasing their efforts toward risk education with their clients.

If you see that a new client has risky investments in his or her portfolio, does that mean there is a high risk tolerance? Or, could it be the client is simply risk-addicted, reckless, or ignorant? Many advisors go on to recommend higher risk investments when they see the presence of others in the portfolio. David Cordell, Ph.D., writes that a portfolio can be a misleading indicator for many reasons, including:

- The client may not have understood inherent risk in specific investments.
- Assets may have come from a spouse or inheritance.
- The client's financial situation may have changed since assets were obtained.
- Riskiness of assets may have changed since they were obtained.
- Retention of assets may be for sentimental or family reasons.
- Retention of assets may be for tax reasons.

(Cordell, David M. "RiskPack: How to Evaluate Risk Tolerance," *Journal of Financial Planning*, June 2001.)

The best approach is using thorough discovery and doing your best to educate each client on the specific risks of each investment decision.

For the purpose of raising MQ, it is important for clients to seek the middle ground on the risk tolerance continuum and to commit to becoming a calculated risk taker. In making financial decisions, a calculated risk taker does not avoid risk or exploit risk, but learns to manage risk.

To become a calculated risk taker, clients must first become aware of the underlying emotional motivators that repel or draw them to financial risk. The next step is for them to be educated so that they can replace irrational responses with rational decisions. They will reap high returns by investing in themselves through financial education.

In addition, by utilizing educational resources at your disposal, your conversations can address the following.

- Help clients learn the features and dynamics associated with common savings and investment vehicles, from money markets to bonds, mutual funds, stocks, and any other vehicles your firm promotes.
- Teach clients how to categorize investment vehicles as cash equivalent, income producing, growth producing, or speculative.
- Help clients learn how to match goals and investments properly: short-term goals to cash equivalents, mid-term goals to income producing, and long-term goals to growth producing. Clients should think thoroughly about putting anything other than "extra" investment dollars in the speculative category.
- Do your best to educate your clients on asset allocation. See my book *Storyselling for Financial Advisors* for easy-to-relate metaphors and illustrations useful for educating clients on this all-important issue. Clients need both a logical and emotional understanding of why we spread savings and investment dollars across investment categories and in a variety of vehicles.

BUILDING BLOCK 4: EVALUATE SATISFACTION WITH FINANCIAL LIFE

Satisfaction describes a feeling of fulfillment or contentment. In our financial lives, satisfaction is as much emotional as practical. In addition, satisfaction is arbitrary and subject to the interpretation of each individual. For example, one person can be completely satisfied with an annual income of $50,000, while another person could feel completely distraught about this level of income.

Another example is the use of credit. One person could be very comfortable carrying an ongoing credit card balance of $5,000 while another person would be totally stressed out about it and not satisfied until that credit card balance was zero. Values and priorities vary from person to person and can also change over time. One person could live with disorganized financial records for years and then one day become discontent with the disorder and say, "I can't live this way anymore!" The exercise on assessing financial satisfaction in Figure 19.3 can act as motivator in getting clients to work with the advisor's plan to organize, allocate, and constantly review their financial lives. There is an instant connection between the statements that stir satisfaction and the services advisors offer that could placate that sense of satisfaction. The advisor in this way becomes a source for emotional calm and assurance that life goals and financial goals will merge and flourish.

Once the groundwork of recognition is laid, the client is ready to move forward with other critical education issues such as resilience, resourcefulness, relationships that affect personal wealth, and how to live wisely in terms of material management. If clients can identify the source of their financial mores, summate, prioritize and calculate the cost of their life goals, come to grips with their true level of risk tolerance, and begin to address areas of financial dissatisfaction, they are well on the way to building wealth—fiscally and emotionally.

FIGURE 19.3   Financial Satisfaction Survey

Directions: The statements below will help you to think about and assess how satisfied you are with the many aspects of your life. On a scale of 0 to 10, indicate your level of satisfaction for each statement. Zero equals "no satisfaction" and 10 equals "perfectly satisfied."

Statements	Score 0–10
1. I am satisfied with my ability to meet my financial obligations.	
2. I am satisfied with the level of credit card debt I carry.	
3. I am satisfied with the working relationships I have with my financial service providers (i.e., insurance agent, banker, broker, financial planner, and accountant).	
4. I am satisfied with the level of personal financial education I have attained.	
5. I am satisfied with my level of income.	

FIGURE 19.3 Continued

Statements	Score 0–10
6. I am satisfied with the income potential my current job or career provides me.	
7. I am satisfied with the level of employee benefits I receive.	
8. I am satisfied with the amount of money that I save and invest on a regular basis.	
9. I am satisfied with my current investment choices.	
10. I am satisfied that I am on track to build a sufficient retirement nest egg.	
11. I am satisfied with the "extras" that I am able to buy for myself and/or loved ones.	
12. I am satisfied that financial issues do not cause stress or strain in the relationships that are important to me.	
13. I am satisfied with how I respond emotionally to my personal finance issues.	
14. I am satisfied that my charitable contributions are directed to the right recipients.	
15. I am satisfied with my level of charitable giving.	
16. I am satisfied with my level of knowledge of personal finances.	
17. I am satisfied with the feelings I have about my money life.	
18. I am satisfied with my style of personal bookkeeping and financial records management.	
19. I am satisfied with my spending habits.	
20. I am satisfied with the amount I save on a regular basis.	
21. I am satisfied with the level of time and attention I devote to my financial matters.	
22. I am satisfied with my ability to communicate my financial matters.	

Chapter *20*

Resilience: Being Prepared for the Storms of Life

> Within a day or two of losing my job, I began taking inventory of the skills I had developed in this job and the know-how I had accumulated. It began to occur to me that I possessed some exact knowledge that was in short supply in that industry. With the contacts I had in the industry, I felt I might be able to parlay that knowledge into a consulting career. Fortunately for my family and me, my financial advisor had stressed the importance of being prepared for times like these—and I had enough to allow myself four months to get this idea up and running. I watched friends of mine go into a funk or back into the same old grind somewhere else because they did not have the time that such a buffer provides.

—*Hannah, executive, age 38*

People seem to naturally possess varying degrees of this critical emotional competency known as resilience. The story is told of Winston Churchill's wife trying to console him after a crushing political defeat by saying, "Well, it's probably a blessing in disguise." To which Churchill responded, "Well it certainly is effectively disguised." Not all people respond the same to adversity. Resilience provides the ability to navigate life transitions and to bounce back from financial setbacks. We all encounter both expected and unexpected transitions in our personal and work lives.

The Money Quotient approach helps clients learn to bounce back by addressing both practical and emotional factors which are equally weighted. Successful transitions require practical strategies and emotional fortitude. From a practical viewpoint, financial resilience involves laying a foundation of economic protection. From an emotional perspective, financial resilience involves increasing an individual's confidence in preparing for and dealing with financial challenges. This factor of a client's money quotient can be strengthened by laying four building blocks.

1. Build a foundation of financial protection.
2. Expand income earning options.
3. Gain a sense of control of financial destiny.
4. Increase financial skills and knowledge.

BUILDING BLOCK 1: BUILD A FOUNDATION OF FINANCIAL PROTECTION

The bedrock for building a financial life is establishing a foundation of economic security for you and your loved ones. There are several tools that we can utilize to mange risk and protect ourselves from financial crisis. The better prepared we are to meet financial challenges, the quicker we will recover economically and emotionally.

The checklist in Figure 20.1 helps clients demonstrate their status regarding the most important financial protection tools. The "Have/ Check" column is available for those who have established the item listed, but want to review the adequacy of current provisions. This checklist will help clients make a quick assessment of their current level of financial protection and determine the action steps needed to upgrade their economic security.

BUILDING BLOCK 2: EXPAND INCOME EARNING OPTIONS

What types of people are retiring early? According to an article in *The Journal of Financial Service Professionals* entitled "Earlier Retirement or Longer Work Life? Myths, Realities, and Predictions," early retirees are not the people you would think. Studies have shown that

FIGURE 20.1   Financial Resilience Checklist

Tool	Description	Have	Have/ Check	Don't Have
Emergency fund	Money set aside in a savings or money market account to be used in case of emergency. At the very least, save enough to cover the costs of unexpected car repairs, emergency travel, or replacing a major appliance. Ideally, this account should grow to the equivalent of three to six months living expenses in case income is lost or reduced.			
Auto insurance	This insurance is purchased to cover: (1) legal liability resulting from ownership and/or operation of an automobile and (2) physical damage to and loss of an automobile.			
Homeowners insurance	This insurance protects against financial loss related to home ownership. Typically, a policy will cover the structure and contents of the dwelling and out buildings, landscape materials, and personal liability.			
Umbrella liability insurance	This insurance covers financial loss due to personal liability that exceeds the personal liability coverage offered through other insurance such as auto or homeowners policies.			

(continued)

FIGURE 20.1 Continued

Tool	Description	Have	Have/ Check	Don't Have
Life insurance	This insurance is typically purchased by individuals who have dependents. At the time of death of the insured, the death benefit is available to the designated beneficiary immediately and automatically.			
Health insurance	This insurance helps individuals pay the costs of regular health care and protects them against the catastrophic health care costs that can result from treating illness and/or injuries.			
Disability insurance	This is a form of health insurance that provides periodic payments to partially replace income lost due to illness, injury, or disease.			
Long-term care insurance	This insurance pays for the long-term care of an individual who, as the result of physical or mental disabilities, can no longer accomplish the tasks of everyday living such as bathing, dressing, or eating.			
Durable power of attorney	This legal document gives direction as to whom you choose and trust to make your health care and financial decisions in the event that you are temporarily or permanently unable to do so.			

FIGURE 20.1:   Continued

Tool	Description	Have	Have/ Check	Don't Have
Will	A will is the first step of estate planning. It is a legal document that specifies how and to whom you would like to have your assets distributed at the time of your death.			

the people over 60 who remain in the workplace are the ones who are better educated and in better financial shape.

The article states: "According to a recent study, poorly educated and low-skilled workers withdraw from the labor market at younger ages than their better-educated and higher-skilled peers, often before they are eligible for Social Security and in spite of low retirement incomes. Many work in unstable industries and find themselves looking for work more frequently. Because of the type of work, they might also find that their skills become obsolete and they are no longer marketable."

The survival of the fittest in today's rapidly changing and volatile workplace means possessing a versatile and fluid set of marketable skills. Those who have mastered a number of portable skill sets through education and diverse employment through the years are more likely to demonstrate employment resilience. Those who have but one skill will discover very little "bounce-backability" when their industry or the economy is tested.

People need to think outside of the realm of what they do for a living and begin to see within that job description the other marketable skills they need to nurture. For example, those who manage people well find that they possess a highly transferable skill set that is always in demand somewhere in the working world. Rather than wishing for the world to be fairer to us, we are better off investing in ourselves via learning a variety of skills and broadening our corporate vernacular through education and exposure to as many realms as possible.

Job loss due to termination, layoffs, downsizing, outsourcing, restructuring, and any number of other reasons can be emotionally devastating—and financially catastrophic. In the world of work, if the rug is pulled out from under you, it is reassuring to know that you've laid the groundwork to quickly regain your career and economic footing. It is important for clients to ask themselves, "If my current sources of income are reduced or eliminated, what are my alternatives for making a living?" The suggestions in Figure 20.2 will not only help clients to rebound from job loss or a derailed career path, but also prepare them to grab hold of new career opportunities.

FIGURE 20.2 Expand Yourself

- Take advantage of workplace educational opportunities that will increase your skills and knowledge.

- Keep an up-to-date list of your work-related achievements and professional activities.

- Welcome opportunities to increase your computer skills and knowledge.

- Ask for projects that challenge and stretch you.

- Make an honest self-appraisal of how well you relate to others, and your oral and written communication skills. Ask a supervisor and a peer to also make that appraisal and discuss with them your strengths and weaknesses in these areas.

- Do you have an outside interest or skill that could be used to make money? If so, establish a sideline business. This could be your ace in the hole if you lose your current job or decide that you want to leave your current workplace.

- More important than job titles on a resume is your "portfolio" of transferable competencies and skills. What competencies and skills do you possess that are currently in demand in many workplace settings and industries?

- Keep abreast of workplace trends in general and developments in your specific areas of expertise.

- Adopt an attitude of personal responsibility for your career management, growth, and satisfaction.

- Take a proactive stance in expanding your career opportunities.

Attracting Greater Wealth

David Bach, in his book *Smart Women Finish Rich,* tells about coaching a client with her finances and her career. As a result, this client was able to double her income to six figures and significantly expand her career fulfillment. Bach boils down the essence of what he taught this client into what he calls the *12 Commandments of Attracting Greater Wealth.* They are:

1. Whatever you earn right now is whatever you have accepted.
2. Society rewards people who add value.
3. Discover what makes you uniquely valuable.
4. Don't waste your time on things other people should be doing for you.
5. Clean up the messes in your life.
6. Post your goals in your office for everyone to see.
7. Invest in yourself; set aside money annually to somehow improve yourself.
8. Learn to be a "go-giver"; successful people add value and give back.
9. Make a decision; your financial future can be shaped the moment you make a decision.
10. Focus on being a "go-to" person.
11. To make money, you have to ask for more money.
12. Live by the philosophy of MTHN (make things happen now).

BUILDING BLOCK 3: GAIN A SENSE OF CONTROL OF YOUR FINANCIAL DESTINY

How many people do you suppose feel in charge of their financial lives? How many feel like they are being swept along by a set of personal and financial circumstances that are beyond their control? Are such people taking responsibility for making their own financial decisions or do they acquiesce to the plans and opinions of others? Many people need to assume a greater sense of leadership over their financial future—and loosen the grips of denial, fear, and complacency in the process.

The degree of power people feel over shaping their financial lives is both objective and subjective in nature. This sense of empowerment is determined by three important characteristics: locus of control, personal responsibility, and self-confidence.

Locus of Control

Locus of control is a psychological term that describes the belief system of individuals regarding the primary point of control in their lives. Those who believe the primary point of control is outside of them have an external locus of control. These individuals feel that outside forces (such as luck or fate), institutions (the government), or other powerful individuals (boss) have more control over the direction of their lives than they themselves do. Consciously or subconsciously, they believe that they are victims of their circumstances and are bystanders to the course of events that surround them. In other words, they don't believe they can have much impact on outcomes in their own lives.

On the other hand, individuals who believe the primary control of their lives is within themselves are described as having an internal locus of control. They feel they can influence the course of events that surrounds them and the outcomes of their own lives. Because they have a strong sense of personal power, they tend to not give in to trials and tribulations and instead are proactive in making the "right things" happen for themselves. Individuals that possess an internal locus of control are more likely to see how they themselves have shaped their own financial life and understand how they can affect and improve their sense of financial well-being.

Personal Responsibility

Encourage clients to look for evidence in their own lives that indicates whether they possess an external or internal locus of control. If they want positive change to take place in their lives, they will want to be open to the truth about themselves. As people become more aware of their own personal power and potential, they will mentally shift to an ever-stronger internal locus of control.

Along with this change will come a greater sense of personal responsibility in all areas of life. This is the attitude that if it is to be, it is up to me. They must be continually reminded that if there is any aspect of their financial lives that is successful or unsatisfying, they have the power to bring about change. Rather than blaming other people, their background, the economy, or whatever for the state of their financial lives, they can focus on what it is they can do to raise their Money Quotient scores and gain a sense of financial well-being.

Self-Confidence

Self-confidence is an individual's evaluation of his or her abilities to accomplish a given task. "Stepping outside my comfort zone" is a phrase many of us use to describe how we feel in situations where we don't know how well we will perform or how others will respond to us. It is the level of your self-confidence that is likely to determine what goals you will set and actions you will take.

Many individuals can be self-assured in other areas of their lives, but not confident when it comes to money management and financial planning. They say, "I was never good at math" or "I'm just not good with numbers." Other emotional responses might include feeling intimidated by confusing financial lingo or feeling uncomfortable talking about financial matters. In addition, they may hesitate to get the help they need because they are embarrassed by their financial situations or lack of financial acumen.

The best way to build self-confidence in any area of life is to take action. Each step your clients take will give them confidence to take the next steps. If clients lack confidence in their financial lives, they should start with first things first. Whether that is balancing their checkbooks, organizing their records, or opening an IRA account, encourage them to just do it! Simple action steps will give them the courage and motivation to tackle other areas that are obstacles to their financial well-being.

Clients can break down big goals like refinancing their mortgages into small action steps. To the uninitiated, the whole process can seem confusing and overwhelming. However, when viewed step by step, the task is not intimidating. Here is an example of the steps toward refinancing. Suggest the client starts by reading about refinancing in a reputable reference such as Jane Bryant Quinn's *Making the Most of Your Money*. Next, the client can evaluate the relative benefit of refinancing by effortlessly running figures using financial calculators such as those available at <www.financialengines.com>. These tools, once only available to financial professionals, are now available to everyone and incredibly easy to use. Next, start calling mortgage companies for current rates, and so on.

In your clients' financial lives, success begets success. Successful completion of one step toward a financial goal is what gives them the confidence and motivation to move on to the next step.

BUILDING BLOCK 4: INCREASE FINANCIAL SKILLS AND KNOWLEDGE

Our educational system continues to send forth our young with so little information about financial matters that they are like time bombs about to destroy their own and their family's economic futures. We equip them to earn good incomes and to live the good life, but we fail miserably as a nation to prepare them to know what to do with the money they earn.

—*Venita Van Caspel, author of* Money Dynamics For The 1990s

Financial knowledge not only gives your clients the facts and the framework they need for making financial decisions, it also counteracts the money messages that sabotage their financial success. Because financial literacy is rarely acquired at school or at home, the burden of responsibility falls to individuals to seek out educational opportunities and to find advisors to provide them with the financial help they need.

As individuals, we are seldom taught about personal finance at home or at school, so it is necessary to take personal responsibility for learning in this area. Keep in mind that clients don't have to become financial experts in order to achieve financial well-being. Instead, they should strive to build a solid foundation of basic financial knowledge. Knowing only the fundamental principles of money management and financial planning will equip them to make sound day-to-day financial decisions, comprehend and evaluate financial advice, and distinguish between different investment options and opportunities. Luckily, there are a plethora of financial education opportunities available including books, classes, and Web sites. Just make sure the sources you recommend are sound and reliable, stick to proven fundamentals, and promote knowledgeable financial decisions.

Books

Encourage clients to select books that promote sound money management and investing practices, not get-rich-quick strategies. Here are a few suggestions.

- *The 8 Biggest Mistakes People Make with Their Finances Before and After Retirement* by Terence L. Reed
- *Everyone's Money Book* by Jordan Goodman
- *Managing to Be Wealthy* by John Sestina
- *Financial Independence the Smart Way* by Stephen Littauer
- *Saving on a Shoestring* and *Investing on a Shoestring,* both by Barbara O'Neill
- *Personal Finance for Dummies* by Eric Tyson
- *Making the Most of Your Money* by Jane Bryant Quinn
- *Beyond the Basics* by Mary Farrell

Web Sites

Noncommercial sites are usually a good bet. Here are some sites focused on financial education rather than product sales.

- <www.sec.gov> The primary mission of the U.S. Securities and Exchange Commission (SEC) is to protect investors and maintain the integrity of the securities markets. In addition to being an industry watchdog, the SEC promotes investor education and offers a wealth of educational materials on its Web site. Peruse all that is available in the Investor Information section; and in particular, check out the Financial Facts Tool Kit that is available via the "Online Publications" link.
- <www.rightonthemoney.org> *Right on the Money* is a how-to public television series. Each episode offers straightforward advice for people who want to make better financial decisions for themselves. Topics cover every area of one's financial life such as "Understanding Health Insurance," "How to Ask for a Raise," "Adopting a Child," "Garden for Less," and "Following Your Dream." Click any of the episode titles for complete program transcripts, extended interviews with experts, and links for more information. In addition, *Right on the Money* will answer questions related to personal finance submitted via this site.

- <www.ihatefinancialplanning.com> This lively and humorous Web site is for everyone who loves money, but hates planning. For clients who are intimidated by financial lingo or think learning about personal finance is boring, this site is a good place to start their journey to financial well-being. They will painlessly learn how to sort through the maze of financial options, analyze their own situation, and get their money life on track in the simplest way possible.

The amount of information available on investing is overwhelming. Equally intimidating is the number of investment products from which to choose. In addition, there are hundreds of "experts" proclaiming to know the only right way to invest. At first, the journey to financial freedom can seem daunting. The first step in your clients' journey will be to set a course which will act as a basis for making financial decisions, judging the credibility of investment advice, and evaluating investment options. Remember that your clients don't need to be financial experts. But they do need to know enough to have a foundation for making wise financial decisions and for working effectively and confidently with you and other financial service providers.

The more clients learn about financial planning, the more empowered they will feel. Empowerment is the noblest goal and highest compliment that can be paid to any educational process.

Chapter 21

Resourcefulness: Making the Most of the Money That You Have

In a recent *Forbes* article ("Do You Really Need That?" March 19, 2001), writer Joanne Gordon marveled at how financial services advertising had begun to sound like someone's mother talking. She cites Citibank which is distributing a print ad that shows a couple stuffing shopping bags into the already packed trunk of a taxi with the tag line, "Just because you can doesn't mean you should." Another ad reads, "The word *splurge* loses meaning if it becomes a regular daily event." According to Gordon, Citibank's estimated $100 million effort—which is themed "Live Richly"—is the first national campaign from the $77 billion firm since the early 1980s when its slogan was "The Citi Never Sleeps." Gordon writes, "It positioned itself as a workhorse. Now, it's a mother hen."

Other firms like Fidelity echo the same theme with a campaign that urges the public to "Invest Responsibly." These branding themes reveal that the industry has made an observation that the baby boomers often have jumbled priorities and an apparent lack of discipline and prudence with resources. Resourcefulness is the desire and ability to maximize your resources. Resourcefulness is the process of making the most of what you have. Resourcefulness also involves looking for effective and creative ways to reach your goals. Resourceful individuals recognize that money in and of itself is not a goal, but rather a tool to achieving goals and increasing life satisfaction. The four building blocks for increasing resourcefulness are:

1. Organize financial records and activities.
2. Set financial goals based on life goals and values.
3. Develop a money management strategy that includes debt reduction and a spending plan.
4. Take a proactive approach to reaching financial goals and building financial independence.

Note that the first and third cornerstones are centered on the left brain-oriented tasks of organizing and developing a strategy for both spending and debt. The second and fourth cornerstones are focused on the right brain-oriented tasks of integrating life goals and values, and developing a proactive attitude toward wealth building. It is this sort of integrative approach to education that will help ensure that clients follow through with their plans for prudent resource management. The odds of follow-through rise exponentially once a client has leveled the emotional obstacles that can impede compliance with the best of plans.

BUILDING BLOCK 1: ORGANIZE FINANCIAL RECORDS AND ACTIVITIES

Positioning statement:

Once I discover a person's goals and ambitions, I then need to see all his financial records. The reason for this is simple; once we understand the end point (the client's goals) we must then establish the starting point. Gathering financial records together is how we establish that starting point. Many times I encounter people who either don't know what they have or don't want to reveal all that they have. I tell both types of individuals that I can't chart out a journey from here to there if I don't know where here is.

Clients need to understand the importance of establishing a starting point in order to give their financial lives a point of reference. Advisors often learn much about their clients' propensity for organization when they ask to see their financial records. Those clients who either can't find them or who bring in a scattered array of statements—some current and some not—reveal all the advisor needs to know. Advisors can help clients facilitate better organization by giving their clients some guidelines for record keeping and sorting.

We begin by teaching clients that the process of gathering and organizing their financial records in a simple but efficient manner will allow their advisor to get an accurate picture of their financial status and provide a basis for developing an action plan. Initially, getting organized can be a tedious and time-consuming task, but the rewards will be well worth the effort. The emotional carrot to hold before your clients is the idea that they will have a clear picture of where they are, where they're going, and how long it will take to get there. In the long run, getting organized is the best time saver. The biggest benefit will be the sense of being in control of their own financial lives. Here are a few suggestions to help clients set up an easy filing system.

- Gather all financial records.
- Sort records into six categories and place them in files labeled: debts owed, assets owned, insurance policies, tax documents, estate plans or documents, and investments.
- Within each file, sort papers chronologically with the most recent records and correspondence on top.

If you really want to spur such organization, you could provide them with the empty labeled files and ask them to return the files at your next meeting. What they bring or fail to bring in those folders will tell you what you need to know and where you need to concentrate your efforts.

BUILDING BLOCK 2: SET FINANCIAL GOALS BASED ON LIFE GOALS AND VALUES

Positioning statement:

The questions of investing, saving, insuring, and reducing debt only have relevance if we have articulated why we are going into this process. Vague answers will not suffice here. Why do you want to invest? "To have more money," most people will say. Why do you want more money? What will you use it for? These sort of questions help clarify our purpose and help motivate us to stick to the wealth-building process. Consequently, I may ask some questions you didn't expect but my reason for doing so is to help clarify the reasons we are doing this work.

By using the questions in Chapter 5, "Questions about Life," and processes like the Life Transitions Survey, we can help clients clarify what is important to them in each area and each phase of their lives. Priorities are a very personal matter and clients should be encouraged to disregard messages from society, parents, friends, or anyone else when deciding what their spending priorities are. This is a process where each person should listen to his or her own heart. Ask your client, "What is it that *you* value most and what do *you* want to achieve in each facet of life?" Whatever the client identifies should become the basis for establishing life goals.

In the "Raising Your MQ" workshop, we have participants fill in the chart, shown in Figure 21.1, in order to articulate their goals in eight aspects of their lives.

Most people do not initiate a goal-setting process for themselves without some assistance or prodding from another source. It may be that clarity does not come to us regarding our goals until we are forced to write them down or verbalize them. Once our goals are on paper and staring back at us, we are compelled to wrestle with their viability and feasibility.

If you can play a role in facilitating the personal goal-setting process, the client will be more likely to discover a greater degree of

---

FIGURE 21.1   Goals for Life

My Work Goals	My Home Goals	My Health Goals	My Family Goals
My Community Goals	**My Leisure Goals**	**My Learning Goals**	**My Personal Growth Goals**

intrinsic motivation regarding the financial plan you offer. Until clients specify what they want and why they want it, they will be vulnerable to the changing winds of whim that control those trying to operate on extrinsic motivation—that which comes from an outside source. We believe that every person needs to discover the power of resolute, unshakeable motivation as it pertains to this process. They will do what they should do when they fully comprehend why they are doing it. We cannot assume that the average person has thought through this process.

Educational self-discovery also offers the opportunity to help clients understand how their money is integrated into all areas of their lives. Once clients have articulated their life goals, they should be challenged to think about what role money can or will play in helping them to achieve each life goal. How will having sufficient financial resources give them more options for realizing their goals? Will economic security give them more time to focus their attention on what is most important to them?

There are simple, direct lines that can be drawn between each client's goals and the dollar sign. Many clients have expressed greater financial satisfaction when they see a direct link between their financial planning activities and their life goals. They also articulate feeling more motivated to make improvements in their money matters when they view financial resources as tools to support their own values and priorities.

BUILDING BLOCK 3: DEVELOP A MONEY MANAGEMENT STRATEGY THAT INCLUDES DEBT REDUCTION AND A SPENDING PLAN

> My wife and I seem to go through the same routine every six months or so: we sit down, add up our debts, and wonder how we got into this predicament again! Each time, we make a plan to pay down those debts and then vow to not let it happen again. But the scenario just keeps repeating itself like a bad dream.
>
> —*Thom, client, age 44*

The first step to helping clients reach their financial goals is to develop a money management strategy. Often, it is the small financial decisions we make on a day-to-day basis that have the most influence on our financial well-being and future economic security. For example, we have all heard the stories of famous stars and athletes who make outrageous amounts of money, yet end up in financial ruin. We have also heard the stories of barbers with modest incomes who have amassed wealth. The point is this: *reaching financial goals is as dependent on the choices we make with the money we have as it is on our level of income.*

Whether a client's annual income is $20,000 or $20,000,000, the most important step to financial wellness is spending less than what is being made. Clients will never reach their financial goals if they have a negative cash flow or just break even from month to month. Many individuals just can't wait until they get a raise or win the lottery. Now is the time to encourage your clients to get real and to develop a plan that will get them from where they are financially to where they want to go.

Individuals must first analyze their spending habits and decide where to reduce expenditures. Next, it is important to develop a spending plan instead of a budget. That is because the term *budget* makes people feel like they are going to go on a "money diet." They immediately start to focus on what they can't have instead of what they are working toward. On the other hand, the term *spending plan* makes people feel like they have a road map that shows their destination—and they get to pick the route. When clients are focused on the benefits of reaching their goals, they will be motivated to take the most expeditious path to get there and to stay on course.

Their next important step is to take a look at their credit card debt. What is the total amount they owe? How much interest do they pay on a monthly basis? They must do whatever they can to reduce their credit card bills, reduce the interest rates, and accelerate payments. When they bring their credit card debt to zero, then they can start investing in their futures. It is also helpful to remind clients that one credit card is all that is necessary for convenience and emergencies. Encourage clients to never charge more than they can pay off each month.

In *Behavior Finance: Past Battles and Future Engagements,* Meir Statman wrote: "Rules are good self-control tools. 'Not one drop' is a good rule for people whose self-control problems center on alcohol. 'Consume from dividends but don't dip into capital' is a good rule for investors whose self-control problems center on spending . . . investors with imperfect self-control are afraid, as recovering alcoholics are, that one dip might lead to another."

It is important for each individual to establish some ground rules for spending, saving, and borrowing. These ground rules—whatever they may be—vary from person to person, and are the cornerstones for successful money management. How do you help individuals determine appropriate ground rules for themselves? If an advisor asks a client or a prospective client, "What rules do you try to follow with your money?" and promptly witnesses a blank stare, this is a good indication that this individual follows one rule with his money—the rule of whim. If, however, you sense that a client could benefit by establishing some ground rules regarding saving, spending, and debt management, you might ask the client to articulate what ground rules she feels are necessary for succeeding in these areas.

It is far better to draw out the ground rules from your clients than to designate the rules for them. The original picture behind the Greek root word for educator is that of drawing water from a well. The idea is that the students already have the water in them and it takes a wise teacher to draw out or reduce the water. While some believe that education involves simply opening up an empty vessel and pouring water into it, education that possesses staying power is drawn from within each individual. So it is with educating clients on how to manage debt and discipline their spending patterns.

Many advisors have told us of clients who say, "I know you'll think my money is all messed up," or some other statement that displays their anticipation of disapproval. Many people have told us that one thought that has dissuaded them from visiting an advisor is that the professional might look down on their spending habits. The easiest answer for this problem is to help clients define a framework for discipline without sounding didactic. Simply facilitate the process by which clients define the rules they want the financial strategy to follow. Here are some sample questions.

- What has been your experience with debt and what rules do you now strive to follow?
- What has been your pattern of spending and what rules have you instituted there?
- What has been your experience with saving and investing, and what rules do you apply?

If you have some clients who do not want to impose discipline upon habits which are preventing the building of wealth, all your efforts will be like pouring water into a broken cup. You might tell them of rules others have come up with such as, "No borrowing over *x* amount without talking it over with our advisor or accountant" or "Save at least 75 percent of all unexpected gains, windfalls, or unexpected income" or "Wait at least two weeks after we decide we want something to actually make the purchase." These rules constitute psychological fences that will prevent assets from slipping away—as long as clients keep their fences mended. The road to wealth is actually quite elementary: *spend less than you earn, avoid debt, and invest for growth.* There is no need to make it any more complicated than that. Your clients may also find the following resources helpful.

- *How to Get Out of Debt, Stay Out of Debt and Live Prosperously,* by Jerrold Mundis
- *Saving on a Shoestring: How to Cut Expenses, Reduce Debt, and Stash More Cash,* by Barbara M. O'Neill
- Quicken or other financial software which simplifies and speeds tasks like tracking spending, creating a spending plan, monitoring debt, and reconciling checking accounts

BUILDING BLOCK 4: TAKE A PROACTIVE APPROACH TO REACHING FINANCIAL GOALS AND BUILDING FINANCIAL INDEPENDENCE

The number one enemy of personal finance is procrastination.

—*Dave Chilton,* The Wealthy Barber

How long can people afford to wait before putting together a financial plan for life? Without a plan, transitions will come and blindside them financially. Without a plan, their dreams and goals of retirement living will get filed away under "woulda, coulda, shoulda." Advisors need to use persuasive examples to convince clients of the importance of acting now. Clients need a better understanding of how expensive delays are. Start an IRA with $2,000 a year at age 25, earn an average of 10 percent, and at age 65 you have just over a million dollars. Wait until you are 40 to start, and your contribution will have to be over $9,500 a year to get to the same place by age 65. For each year people delay saving, they place more fiscal pressure on themselves for later in life. Can their health and mental well-being afford the extra pressure later in life?

Resourceful individuals are proactive. They take responsibility to make things happen in their own lives. They make plans that make the best use of their time, talent, energy, skills, intellect, and resources to overcome obstacles and reach their goals. Being proactive involves

- making a plan for all areas of life that require financial attention,
- following up and monitoring progress on a regular basis,
- aligning spending and saving behaviors accordingly, and
- getting the necessary help for matters they do not understand.

Resourcefulness is as much an attitude as it is a skill. Resourceful people find ways to save, regardless of income level. For example, a person who earns six figures and saves nothing is the antithetical example of someone earning less than $30,000 and putting away an impressive nest egg. The final cornerstone for resourcefulness is being proactive in reaching goals and achieving independence. Those who wish to make excuses will never lack for the opportunity throughout their lifetime to make them. Figure 21.2 details examples of the rationale people use throughout their lives.

According to the 1999 Consumer Survey by the Certified Financial Planner Board of Standards, Inc., when it comes to attitudes regarding planning and managing one's financial affairs, upper income consumers divide into three camps: worriers, independents, and help wanteds. Figure 21.3 details the characteristics of each of these groups.

The independents in all probability aren't going to come to see you. What are left are the worriers and the help wanteds. Everything you do to help these groups become more proactive will empower them. Help them articulate their goals. Help them define the boundaries and ground rules for debt, spending, and saving. Help them to think ahead and prepare accordingly. This is what the attitude of being proactive is all about. Clients are empowered and invigorated by the fact that they thought ahead and prepared—now, they can reap the peace of mind that comes as the first dividend of the process. Proactivity must become a habit and a way of life.

Resourcefulness is, in short, making the most with what we have. The opposite of resourcefulness is wastefulness—failing to appreciate the value of what we have. We must do our best to teach clients the tricks of the resourcefulness trade. We must strive for resourcefulness with our money, our time with that money, and the opportunities made available for our money and time.

FIGURE 21.2   I Can't Save Now

20s   **I CAN'T SAVE NOW.** I'm just getting established. I've got school loans to pay back and a car loan, too. I'm not ready to make commitments yet and I want to have fun while I can. There will be time to think about saving later on, then I'll save.

30s   **I CAN'T SAVE NOW.** I've got family and responsibilities. It costs a lot to raise children and there's the mortgage on the house, too. It takes all I have to make ends meet. When I'm making more and the kids are older, then I'll save.

40s   **I CAN'T SAVE NOW.** I've got kids in college and costs are out of sight. Then, there are the weddings. I want to help the kids get started. Expenses are at their highest and it's the hardest time to save, but things will ease off soon, then, I'll save.

50s   **I CAN'T SAVE NOW.** Things haven't worked out like I thought they would. It's not easy when you are locked in and there's no opportunity to move up the ladder. I can't just make a break and start a new career. I'm helping the folks, too, now that they need assistance. I'm just barely making ends meet. Something will open up, then I'll save.

60s   **I CAN'T SAVE NOW.** I thought things would be better. I wanted to retire earlier but I just can't do it. I'm trying to pay off the last of the mortgage and take care of other bills, but things mount up. Remembering the grandchildren and other things take all I have. I guess that's the way it is. I wish I could save.

70s   **I CAN'T SAVE NOW.** I'm too old to save. My Social Security check and my pension just don't go far enough. Medications and long-term care expenses really worry me. I hate being such a burden on my kids. I wish I had saved when I should have.

The resourceful achiever has greater pleasure at the end of the race—much like the kid who built his own soapbox and beat the kid whose wealthy daddy bought him the best money could buy. One built his vehicle piece by piece and understood the value and function of each piece. He took pride in what he built, how he kept it in

FIGURE 21.3   The Three Types of Upper-Income Consumers

Worriers *(42% of upper-income consumers)*	• Fret about financial decisions • Are not confident in their control over their financial future • Do not enjoy planning and thinking about financial matters • May have a financial plan, but admit that they don't really follow it • Are their own primary financial advisors, despite their discomfort
Independents *(33% of upper-income consumers)*	• Are satisfied with their financial decisions • Feel more knowledgeable and successful than other consumers • Devote more time each month to financial matters than the average consumer • Use the Internet for financial purposes • Prefer to make financial decisions without professional help
Help Wanteds *(25% of upper-income consumers)*	• Enthusiastically seek professional financial advice • Are confident that they are in control of their financial lives • Feel their investments meet or exceed their expectations • Have benefited from having a financial plan

Source: 1999 Consumer Survey, Certified Financial Planner Board of Standards, Inc.

running order, and what he was able to achieve with it. This is precisely why we want to engage clients in as much of the process as possible. Resourcefulness training will teach them to take ownership of the process. Empowerment comes when they see the process working.

Chapter 22

Relationships That Affect Personal Wealth

Everywhere I look it seems like I have tension around my money. My wife and I can't talk about it without getting into a shouting match. I worry if I'm doing too much for my kids and not enough for my parents. And to top it off, I have serious questions about the advisor I'm using. I wonder if he's really concerned about my interests. I'd probably take a little less money if it meant a little more peace of mind with all these money issues.

—*Isaac K., client, age 51*

It is nearly impossible to adequately address the topic of financial intelligence and financial satisfaction without talking about the many relationships that are directly affected by our prosperity—or lack thereof. Marriages crumble because couples can't talk about money without going into emotional debt. Millions are sandwiched between obligations to progeny and parents. Many want to help charitable causes but are not sure whom to help and how much to give. Millions sense the need to partner with an expert but are fearful of being taken advantage of—and having only their own ignorance to blame for it.

In this section of the money quotient education program, we address the relationships or connections with others that have a direct bearing on our wealth-building and wealth-distribution processes. The four building blocks for the this particular cornerstone of money intelligence and satisfaction are:

1. Improve communication skills and relationship dynamics regarding money issues.
2. Evaluate financial responsibilities across generations.
3. Build good working relationships with financial professionals.
4. Participate in giving and philanthropy.

This chapter will outline the steps necessary to create a sense of money harmony and satisfaction within the context of the myriad relationships that affect money coming in and money going out. In the MQ program, our stated goal with clients is to bring them to the place where they establish the ground rules for diminishing financial tension with spouses, family members, and advisors. We also build a framework for giving and philanthropic decision making.

BUILDING BLOCK 1: IMPROVE COMMUNICATION SKILLS AND RELATIONSHIP DYNAMICS REGARDING MONEY ISSUES

> Insanity is doing the same thing over and over and expecting a different result.
>
> —*Rita Mae Brown*

Karen Ramsey, author of *Everything You Learned About Money Is Wrong*, believes that many people harbor the deep belief that they are the only ones who are screwed up about money. When she asks her audiences how many of them believe that everyone besides them has their money figured out, without fail, hands fly up across the room. This belief that other people know more than they do causes many to avoid talking about money for fear that their ignorance will be exposed.

This mental trap of exposing financial ignorance is what keeps many people firmly bound in financial insanity. They continue the same actions yet expect different results. The first step to freeing clients from their financial shackles is to teach them how to communicate with professionals and significant others in their lives.

Ramsey writes: "If you are confused or intimidated or frustrated about money, the place to start is to realize that you need to find someone you can talk to about it. Who is this someone? If you are concerned that your finances are not heading in the right direction, it may be time to seek out a professional. Tell this advisor that you really don't know anything about investments and that you need some answers to basic questions about your options. *Tell him or her that you need help.* In my experience, any time you start a conversation like that, people will be more than willing to help you. You need to talk to someone with whom you are comfortable, if that person leaves you feeling like you should know all of this stuff already, then that is not the person for you."

The inability to communicate our own areas of ignorance and need can be fallow ground on which to develop relationships where money harmony is essential. It is no wonder that many couples cannot find agreement in money goals and management. This financial tension often expedites a trip to the divorce lawyer's office—which will all but decimate their financial prospects for years to come.

Opposites truly seem to attract in regard to personality. This is especially true of financial behaviors. It is rare to find two people together who approach money in identical manners; consequently, each will assert that the other person's thinking is wrong and his or her behavior is at fault. Marital problems often occur when one partner tries to change the other's behavior regarding money, rather than setting up a structure that will meet the needs of both partners.

Most couples desperately need an agreed upon plan and structure that will accommodate both partners' automatic behaviors. If the structure is not realistic in this regard, the plan will be instantly violated and result in amplified tensions. When couples learn to accept and understand that they cannot change one another's financial behaviors, then they can commence to develop a plan that accommodates both and calls both to make concessions. Learning to recognize and accept one another has the potential to remove many layers of fiscal conflict. As couples resolve these conflicts, they avoid the dread surrounding money talks and lose their sense that finding financial satisfaction is hopeless.

Many advisors agree with Karen Ramsey's synopsis of the four major types of money personalities.

1. *The saver.* Savers must save money no matter what the circumstance and cannot save enough to quench their desire for more. Even if they agree with their partner on how much they

will save, they will constantly raise the bar to new heights and apply more saving pressure.

2. *The spender.* The spender is the saver's worst nightmare. Spenders need to spend to keep their emotions from feeling too confined. Their spending is linked to their mood. Whether it is spending $5 here and $10 there or making major purchases on a periodic basis, it is the act of purchasing that elevates them. To spenders, their behavior is perfectly justifiable.

3. *The worrier.* The worrier is always vigilantly awaiting disaster. If worriers have enough to cover their needs they are afraid it won't last. They constantly fear the loss of their job or their spouse's job. Money fears keep them up at night.

4. *The avoider.* The avoider would rather do anything than have to talk about or deal with money matters. Avoiders procrastinate, pay bills late, file extensions on tax returns, and get into trouble with creditors—even when they have sufficient funds. They are simply uncomfortable with money matters and go to great lengths to avoid dealing with them.

In his book *Smart Couples Finish Rich,* advisor and author David Bach gives couples exercises to help find agreement on financial goals and the agreed-upon processes for attaining those goals. Advisors would do well to facilitate similar processes for their clients who struggle with synchronizing their financial habits. Tension is released when a system is created that accommodates both parties' habits and desires within the bounds of reason. Through give and take both parties can feel like they are getting what they need without stifling the financial needs of their partner.

BUILDING BLOCK 2: EVALUATE FINANCIAL RESPONSIBILITIES ACROSS GENERATIONS

The term *sandwich generation* has been adopted to describe the large contingency of baby boomers who feel a sense of financial obligation to provide opportunity for their children, and care or creature comforts for their parents during their aging years. We will now discuss how advisors can help clients fulfill these three obligations: education and advancement for their children, retirement comfort for their parents, and caregiving for loved ones.

Sending Junior to Harvard

There has been some consumer backlash in recent years to the liberal projections (some would say hyperbolic) of the future costs of higher education. Two assumptions are being challenged by many consumers. First, that it will take $250,000 to put a child through college—more money than most people could ever save. Second, that consumers will need to pay the entire bill themselves. The parents challenging these assumptions may well be wrong on the first issue (college tuitions are escalating rapidly), but many are coming up with creative ways to split the bill.

My wife and I have set up matching funds college accounts with our children. We have found many other parents who are creating other sorts of resourceful arrangements with their children. Our family program works like this: for every dollar each child earns and saves toward college (scholarships included), we will match the amount. The children's obligation is to then earn and save half of the actual amount needed to complete their education. I am happy to report that our first child has saved enough money for his first two years of college.

Whether using 529s (tax-advantaged college savings plans) or matching grant savings accounts, advisors should allow clients to design an approach that fits both their values structure and resource capabilities. We chose to approach the issue of college savings in a way that would test our children's work ethic and intrinsic motivation so that we would not end up subsidizing a sorority slacker. Ask your clients how they feel about the issue before giving a prescription. Don't sow seeds of hopelessness by focusing on education cost projections that far supercede the client's earning potential.

Paying Back Mom and Dad

Many prospering baby boomers, who have had earning opportunities unfathomable during their parents' prime working years, are looking for ways to repay a debt of obligation to their parents for the sacrifices made in their behalf. Advisor Bruce Bruinsma observes that as little as $300 to $400 per month can make a substantial difference in providing a margin of comfort for many aging retirees. Many baby boomers—who now find themselves with more abundant resources—are reexamining their personal values, like the idea of blessing their own aging parents in this way.

In *The New Retirementality,* I apply the term *parental pension* to this investment idea. I have talked to clients who, along with siblings, have pooled their funds into an annuity type of account—spinning off a few hundred dollars each month to a parent or parents. Scenarios such as these affirm Bruinsma's assertion that a few hundred dollars a month does go along way toward providing easier breathing to those on fixed retirement incomes.

The autumn years of life are propagandized as being the golden years. The gold can quickly lose its shine due to ailing health and dwindling spending power. Children who wish to pay a debt of gratitude—and have the resources to do so—will welcome a conversation that focuses on using their wealth to improve the quality of their parents' lives. Some could only afford to make such an arrangement by combining their funds with the funds of their siblings to create a parental pension. Some siblings have also pooled their resources to pay off their parents' mortgage in order to open up breathing room for their parents. These ideas can be an innovative means of connecting your services to the family lives of your clients.

The Cost of Caregiving

Caregiving is beginning to exact quite a toll on the financial lives of millions of Americans according to *The MetLife Juggling Act Study—Balancing Caregiving with Work and the Costs Involved.* (The MetLife study was based on the findings of a national study by the National Alliance for Caregiving and National Center on Women and Aging at Brandeis University). Nearly 25 percent of all households include at least one adult who has provided care for an elderly person at some point during the last 12 months. Over the next ten years, the total number of employed caregivers in the United States is expected to increase to between 11 and 15.6 million working Americans. This landmark study was the first to examine the long-term care costs these caregivers face when they disrupt their work to accommodate the needs of their older loved ones.

The MetLife study found that, in addition to their caregiving responsibilities, 64 percent of these caregivers are employed and must find a balance between work and caregiving obligations. The research revealed that these working caregivers often incur significant losses in career development, salary, and retirement benefits, in addition to out-of-pocket expenses that result from their caregiving. Promotions and salaries are compromised as working hours are sacrificed to meet the caregiving obligations.

Caregivers often find themselves in a place of stalled careers and scaled-down wages as a result of their responsibilities. Forty percent of the survey participants reported that caregiving had affected their upward mobility in the workplace in the following ways:

- 29 percent passed up a job promotion, training, or assignment
- 25 percent passed up an opportunity for job advancement
- 22 percent were not able to acquire new skills
- 13 percent were not able to keep up with changes in necessary job skills

Income can also be severely affected in the work versus caregiving scenario. In the study, 67 percent of the respondents stated that their caregiving activities had hindered their earning power. The wage wealth impact was significant for those who could provide information to quantify the economic impact. Wage wealth is defined as the present value of lifetime wages calculated as of the date of retirement. The average loss of wage wealth per respondent was $566,443.

In addition to their current income, the caregivers' retirement savings were adversely impacted. The average decrease in Social Security benefits was $2,160 annually, for an average total of $25,494. Among those eligible for pensions, their average benefits fell $5,339 annually, or a total of $67,202 in lost pension wealth for their retirement years. Add lost wages, Social Security benefits, and pension payouts, and the price of caregivng rises to an average of $659,139 over a lifetime.

The numbers assume that the caregiving process will continue into the retirement years of the caregiver, which is not all that unreasonable when a 52-year-old child begins caring for a 78-year-old parent who may well live to be 90 or more. The first place that caregivers reach for caregiving expenses is into the purse they once used to fund investments and savings.

Advisors will need to act as guides and educators in helping clients anticipate such circumstances before they are blindsided by them, and help clients financially navigate through these scenarios. This is a life issue that faces many future retirees who will need an earning or investment revolution to meet the costs of the aging revolution.

BUILDING BLOCK 3: BUILD GOOD WORKING RELATIONSHIPS WITH FINANCIAL PROFESSIONALS

In the Money Quotient approach to financial education, we have chosen to swim upstream against the tide of popular media that suggests that the public can and should do much of its financial and retirement planning on its own. The plain fact is that most people are underqualified for the task and too overworked to be able perform due diligence even if they did possess sufficient knowledge.

Andrew Tobias, in his book *The Only Investment Book You Will Ever Need*, addresses the question "Do you need an advisor?" Encourage clients to learn as much as they can, but remind them there will be times when they will need an expert's personalized advice. Here are some examples.

- Help with tax strategies or retirement planning where a mistake or oversight can prove to be very expensive in the long run.
- Create an estate plan, write a will, or review an existing one.
- Review a current financial situation and asset-allocation.
- Help whip a disorganized financial life into shape.
- Choose a long-term care policy.
- Help navigate a financial transition, such as divorce, retirement, or death of a spouse.
- Develop a plan for minimizing the cost of children's college education.

Tobias goes on to say that "a good advisor will empower you by helping you learn." What this tells us is that even advocates of do-it-yourself financial literature recognize the limits and shortfalls of the approach, given the average level of financial education and discipline in our populace. This leads them to recommend the financial profession—howbeit with caveats—and to tell the public what sort of advisor to look for. Advisors who educate will find that the clients will be more likely to refer the advisor's services because of the emotional empowerment they gathered while being educated.

The public intuitively recognizes its inadequacy when faced with the financial tasks, but it wonders if it will be able to discern which advisor is right. People want help but are not sure of the criteria to use when looking for help. In a chapter in *The New Retirementality* entitled "Finding the Right Wealth-Building Partner," I use an illustration to guide consumers on why they need an advisor.

> When I was building an addition in my home for our new baby boy, I decided I wanted to do the some of the work myself to save some money. I had some experience doing electrical wiring and decided to tackle it with some consultation. The builder agreed to inspect my work before the official inspector came in. When I was done with the wiring, the builder came to check my work. When he came to the last connection I had made, he showed me how I had erred and informed me that it could have easily started a fire in that room. Then and there I decided that there are some projects that are far too important to try to tackle alone with a limited degree of experience. I believe that retirement or emancipation planning is one of those projects.

Here are some questions your clients can use when seeking other financial service providers, such as state attorneys, insurance agents, accountants, and bankers. Also ask yourself if you provide your clients with this level of service.

- *What was your first impression of the individual?* Was the individual personable and respectful, or officious, distracted, or arrogant? This will provide a good indicator of the kind of service and attention you can expect to receive down the road should problems or concerns arise.
- *What kind of questions did the financial professional ask you?* Did the advisor ask more about your money or about your life, values, and goals? The best people in the business know they cannot do right by you if they do not have a clear understanding of where you've been, who you are, and where you want to go. Those who only inquire about your assets are only interested in your assets.
- *Did the financial professional demonstrate good listening skills?* Did he or she carefully summarize your concerns, goals, and level of risk tolerance? If you get the feeling you are not dealing with a good listener, move on. If the individual is paying close attention now, you know that is what you can expect later. If the individual pretends to listen but just charges ahead with an agenda that seems to miss the point of what you explained,

move on. If the professional dominates the conversation, get out as fast as you can!

- *Did the financial professional explain matters in a language you could understand or use jargon and talk over your head?* Those who talk over your head probably want to keep you in the dark or simply aren't smart enough to make matters understandable. Anyone who makes you feel stupid is not worthy of your business. A sure sign of competence is the ability to make complex matters seem simple and understandable. A good advisor will also be a good teacher and will help you raise your MQ.

- *Is the financial professional willing to disclose a personal portfolio?* Find out if the professional is buying what is being sold. If a financial professional is trying to sell something that he or she does not own, you want to know why. If you find an advisor who handles personal matters like his or her own, you have a greater potential for trust.

- *Does the financial professional have a track record that can be documented?* Unless you want to be somebody's guinea pig, you should ask to see the professional's performance record. Check to see that the individual has done well in down markets as well as in up markets. Ask for references and talk to those who have been clients for a long period of time (beware of shills when asking for references).

- *Does the financial professional articulate a clear philosophy regarding investments and wealth building?* If the professional does not have a clear philosophical compass that has been fine-tuned through experience, it is more likely to be one of those people who just follows the crowd. The dime-a-dozen advisor that sells whatever he or she is told to sell is not the person you are looking for. I like to see advisors who are comfortable talking about their mistakes as well as their victories because a good investment philosophy borrows from the lessons of both failure and success.

- *Ask the financial professional why he or she got into this business.* Here you will hear answers ranging from being on a mission to help other people, to those pretending to be on a mission to help other people but really on a mission to help themselves. I read between the lines on this answer. I want to get the sense that the financial professional is fascinated about money matters, curious about people, and motivated by the work.

If clients walk out of an interview satisfied that these bases have been or could be covered, they will feel like they are partnering with a trustworthy individual. People want to work with a concerned and competent professional who is in the business for the right reasons. The prospective clients know they need someone to help. It is up to you to prove that you are that someone.

BUILDING BLOCK 4: PARTICIPATE IN GIVING AND PHILANTHROPY

Jack McConnell, M.D., used to be a retired doctor until he started remembering the question his minister father used to repeat each night around the dinner table. (Source: "My Turn," *Newsweek,* June 18, 2001.) Each day when he and his brothers and sisters arrived home, they would sit around the dining room table and take turns answering their father's question, "And what did you do for someone today?"

McConnell lived the definitive successful life before retiring to a posh gated community on Hilton Head Island. But when he left his luxurious buffer zone to travel to the other side of the island, he was stunned by the disparity between what he had and what those on the other side of the island did not have. McConnell soon discovered through interaction with maids, gardeners, waitresses, and construction workers that they had little or no access to medical care. He thought it was an unfair and inequitable situation, especially given the abundant population of retired doctors on the island.

Soon McConnell started working on a solution. He started approaching the legions of retired doctors to see if he could persuade them to work a few hours a week volunteering their services. Most of the doctors he approached liked the idea—as long as they weren't putting their life savings at risk through malpractice suits. After one year of preparation, McConnell paved the path for these doctors to be relicensed and insured. He then opened the Volunteers in Medicine Clinic, which is fully staffed by retired physicians, nurses, dentists, and chiropractors, as well as 150 lay volunteers. The first year they treated 5,000 patients, which quickly grew to 16,000 patients the following year.

McConnell's example inspired others. Today, there are 15 other Volunteers in Medicine clinics up and running. As a result, his golf handicap has gone from 16 to 26 and his leisure time has evaporated into 60-hour work weeks with no pay, but his energy and life satisfaction are *up*. This is not the retirement that this doctor envisioned, but he is far from disappointed.

In the coming years, as many prosperous achievers head toward the retirement they think they want, many will experience a similar epiphany and inclination to start investing their time, money, and energy into channels of giving and philanthropy. These inclinations will lead them into relationships with causes that will have a direct bearing on savings and disbursements. This is an important philosophical inclination for the baby boomer set—many of whom will find themselves wanting to make up for lost time as they reach the level where they have all they need to maintain the lifestyles they desire.

Many will want to invest both time and money in causes near their to hearts. Like the doctor, many will want to utilize their professional skills in charitable environs. By using the benevolence profile in Chapter 15, "Leaving a Legacy," you can help clients start the thought process of how they might best apply themselves, once they come to the realization that soaking in the gated community pools for the rest of their days may not lead to perpetual satisfaction.

Financial satisfaction is deeply and intricately affected by a number of relationships in our lives—those we live with, those we once lived with, and those who once lived with us. An important aspect to consider is how these various relationships play in and out of our financial lives and how they can accelerate or slow down on our investment plans. At the end of the day, it is meaningful relationships—more than account balances—that determine a client's satisfaction with life.

Chapter 23

Wisdom: Putting Money in Its Place

There is an ancient eastern parable entitled "The Wealth Is Nearer than You Think." The story is about a wealthy merchant who embarked on a long journey and brought along his most valuable jewels. Along the way, another traveler befriended him by feigning a chance meeting—with the sole intention of getting his hands on the precious stones. At the end of each day's travel, they would share accommodations at an inn. As was the custom when they arrived at an inn, each would receive a mat, a pillow, and a wash basin with a towel for nightly cleaning.

Suspicious of the intentions of his new friend, the wealthy merchant worked out a scheme to guard his valuables which left his conniving companion completely riddled. Before turning in for the night, he kindly offered the would-be-thief the opportunity to bathe first. As soon as the thief left the room, he placed his bag of precious stones under the thief's pillow. When the thief returned and the merchant left for his ablution, the opportunistic scoundrel enthusiastically rifled through the merchant's belongings, throughout the room, and even under the merchant's pillow. Having failed to locate the all-too-close treasure, his frenzied search left him exhausted but too frustrated to sleep.

On the last day that they were to spend together, the rich man began his salutation by informing his dumbfounded companion that he was privy to his intentions all along. The merchant increased the thief's agony by informing him, "You poured all your energies into looking everywhere—except under your own pillow. The wealth was nearer to you than you realized."

This plain but profound allegory has much to teach us about the relentless pursuit of riches and easy wealth. What we learn about money is futile if we do not come to grips with placing money in its proper posture. Money is meant to be a servant—not a master. No one can claim exemption from the temptation to make unwise compromises and bow to our intended servant. When we do bow, we experience as Fielding once said, "If you make money your god it will plague you like the devil."

The closing context, therefore, of the Money Quotient approach to financial literacy and financial satisfaction is to examine the meaning of money and to negotiate our lives back to a point where money is serving us—not vice versa. The four building blocks of wisdom as related to the wealth-building process are:

1. Engage in meaningful "work."
2. Seek to understand and achieve true "wealth."
3. Pursue a balanced and meaningful life.
4. Make a lifelong commitment to raising our MQ.

BUILDING BLOCK 1: ENGAGE IN MEANINGFUL "WORK"

A good cause makes for a strong arm.

—*Anon*

In her book *Everything You Learned about Money Is Wrong*, author Karen Ramsey wrote a chapter entitled "*I Don't Like My Job but I Can't Afford to Leave It.*" In this chapter, Ramsey shares the story of telling a client he was going to have to work 12 years longer than anticipated if he hoped to have what he wanted at retirement.

"What can I do?" her client asked.

"Look," Ramsey answered, "12 years is a long time. For you, it's going to feel like an especially long time because you hate your job. I'm guessing that it's not the length of time you dread, it's the prospect of spending the next 12 years doing something you do not want to do."

"I don't have any choice," her client responded.

"What about doing work that you like?" she asked. "Since it's going to take you longer to get to retirement than you hoped, you might as well do something you enjoy."

We cannot help but believe that this conversation will become more common given the economy and events of recent times. Many retirement nest eggs have contracted to the point where many clients face the same dilemma that Ramsey's client articulated. People have the following choices when their resources fail to keep pace with their retirement plans.

- They can sit with static plans and hope that the market will give back what it took away.
- They can make arrangements to work longer where they are, if they enjoy their work scenario.
- They can work longer in a negative work scenario and extend their misery.
- They can start working on a transition to work they will enjoy and increase the enjoyment factor of their extended work life.

This is not to say that the rule of following your bliss is a safe guidepost for every person who is dissatisfied with his present working circumstances. Many have gone on a quest to start a business or shift careers only to find the new evil to be worse than the first—especially if it entails an unpredictable income stream. Many have found that the stress they had with their old jobs was much more bearable than the stress they now live with.

However, the idea that we must struggle through years of occupational misery to get to the Shangri-La of retirement is equally as foolish as chasing frothy dreams because we might have nothing left in us when we reach the gate to Shangri-La. Before clients can make a transition to a more fulfilling work life, they must open themselves up to the possibility that the words *work* and *fulfilling* can be congruous.

For some, the theft of fulfillment is the environment they work in. For others, it is the people they work with. For others, it is the nature of the work they do. The client must identify the culprit before pressing toward a change. Using some of the tools and ideas in Chapter 14, "Offering Guidance in Times of Career and Retirement Transition," can help you facilitate such a conversation.

Many people have been wrongly conditioned to think of work as a burden. How many people do you know whose eyes sparkle when they talk of their work? It is not a Pollyannaish idea to do work that you like, to work with people you enjoy, and to engage in work that intrigues you to your dying day. In fact, these were the hallmarks of wise career choices before the industrial age introduced the idea of a "job"—simply performing routine tasks we hate and counting the days until we can quit. The need to earn enough money is not the root of this problem. It is the belief that the only way to earn the money is to continue in miserable employment. The wise person works toward a place of unity and synchronicity between working life and inner life. The wise advisor is positioned as a partner and guide in the discovery and transition phases of this process of change.

BUILDING BLOCK 2: SEEK TO UNDERSTAND AND ACHIEVE TRUE "WEALTH"

Give careful thought to your ways. You have planted much, but have harvested little. You eat, but never have enough. You drink, but never have your fill. You put on clothes, but are not warm. You earn wages only to put them in a purse with holes in it.

—*Haggai 1:5-6*

Warren Buffett was once quoted as saying, "The only things that truly make you happy are having your health and people that love you and you can't buy either one of those." It may also be true that the realization of wealth immediately exposes money's inability to satisfy. There is no sure time, age, or experience that will drive this point home; but, hopefully, the coin drops for everyone at some time or another.

I recently heard a story of a couple in an extended family tree who deceptively persuaded an older relative stricken with Alzheimer's disease to change her will and make them the sole beneficiaries. Not surprisingly, there was an outrage among the relatives after this woman's death—especially when they observed the couple building a new home and purchasing new vehicles. What was surprising, however, was that the couple who did this were in their early 80s. Obviously the coin of wisdom and the meaning of money doesn't drop at any particular stage of life.

FIGURE 23.1   True Wealth

1. How do you define success in your *working* life?

2. How do you measure success in your *family* life?

3. How do you define balance in your life?

4. How do you define success in your *financial* life?

5. How do you hope to be remembered someday?

Advisors who wish to broach the conversation of true wealth with their clients may find the questionnaire in Figure 23.1 helpful.

As important as building wealth is to our lives, it is also important to remember that building wealth does not define our lives. Our desire is to connect with the values that drive the wealth-building process for each client. Your clients' answers to the questions in Figure 23.1 will help you understand how they define true wealth.

Once your clients have articulated their values, you can begin to help them navigate their journey to true wealth—rather than mindlessly accept the societal and cultural definitions that leave most feeling like we're never quite where we need to be. Measuring success by material standards distributes a sense of inferiority to some and a sense of superiority to others yet rarely leaves a mark of contentment in the people who live by the standard. Author Suze Orman put it this way: "The quality of our lives does not depend only how we accumulate, save, and spend our money. True financial freedom lies in defining ourselves by who and what we are, not by what we have or do not have. You are the person you are right now. We cannot measure our self-worth by our net worth."

BUILDING BLOCK 3: PURSUE A BALANCED AND MEANINGFUL LIFE

Most of us go to our graves with our music still inside us.

—*Oliver Wendell Holmes*

The greatest investment challenge facing our culture is not centered on how to attain material resources but on how to invest our lives. Survey after survey affirms the idea that the limited bucket of time carried by most Americans has a noticeable leak. The majority of respondents feel a constant stress and list personal time as a top priority. As people mature (when their "time" bucket is less than half full), they begin to notice this perforation in their reservoir of time (an awareness of their mortality). When asked what they would do with their increased personal time, most respondents pointed to family, leisure, and activities that give them a sense of connectivity and meaning. Many midlife professionals speak of being tired of deferring satisfaction to a later date in life. Some are on their second family—having seen the price one often pays in all-consuming careers.

Advisor and author, Karen Ramsey, has captured this sentiment.

Few people are able to find total satisfaction and contentment in work alone. We also need relationships with others in our lives—and the time needed to invest in those relationships. We often find ourselves too busy to spend time with those we love, and the rewards of our long hours of toil are rarely sufficient to fill the resulting void. To find harmony and balance in our lives, we may need to implement changes. That may mean doing what we want, rather than what everyone else expects.

A job can be defined as a trade in which we exchange our time for someone else's money. The fairness of that trade should be under constant scrutiny. The impact of that trade on other important aspects of our lives should be a point of perpetual examination. When people say they are feeling stressed and need more balance in their lives, they are really admitting that they have surrendered the locus of control of their most precious commodity—time. Would these same individuals give up control of their material assets and complain about the resulting stress and hopelessness of their predicament? Wise investors understand that their time and energy also contain the seeds of compounding wealth. What is the point of putting your money in aggressive growth funds while your time and energy are in the equivalent of passbook savings or, worse, a losing enterprise?

Maybe what people are saying is that they are waking to the realization that it is not just the money that they want—there are more lasting prizes to be had. We have found that oftentimes these people are waiting for someone to "give permission" to think this way.

Author Mark Eisenson demonstrates that the investment metaphor cuts incisively to the soul of the materially focused but perplexed individual. He writes:

> Quality of life means different things to different people—each person's definition is unique. But the important thing to realize is that your life is multifaceted and each facet contributes to the quality of life you experience. Each facet is an integral part of your "life portfolio" and your investments of time and energy are how you make that portfolio grow. Are they experiencing the "value" for your investment that you should expect? If not, it's time to reevaluate and rebalance your portfolio. In the same way that Wall Street investment appreciates in value, you want your investments of time and energy to offer high yields. They should make you feel good—happy, satisfied, energized, or relaxed. If you're really lucky, they may even make you money.

Something Worth Doing

Like a sense of balance, our sense of meaning is also affected by our time investments. The word *meaning* can be abstract and difficult to define leading to deep philosophical questions such as, "What is the meaning of life?" However, in terms of financial life planning, the more practical question is, "What is meaningful to me?" In other words, as clients design their future, the top criterion for investing time should be to spend time in a way that is meaningful.

Whether paid or unpaid, it is especially important that each individual's work enhances his self-worth and personal identity. Do you know of any advisors who, although successful, seem to not be enjoying what they do? Such demeanors are often symptomatic of a disconnect at this level. Author Barbara Sher explains that the first step to finding work that "fits" you—in other words, matches your skills, interests, values, and preferences—is to understand the connection between doing what you love and doing something worth doing. At that intersection you will find meaning. Sher writes: "When something really matters to you, you must bring it into your life. It's a tribute to the success of our culture that so many of us have freedom to search for our own life's work."

We have found that a majority of those who do not possess this freedom have also compromised their freedom in the realm of financial decisions. By borrowing and spending too much, by making ill-guided investment choices and strategies, and by neglecting to bring their financial lives under analysis and control, these individuals have delayed or abandoned their quest for meaning. This is where a good financial life planner can make all the difference in the world. First, help clients think about locating the intersection where meaning will be found. Second, help clients align their financial lives with the objective of reaching that destination. Without a clear vision of the destination, the process rings hollow and will be compromised by every impulsive whim and wind of influence.

BUILDING BLOCK 4: MAKE A LIFELONG COMMITMENT TO RAISING YOUR MQ

Raising one's MQ is about developing a better sense of reasoning regarding money. Most people fail to understand that reasoning and intellect are not the same things. Intellect is concerned with grasping the meaning and context of terms and figures. We could educate every American intellectually about money, investments, and markets yet see very little noticeable change in their financial behaviors. What we are distinguishing here is the difference between the brain and the mind.

There is an undeniable "soulish" aspect to financial thinking and behavior. Intellect is impotent in the face of financial reasoning rooted in values, family patterns, fears, and beliefs. As we look to raising our own money quotient, we must understand at the outset that being smart *about* money does not necessarily translate to being smart *with* money. Raising our MQ is about changing our reasoning on money matters. Being able to spew out facts and definitions of financial mechanisms is of little help here.

Many approach financial education as if it is little else than a mathematics or personal economics course. Anyone who follows the markets, however, knows that to understand its tempestuous gyrations, it is helpful to take a number of courses in psychology. The same is true of personal financial education. Although our tempestuous financial gyrations on a personal level will never make the headlines on CNBC, they can be explained more clearly by the vernacular of psychology than they can by the vernacular of mathematics.

To succeed as an investor is difficult emotionally. Mr. Market (the manic-depressive metaphor for the market's behavior created by Benjamin Graham) is seductive in his offers based in naked fear and greed. It sometimes takes emotions overdosed on Novocaine to ignore his panicked offers to buy and sell. As Warren Buffett, a student of Benjamin Graham, exhorts, you must pay absolutely no attention to Mr. Market, no matter what happens.

Controlling our emotions usually means doing nothing when Mr. Market is shouting his offers from the business page or the financial channel. Columnist Jason Zweig says, "If you can't control your emotions, being in the market is like walking into a heated area wearing a backpack full of explosives." Perhaps you have clients who walk into your office wearing that same backpack. If you do, you might first ponder the issue of suitability. Some people do not possess the emotional resistance to keep from following Mr. Market's ill-timed advice. They are like the alcoholic who will end in ruins if he does not follow the dictum "not a single drop." For this man, a single drop becomes the Niagara Falls over which he will soon barrel.

Clients need a financial education process that allows them to get in touch not only with the mechanics of finance but with the emotional machinations that play out in their reasoning processes. They need to recognize where they are strong and where they are weak and vulnerable in organization, practice, and emotion. In the words of the Andrew Tobias, author of *Financial Planning Made Easy,* "The idea is to get your heart and your mind thinking in ways other than pure dollars and cents."

Wisdom is the product of knowledge and experience, which in turn leads to self-knowledge. Clients who have discovered this self-awareness will understand the issues that they must watch for vigilantly in their lives to keep from sabotaging their financial lives. Clients will learn to safeguard their wealth-building process from ignorance, denial, lack of self-control, resilience, and counterproductive relationships. By putting money in its proper place—as servant and not as master—your clients will hopefully discover that true wealth was indeed closer than they suspected.

Chapter 24

Continuing the Education Process

J. D. Powers, a marketing research firm, recently polled 100,000 households to determine the factors that promoted investor satisfaction with financial services providers. The study, which was sponsored by *The Wall Street Journal* and Dow Jones Newswires, revealed surprising results. Across the wealth spectrum (assets ranging from under $50,000 to over $1 million), investors identified education and information as the most important driver of their level of satisfaction with investment firms and investment professionals.

However, the J.D. Powers research also found that the information and education opportunities that firms provide to clients is not the right type. Nancy Salk, director of the study, explained, "The customer is deluged with material, but the broker doesn't have the time and isn't really incentivized to provide the kind of guidance the customer wants." Salk also reported that clients like the financial planner model as she continued, "and unless brokers are at least perceived as being financial planner-like, customers will go elsewhere and brokers will miss out on lucrative opportunities." ("Unsatisfactory Satisfaction," by Editorial Staff, *On Wall Street*, April 1, 2001.)

Clearly, investors prefer to work with professionals that offer a more comprehensive approach to money management and those who will also help build their financial knowledge. However, the majority of clients neither want nor need an information dump that is heavy in industry jargon, technical analysis, and economic forecasts. As

Arthur Levitt, former chairman of the Securities and Exchange Commission, observed, "Today there is a glut of information. But the irony is: Do people have the foundation in the financial basics that will allow them to use that information?"

In the fall of 1999, the Fannie Mae Foundation commissioned the Institute of Socio-Financial Studies (ISFS) to study the current state of financial literacy education in the United States. In the final report, *Personal Finance and the Rush to Competence: Financial Literacy Education in the U.S.*, the researchers beseech financial services providers to respond to consumer needs and, as a result, realize greater market share.

> Personal financial education for every socioeconomic and sociocultural level is challenging. Yet, there must be a willingness by the financial services industry to meet the document literacy needs of the public by producing clear, plain English contracts, and other documents. We see this as a marketing opportunity for financial services firms who can become "lifestyle allies" in the escalating competition for the business of increasingly savvy consumers.

What clients (and prospective clients) want from financial services providers is education that addresses basic financial principles communicated in understandable terms. In addition, this information will be more effective and engaging if it is delivered in a context that is personally relevant to them as individuals. Herein lies the challenge—and the opportunity—for financial life planners to meet client needs and also distinguish themselves from the competition.

With each client, your education efforts as a financial life planner will start with your initial one-on-one meeting. From that point, this holistic education process can continue in a number of ways: the books that you recommend, the materials that you include with monthly statements, the newsletters that you send out, and the information and resources that you feature on your Web site.

EDUCATIONAL WORKSHOPS

In addition, workshops, and seminars are effective ways to serve your current clients and attract new clients. Beside the measures of financial intelligence that were discussed in Chapters 18 through 23, the financial and nonfinancial aspects of retirement planning are particularly popular topics. At the conclusion of the ISFS financial literacy study, the researchers observed that a holistic approach is an especially effective model for retirement planning workshops.

Life planning approaches should increasingly be built into curricula in order to help preretirement populations learn proactive ways to think about the future. Retirement planning approaches should be expanded beyond the financial to include lifestyle choices and other so-called "soft" course topics and materials that are so meaningful to seminar participants when they are included.

The New Retirementality workshop is one example of curricula that looks beyond the numbers and examines the value of meaningful "work" both before and after retirement. The content also addresses health, wellness, and relationship issues. An advisor can license this program for use with clients or for presentations in community organizations and corporations. In addition, *The New Retirementality* newsletter, a print or electronic bimonthly publication, can be delivered to seminar participants as a follow-up piece. The newsletter also serves as a value-added benefit for clients and as a marketing tool.

George Mundy, financial advisor with Morgan Stanley, doesn't conduct retirement planning workshops, but gives his clients who are within five to ten years of retirement a copy of *Designing Your Life in Retirement: A Guide to Planning Your Future*. This workbook addresses the six keys to a successful and satisfying retirement experience: change, balance, potential, meaning, prosperity, and purpose. To stress the value of this perspective and the strength of his convictions, Mundy includes the following personal message with each copy of the workbook that he gives to his clients.

Many of us tend to think of retirement in the traditional sense. Long ago, an individual would work until the age of 62, retire after 30 years of loyal service with a gold wristwatch, apply for Social Security benefits, and then for the remaining ten or so years of life, relax, play some golf, travel a bit, and simply try to enjoy the "golden years" of life. Needless to say, that model of retirement no longer exists. People are retiring earlier and living longer lives. It will not be uncommon for today's retiree to spend 35 or 40 years in retirement. While this paradigm shift has tremendous financial planning implications, the total "life planning" considerations are equally, if not more, important. The concept of retirement is changing and many individuals are inadequately prepared for what lies ahead.

What does it mean to be "retired"? Many retirees are opting for second careers or starting new small businesses. They're devoting their time to charity and community events. They're out there every day making a difference in the world in which we live. As 80 million baby boomers approach retirement during the next ten years, the face of retirement as we have known it will forever be changed.

For many years, I have assisted preretirees in planning for the financial challenges associated with retirement. I have learned that in advising my clients, I can no longer offer financial planning and investment advice "in a vacuum." There is so much more to retirement planning than simply addressing the numbers. Success in retirement, as in life, consists of more than just a hefty investment portfolio. An effective retirement planning strategy must take into consideration all areas of life—spiritual, physical, mental, and social. As a retirement advisor, helping my clients formulate a "holistic" retirement strategy is, without question, the greatest value and highest level of service that I can offer.

I have found this workbook to be an invaluable resource for today's retiree. It will help you carefully examine all facets of your life as you make the transition into retirement— whatever retirement may mean to you! Consider your retirement a new adventure. As you approach this phase of your life, develop a "life strategy" that is in alignment with your long-held dreams. I welcome the opportunity to discuss these thought-provoking issues with you and to help you devise a truly comprehensive life plan.

Live life to the fullest!

NICHE MARKETS

Workshops and seminars with a life planning focus are also very successful in reaching niche markets. For example, women are particularly receptive to this client-centered, values-based approach. Van Kampen Mutual Funds has produced a 90-minute advisor presentation and supporting materials based on David Bach's best selling book, *Smart Women Finish Rich*. The content explains financial basics like the time value of money and determining net worth, and also emphasizes more subjective topics such as basing financial goals and personal values. As Bach explains in the program materials, this process starts with the individual really understanding what is "driving" her when it comes to money. This, he says, is the single most effective tool for helping "people create a life plan that will lead them to the ultimate financial security they want."

OPENING THE DOORS TO CORPORATIONS

You can broaden the scope of your education efforts by making presentations in the workplace. In the *Journal of Financial Planning*, Jacqueline M. Quinn wrote: "There's a trend afoot in the corporate benefit arena. Financial education, once a benefit afforded only those in plum executive levels, is moving mainstream." For employers, the main motivating factors have been related to their 401(k) plans. They depend on financial education efforts to increase the number of participating employees, increase contribution levels, comply with the regulations defined under Section 404(c) of ERISA, and avoid potential liability for any losses. More recently, employers are also finding that financial education can be an effective tool for attracting and retaining valued workers.

Deloitte & Touche conducted a survey to 280 benefit specialists to identify their top benefit priorities for the upcoming year. Two of the top five priorities of these benefit specialists were related to financial education: to provide financial/retirement planning tools and information; and to provide increased investment education. (Source: "Top 5 Benefit Priorities for 2001: A Survey of Certified Employee Benefit Specialists," Deloitte & Touche, 2000.)

Another educational opportunity exists in the workplace for those advisors who are in touch with the new retirementality—a trend where mature people are staying in the workplace longer. This trend will have significant impact on retirement planning, savings, and education. In an article entitled "The Transformed Workplace: How You Can Survive," outplacement consultant John A. Challenger writes:

... perhaps the most positive change in the allocation of human capital arises from how employers are using their most experienced workers. Retirement at age 65 in the United States is disappearing. Companies are creating work arrangements that allow seniors to work into their 70s and 80s. Part-time contingency, and consulting work arrangements allow seniors to rebalance work and personal life needs.

Society increasingly values not only youth and energy, but also age and wisdom. The discriminatory thinking that once made it difficult for companies to hire older workers was inherently irrational; such a system is now completely out of sync with current values. Today, large corporations have an open-door policy for over-50 workers. It is no longer the case, if you lose your job in your 40s or older, that there will be no large, well-known companies interested in hiring you. Companies today place high value on experience, corporate memory, and know-how, the traits older individuals are most likely to possess, and these companies have backed that realization by hiring older workers in record numbers. (Source: *The Futurist*, November/December 2001, p. 28.)

This trend will no doubt create a need for education that embraces this shift into retirement planning calculations. Work-related earnings will play a much larger role in the baby boomer's retirement scenario than they currently anticipate. The chart in Figure 24.1 contrasts baby boomers's beliefs and realities projected by current trends.

FIGURE 24.1   **Sources of Baby Boomers' Retirement Income: Beliefs versus Reality**

Source of Income	Belief	Reality
Company pensions	45%	20%
Social Security	26%	18%
Private savings	22%	33%
Other	4%	2%
Work earnings	**3%**	**27%**

Source: U.S. Department of Health and Human Services.

Many boomers are in for a rude awakening on this matter but, fortunately, they will be both healthy and interested enough to keep working as traditional notions about retirement fade away.

DIFFERENTIATE YOURSELF AS AN EDUCATOR

Again, this is where financial life planners can distinguish themselves from the competition because they understand these issues and emphasize a life planning process rather than financial products. Likewise, rather than focusing on making a sale, they focus on equipping and empowering the consumer to make sound financial decisions. In the workplace setting, they win favor with employees and employers alike not by dazzling them with brilliance and puffery, but by presenting understandable and relevant information that can be used to guide and direct life decisions.

THE GOALS

The education efforts of financial life planners should be directed at helping those they reach build financial security in their lives. However, that is not the only objective. You must also communicate that true financial freedom is more than having a lot of money. It is being free of money myths and notions that influence money attitudes and behaviors. And, most importantly, strive to help your constituents align their financial goals with their inner compasses—a point that is eloquently expressed by Karen Ramsey in her book, *Everything You Know about Money Is Wrong*.

In personal financial management, the place to begin is to adopt a realistic perspective. Money will only improve the quality of your life when it is used with clarity. Only when you learn to spend money in concert with your underlying values—the things that you most deeply care about—will it become a tool for creating a more fulfilling life.

Today's advisors, with a financial life planning approach, can build a bridge between having money and having a life. Clients should be able to use their money for finding a life of fulfillment and balance. Advisors who have redefined their role as partner, guide, and educator become invaluable in the life and future of their clients.

Epilogue

After a recent speech, an advisor approached me and asked, "Do you think financial life planning can help me feel like I'm doing something significant with my life?" His comment echoed the scores of calls and conversations I have had with advisors and brokers who confided that they too are burned out, frustrated, tired, and bored with the way their business is going. This particular advisor went on to tell me that he thought a closer connection to the lives of his clients was what he needed to snap out of a routinous, repetition of process. Although he was making plenty of money, he somehow felt disconnected in the process. I told him, "Before you help clients try to figure out what it is that they want out of life, you might want to ask yourself the same questions."

The most successful people in the world can see a transcending purpose beyond the processes in which they indulge. They feel like they are fulfilling a calling in their lives by channeling their energies, know-how, and passion into a practice that they are good at and enjoy doing. If you asked these individuals, they would tell you their work is more than just a job. People sense it when they encounter these individuals and want to be associated with them. This book is written for those who are or who want to be just such an individual.

Take yourself through some of the inquiries prescribed for clients in this book. Check your current temperature regarding life balance, purposeful living, and life values and goals. You'll find that you are no different than the clients you serve. It's about having a life. It's about having time to enjoy the journey. It's about making a difference for the people we love and the things we care about. Money can make or break us in these pursuits. That is why your role is so important. You may be able to help people figure out what it is and where they want to go in life. You may be able to help them get there sooner and stay there longer. That sounds like more than a job to me—it sounds like a calling.

It is by placing purpose at the center of our processes that gives our work meaning. It is by providing greater value to those we serve that we experience a greater sense of significance.

If you would like more information on speeches or training for Financial Life Planning, The New Retirementality, Money Quotient, Inc., or other advisor training programs, contact Mitch Anthony by phone (507-282-2723) or e-mail (Mitch@moneyquotient.com).

Bibliography

"AARP Announces Largest Magazine Launch in History; Betsy Carter Named Editor of New Boomer Title." *AARP, Press Release,* September 25, 2000.

AARP: Money and the American Family. (Conducted for AARP'S *Modern Maturity* Magazine) May 2000.

"AARP Unveils Landmark Report on Economic State of 50+ America." *AARP, Press Center,* May 23, 2001.

"Americans Working Too Hard." *Hilton Generational Time Survey,* January 2001, reported in *USA Today.*

Ammondson, Pamela. *Clarity Quest: How to Take a Sabbatical without More than a Week.* Fireside, 1999.

Anderson, Carol. "Designing Your Life in Retirement: A Guide to Planning Your Future, Money Quotient, Inc., 2001.

Andorfer, James B. "More Planners Using Both Couch and Calculator." *Investment News,* February 7, 2000.

Anthes, William L. and Lee, Shelley A. "Experts Examine Emerging Concept of Life." *Journal of Financial Planning,* June, 2001.

Anthony, Mitch. *The New Retirementality.* Dearborn Trade, 2001.

Anthony, Mitch and West, Scott. *StorySelling for Financial Advisors.* Dearborn Trade, 2000.

Anthony, Mitch and DeMoss, Gary. *The Financial Professional's Guide to Persuading 1 or 1,000.* Dearborn Trade, 2001.

Appleby, Julie. "Health Benefits for Retirees Continue Decline." *USA Today,* May 31, 2001, B-1.

Arzen, Kris. "Values-Based Planning: Seeing the Whole Client—Part I." *Journal of Financial Planning,* March 1999.

Arzen, Kris. "Values-Based Planning: Seeing the Whole Client—Part II." *Journal of Financial Planning,* March 1999.

Baby Boomers Look toward Retirement," *Roper Starch Worldwide Press Release,* Commissioned by the AARP, June 2, 1998.

Bach, David. *Smart Women Finish Rich.* Broadway Books, 1999.

"Boomers on the Brink." *Perspective,* Summer of 2001 (Vol. 6, Issue 3), 1–2.

Bowers, Richard. "Inheritance versus Legacy." *York Daily Record,* February 12, 2000.

Bradford, Michael. "Sabbatical Programs Becoming Valuable Way to Retain Employees." *Business Insurance,* June 25, 2001.

"Brain Drain." *Business Week,* September 20, 1999.

Carlson, Peter. "Ready for the Rocker, AARP Style." *Washington Post,* September 24, 2000.

Challenger, John A. "Workplace Rules in the New Millennium." *The Futurist.* November–December 2001, p. 28.

Chapman, Elwood N., and Haynes, Marion E. *Comfort Zones,* 4th edition. Crisp, 1997.

Christiansen, Tim and DeVaney, Sharon A. "Antecedents of Trust and Commitment in the Financial Planner-Client Relationship." *Association for Financial Counseling and Planning Education,* 1998.

Conlin, Michelle. "9 to 5 Isn't Working Anymore." *Business Week,* September 20, 1999, 94–98.

Cordell, David M. "RiskPACK: How to Evaluate Risk Tolerance." *Journal of Financial Planning,* June 2001, 36–40.

Covey, Stephen. *The Seven Habits of Highly Effective People.* Simon & Schuster, 1989.

Cruz, Humberto and Georgina. "Redefining Retirement." *South Florida Sun-Sentinel,* January 21, 2001, 1E.

Cruz, Humberto. "Take Stock in Time Invested in Post-Retirement Endeavor." *JS Online,* September 2001.

Culver, Barbara. "The Evolution of the Financial Services Industry—From Transaction to Transformation, Part I." *Journal of Financial Planning,* October 19, 1998, 1–2.

Culver, Barbara. "The Evolution of the Financial Services Industry—From Transaction to Transformation, Part II." *Journal of Financial Planning*, October 26, 1998, 1–2.

Dauten, Dale. "Is Your Dream Career Still Only a Dream?" *Star Tribune*, May 23, 2001, D2.

DeBlasio, Libby. "Local Author Asks: Will Retirement Be Prosperous?" *The Boulder County Business Report, Online Edition*, July 1998.

Deloitte & Touche, Top 5 Benefit Priorities for 2001: A Survey of Certified Employee Benefit Specialists. (Conducted by the International Society of Certified Employee Benefit Specialists and Deloitte & Touche LLP) 2000.

Dennis, Helen. "The New Retirement: Its Meaning for Individuals and the Workplace." *Working through Demographic Change: How Older Americans Can Sustain the Nation's Prosperity*. Edited by Zinke, William K. and Tattershall, Susan. Human Resource Services, Inc., 2001.

Dlugozima, Hope, Scott, James and Sharp, David. *Six Months Off: How to Plan, Negotiate, and Take the Break You Need without Burning Bridges or Going Broke*. Henry Holt, 1996.

Eisenson, Marc, Detweiler, Gerri, and Castleman, Nancy. *Invest in Yourself: Six Secrets to a Rich Life*. Wiley, 1998.

Farrell, Paul B. "Yes, You Can Retire on $22,000 a Year: Don't Buy Wall Street's Scare Tactics, Self-Promotion." *CBS MarketWatch*, February 12, 2001.

"Financial Strategies." Securian Financial Services, 2001.

Fichenscher, Lisa. "The New Face of Giving." *Family Money*, November/December 2000.

Franklin, Mary Beth. "Putting a (Rough) Price Tag on Your Dream." *Investing Kiplinger's*, March 2001, 42–46.

Franklin, Mary Beth. "Exit Strategies." *Investing Kiplinger's*, March 2001, 38–41.

Freedman, Marc. *Prime Time—How Baby Boomers Will Revolutionize Retirement and Transform America*. PublicAffairs, 1999.

Freidan, Betty. *The Fountain of Age*. Simon & Schuster, 1993.

Gabriel, Michelle. "Why Clients Leave." *Registered Representative*, February 1, 2001.

Goleman, Daniel. *Emotional Intelligence*. Bloomsbury Publishing, 1995. E.Q.

Gordon, Joanne. "Do You Really Need That?" *Forbes*, March 19, 2001.

Green, James J. "Back of the Book." *Investment Advisor*, May 2001, 12.

Greenberg, Ian. "Billy the Kid Grows Up." *Industry Standard*, June 12, 2000.

Gurney, Kathleen. "Knowing Your Money Personality Can Help You Find the Right Financial Advisor for You." *Financial Psychology Corporation,* 1999.

Hayes, Christopher L., Ph.D. "What's Your Money Personality?" *Working Woman,* February 1995, 35.

Herman, Tracy. "Retirement Concierge." *Supplement to Registered Representative,* October 1999.

Hewitt Associates. "Internet Access Makes Saving, Trading Easier for 401-K Plan." *Businesswire,* November 16, 2000.

"Highly Engaged Investors Put Internet and Financial Advisors on Equal Footing" *Canada Newswire,* 2001.

Hinden, Stan. "Is There Enough for a Nest?" *The Washington Post,* August 26, 2001, H-1.

"His and Her Retirement? The Role of Gender and Marriage in the Retirement Process." *Roybal Issue Brief* <www.applied-gerontology.org>.

Hunt, Albert R. "An Emerging Fundamental Shift in What It Means to Be a 'Senior.'" *The Wall Street Journal Interactive Edition,* March 11, 1999.

Jacoby, Susan, "The Allure of Money." *Modern Maturity,* July–August 2000, 35–41.

Joyce, Amy. "After the Layoff, Time Off." *Washington Post,* August 15, 2001.

Kalajian, Douglas. "Baby Boomers to Change Retirement." *Seattle P.I.,* September 4, 2000.

Kindel, Stephen, and Goydon, Raymond. "The Reggies Are Coming!" <www.2young2retire.com>.

"Leaving a Legacy." *Unconventional Wisdom,* Fall 2000.

Lee, Shelley A. "Why Do Financial Plans Fail?" *Journal of Financial Planning,* June 2001, 60–67.

Leider, Richard. "Are You Deciding on Purpose?" *Fast Company,* February–March 1998.

Leider, Richard. *The Power of Purpose: Creating Meaning in Your Life and Work,* Berrett-Koehler, 1997.

"Less Fun, Less Sleep, More Work." *Executive Summary of the National Sleep Foundation Study,* March 2001.

Levin, Ross. "Enjoy the Process." *Journal of Financial Planning,* August 2001, 32–34.

Levin, Ross. *The Wealth Management Index: The Financial Advisor's System for Assessing & Managing Your Client's Plans & Goal.* Irwin Professional Publishing, 1997.

McConnell, Jack. "And What Did You Do for Someone Today?" *Newsweek,* June 18, 2001, 13.

"The MetLife Juggling Act Study." (Findings from a National Study by the National Alliance for Caregiving and the National Center on Women and Aging at Brandeis University) November 1999.

Moen, Phyllis, Principal Investigator with Agarwal, Madhurima, Fields, Vivian, and Todd, Laurie. The Cornell Retirement and Well-Being Study, Final Report, 2000.

Morgan, Sharon Drew. *Selling with Integrity.* Berkley Publishing Group, November 1999.

1999 Consumer Survey, Certified Financial Planner Board of Standards, Inc.

Opiela, Nancy. "Retirement Mind Games." *Journal of Financial Planning,* April 2000.

Orman, Suze. *The 9 Steps to Financial Freedom.* Crown, 1997.

Owen, Jim. "Taking a Sabbatical from Work." <www.careerbuilder.com>.

Quinn, Jacqueline M. "The Metamorphosis of Retirement." *The Journal of Financial Planning,* April 2001.

Quinn, Jane Bryant. *Making the Most of Your Money,* Simon & Schuster, 1991.

Ramsey, Karen. *Everything You Know about Money Is Wrong.* ReganBooks, 1999.

"Reinventing Retirement, Baby-Boomer Style." *Sage Online,* March 12, 2001, 1–3.

Reilly, Shannon and Tian, Quin. "People Describe Their Workplace." *USA Today,* June 27, 2001, B-1.

"Retirement Revisited: An Index of Optimism Special Report," *The PaineWebber Poll of Investor Attitudes,* 1998.

Roha, Ronaleen R. "Charity Gets Personal." *Kiplingers Personal Finance,* September 2000.

Sher, Barbara. *I Could Do Anything If I Only Knew What It Was.* Dell, 1994.

Smart, Tim. "Not Acting Their Age." *U.S. News and World Report,* June 4, 2001.

"Sources of Baby Boomers' Retirement Income: Beliefs vs. Reality." *Futurist—Supplement Outlook 2001.*

Spiro, Leah Nathans with Edward C. Baig in New York. "Who Needs a Broker?" *Business Week,* February 22, 1999.

Stanley, Thomas J. and Danko, William D. *The Millionaire Next Door: The Surprising Secrets of America's Wealthy.* Pocketbooks, 2000.

Statman, Meir. "Behaviorial Finance: Past Battles and Future Engagements." *Financial Analysts Journal,* November/December 1999, 18–26.

"Stefan, Kara. "Collecting a Monthly 'Playcheck'—More Americans to Work through Their Retirement Years." *CBS MarketWatch,* February 23, 2001.

Stein, Helene and Brier, Marcia. *Financial Planner Interactive,* <www .financialplanning.com>.

Stein, Michael. *The Prosperous Retirement: Guide to the New Reality.* EMSTCO Press, 1998.

Sternberg, R. *Successful Intelligence.* Plume, 1997.

Steuerle, Eugene, and Spiro, Christopher. "A New Approach to Age and Work." *Urban Institute,* No. 6, August 30, 1999.

Stone, Howard, and Stone, Marika. "Retire the 'R' Word Winners!" <www.2young2retire.com>.

Stone, Howard and Stone, Marika. "Top Ten Ways to Reinvent Retirement." <www.2young2retire.com>

Sullivan, Jim, and Piper, Beth. "Retiring Rich/Retiring Well." *BC Solutions,* September 1998, 1–5.

"Taking a Sabbatical." *Unconventional Wisdom,* September/October 2001, 1.

"10 Questions with Elissa Buie, CFP, President, Financial Planning Group, Inc., Falls Church, VA." *Best Practices/Planner Spotlight* <www.journalfp .net>, September 17, 2001.

"10 Questions with Kathleen Cotton, CFP, Cotton Financial Advisors, Lynnwood, Wash." *Best Practices/Planner Spotlight* <www.journalfp.net>, April 30, 2001.

Thomas, Robert B. *The Old Farmers Almanac 2001,* ed. Judson D. Hale. Villard Books, 2000.

Timmerman, Sandra. "Earlier Retirement or Longer Worklife? Myths, Realities, and Predictions." *Journal of Financial Service Professionals,* September 1, 2000, 34–39.

"Tips from Ross Levin: Values in Investing and Giving." *Sound Money,* January 20, 2001. (Sound Money is a radio program produced by Minnesota Public Radio. Ross was a guest on the show on that date, and the article was posted to the Web site <www.soundmoney.org> as a resource based on the radio program discussion.)

Tobias, Andrew. *The Only Investment Book You Will Ever Need.* Harvest Books, 1999.

"Top Performers Conference." *Getting Clients, Keeping Clients* newsletter, April 24, 2000.

"Twenty (20) Moves to Make before New Year's Day." *Modern Maturity,* July–August 2000, 48.

"2000 Phoenix Wealth Management Survey: Millionaire Does Not Mean Wealthy by Today's Standards." Phoenix Wealth Management (Phoenix Home Life Mutual Insurance Company and affiliated companies Web page) 2001.

"2000 Phoenix Wealth Management Survey: Fact Sheet: How Much Do You Know about Wealthy Individuals?" Phoenix Wealth Management (Phoenix Home Life Mutual Insurance Company and affiliated companies Web page) 2001.

"2000 Phoenix Wealth Management Survey: A Snapshot of America's Wealthy." Phoenix Wealth Management (Phoenix Home Life Mutual Insurance Company and affiliated companies Web page) 2001.

"2000 Phoenix Wealth Management Survey: Senior Corporate Executives Are Most Stressed Despite Success." Phoenix Wealth Management (Phoenix Home Life Mutual Insurance Company and affiliated companies Web page) 2001.

"2000 Phoenix Wealth Management Survey: New, Diverse Group of Wealthy Americans Face Different Financial Needs." Phoenix Wealth Management (Phoenix Home Life Mutual Insurance Company and affiliated companies Web page) 2001.

"The 2001 Retirement Confidence Survey Summary of Findings: Fewer Americans Are Saving for Retirement." Employee Benefit Research Institute <www.ebri.org>, May 10, 2001.

"Unsatisfactory Satisfaction." *On Wall Street,* April 1, 2001.

VanCaspel, Vernita. *Money Dynamics for the 1990s.* Simon & Schuster, 1988.

Vitt, Lois, Anderson, Carol, Kent, Jamie, Lyter, Danna M., Siegenthaler, Jurg K. and Ward, Jeremy. "Personal Finance and the Rush to Competence: Financial Literacy Education in the U.S." *A Study Conducted by: The Institute of Socio-Financial Studies for the Fannie Mae Foundation,* 2000.

Wagner, Cynthia G. "Economics—Adapting to the Adaptables." *The Futurist,* March–April 2001, 8–9.

Walker, Lewis, J. "A Look at the Financial Services Revolution." *The Journal of Financial Planning,* October 2001.

Walsh, Mary Williams. "Reversing a Long Trend, Americans Are Retiring from Jobs Later in Life." *New York Times,* February 26, 2001.

Warner, Ralph. *Get a Life, You Don't Need a Million to Retire Well.* Nolo Press, 2001.

Wasik, John F. *The Late-Start Investor: The Better-Late-Than-Never Guide to Realizing Your Retirement Dreams.* Owl Books, 1998.

Zweig, Jason. "Wall Street's Wisest Man." *Money,* June 2001, 49–52.

Index

YOUR CLIENTS FOR LIFE

Finally a book that explains how to become a financial life planner! Order in quantities at deep discounts and watch sales soar.

Life planners: *The New Retirementality* is a book for every client! Don't just make your clients' day—help them transform their way of thinking!

- Call 800-621-9621, ext. 4455
- E-mail bermel@dearborn.com
- Great service, top discounts
- Customize books with your firm's name and logo

Did we mention that our authors are dynamic speakers?